CONFLICT IN LUKE

Fortress Press Books
by
Jack Dean Kingsbury

The Christology of Mark's Gospel

Jesus Christ in Matthew, Mark, and Luke
(Proclamation Commentary)

Matthew, 2d ed. (Proclamation Commentary)

Matthew as Story, 2d ed.

Matthew: Structure, Christology, Kingdom

Conflict in Mark: Jesus, Authorities, Disciples

CONFLICT IN LUKE

JESUS, AUTHORITIES, DISCIPLES

Jack Dean Kingsbury

FORTRESS PRESS   **MINNEAPOLIS**

Kingsbury, Jack Dean.
    Conflict in Luke : Jesus, authorities, disciples / Jack Dean
Kingsbury.
        p.   cm.
    Includes bibliographical references and index.
    ISBN 0-8006-2472-6
    1. Bible.   N.T.   Luke—Criticism, interpretation, etc.   2. Jesus
Christ—History of doctrines—Early church, ca. 30–600
    3. Authority—Biblical teaching.   I. Title.
    BS2595.2.K56   1991
    226.4'06—dc20   90-21896
                                                               CIP

The paper used in this publication meets the minimum requirements
of American National Standard for Information Sciences—Permanence
of Paper for Printed Library Materials, ANSI Z329.48-1984.   ∞ ™

Manufactured in the U.S.A.   AF 1-2472

95   94   93   92   91   1   2   3   4   5   6   7   8   9   10

To
John A. Hollar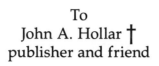
publisher and friend

CONTENTS

PREFACE

As the title indicates, this book is a companion volume to *Conflict in Mark: Jesus, Authorities, Disciples* (Minneapolis: Fortress Press, 1989). In the recent past, the literary, or narrative, approach to the study of the Gospels has proved so fruitful that it has now become, in North America, one of the dominant approaches. As evidence of this, one need only take note of the ever-increasing number of books, articles, and monographs being published utilizing this approach. Still, because the great bulk of these publications tend to be narrow in focus or highly specialized, they often do not lend themselves to ready use in the classroom or pastor's study. As with *Conflict in Mark,* I have written this book not only for instructors but also for pastors and students. In chapter 1, my goal is to introduce the reader to the world of Luke's gospel story and to elements that fill it with life and drama, such as settings, characters, and the plot. In chapters 2–4, I trace and interpret the three chief story lines in Luke's Gospel, that of Jesus, of the religious authorities, and of the disciples. To be sure, the story of Jesus is central throughout Luke's Gospel; nevertheless, intertwined with it are also the stories of the authorities and of the disciples.

The story of Jesus in Luke's Gospel is that of Israel's Messiah and God's Son in whom God inaugurates the time of salvation by fulfilling his scriptural promises to Israel (and the nations) and thus accomplishing his plan of salvation. In his story of the religious authorities, Luke harshly stereotypes them as "self-righteous"; at the human level, they are Jesus' chief opponents. And in his story of the disciples, Luke portrays them as followers of Jesus who are loyal yet spiritually immature. For an overview of the plot of Luke's gospel story, the reader may turn to the end of chapter 1.

It is with no little sense of gratitude and privilege that I follow the time-honored convention of expressing my indebtedness to those who have assisted me in various ways in bringing this book to completion. As the one who commissioned it and to whose memory I should like to dedicate it, John A. Hollar deserves special mention. In addition, my thanks go to his able successor, Marshall D. Johnson, Editorial Director of Fortress Press, for reading the manuscript and overseeing its publication; to Martha Aycock, Associate Librarian at Union Theological Seminary, Virginia, for securing hard-to-get materials; to Jeffrey A. Gibbs, my graduate assistant, for preparing the index; to Michael Compton, my research assistant, for the many hours he labored in the library on my behalf; and to my wife, Barbara, whose good humor and cheerful support bestow on every undertaking a special touch of grace.

J. D. K.

Union Theological Seminary in Virginia
Easter Season, 1990

1 INTRODUCTION

Luke's story of Jesus has often been described as one of the most "beautiful" ever told.[1] To some, this means it has a romantic quality about it: An angel suddenly appears to shepherds announcing Jesus' birth and a multitude of heavenly choristers burst forth in praise of God. As a precocious twelve-year-old, Jesus astonishes the teachers in the temple with the wisdom of his questions and answers. And during his ministry, Jesus champions the cause of persons on the margins of society, reversing their fortunes. In a profound sense, however, Luke's gospel story is in fact beautiful. It is the work of an educated writer whose artistry was that he knew how to draw on tradition to tell a story that is at once aesthetically pleasing and capable of conveying afresh the truth about the salvation God has accomplished in Jesus of Nazareth.[2] To assist us in our understanding of this story, we begin by examining several of its features.

THE WORLD OF THE STORY

When first written around A.D. 85 perhaps in Asia Minor,[3] Luke's Gospel was read aloud to groups of Christians gathered together in house churches.[4] Whether the Gospel is heard or read, however, the reader or hearer temporarily takes leave of his or her own world and, through the use of imagination, enters into the world of Luke's Gospel. It is as one dwelling within this world that the reader or hearer experiences Luke's gospel story and is shaped by it. Accordingly, the first feature we want to explore is the world of this gospel story.

Fundamental to this world is the view shared by all the canonical Gospels that human history constitutes an arena within which

God and Satan are engaged in cosmic struggle. According to Luke, God is powerfully present in Jesus to overcome Satan and evil and to summon Israel to repentance and to salvation in the sphere of God's kingly rule. Following Jesus' ascension, God's struggle with Satan and evil continues as God and the exalted Jesus work through the apostles and Paul, proffering salvation not only to Israel but also to the gentiles. Within Luke's story world, therefore, one sees that human history is not closed but open to supernatural influences: Angels appear to humans; humans are filled with the Holy Spirit; God's voice sounds from above; the Holy Spirit descends upon Jesus in bodily form as a dove; Satan puts Jesus to the test; demons shout aloud in dread of Jesus; Jesus performs miracles and predicts the future; Satan enters into Judas; and the glorified Jesus appears to the disciples, speaks and eats with them, and ascends to heaven. In the world of Luke's story, ordinary human experience is the setting where extraordinary occurrences take place.

Open as human history is to supernatural influences, Luke's story of Jesus nonetheless unfolds within history. Angels may come from heaven and return to heaven, but the reader has them in view only while they are still on earth. At his ascension, Jesus, too, disappears from human sight. True, the reader is given glimpses of heaven and Hades. In the parable of the rich man and Lazarus (16:19-31), Jesus briefly depicts both the bliss of heaven and the torment of Hades. In Acts, Stephen, about to die, is said to gaze directly into heaven, whereupon he exclaims that he sees the exalted Jesus standing at the right hand of God (Acts 7:56). Still, for the reader to be situated by Luke on earth and given glimpses of heaven or Hades is one thing. It would be quite another if suddenly the reader were narratively transported by an angel into the very regions of heaven or Hades and given a guided tour. Such journeys, which occur in contemporary apocalyptic literature,[5] are foreign to Luke's gospel story. In it, earth and human history clearly remain the center of attention.

We have just seen that, spatially, the world of Luke's gospel story is made up of heaven, earth, and Hades.[6] While earth is open to both heaven and Hades (10:15), the boundaries separating these realms are nonetheless fixed. Earth is the dwelling place God has created for humankind;[7] it is the "theatre of history."[8] The history of Jesus' life, for example, is situated within the wider contexts of the history of Israel,[9] of the Roman Empire (2:1-2), of Palestine (3:1-2a), and of the early church (1:1-4).

Hades, in turn, is the underworld, the "deepest depth" that lies at "heart of the earth."[10] It is the abode of the dead.[11] For the wicked, whose souls descend there and remain until the final judgment, it is a place of extreme torment (16:22b-24), of "thirst"[12] and "flame."[13] As the opposite of Hades, heaven is the "highest height." It is the abode of God,[14] his angels,[15] the exalted Jesus,[16] and the righteous.[17] As Lord of heaven and earth, God is the creator and ruler of the universe.[18] In heaven, God dwells in ineffable glory, and because his kingly rule encounters no opposition, peace[19] reigns supreme (19:38). In Jesus of Nazareth, God in his kingly rule makes himself present in the midst of Israel.[20] Through word and deed, Jesus summons Israel to repentance and to discipleship, proffering it peace and salvation.[21] Following Jesus' ascension, the apostles and Paul proclaim repentance and salvation in his name, first to Israel and then to the nations. Still, at a future time God has appointed, the exalted Jesus will return to inaugurate the restoration of all things and usher in God's rule in splendor.[22] At that time, all people on earth will witness the fulfillment of the petitions Jesus teaches his disciples to pray: "Father, let your name be held holy; let your kingdom come" (11:2).

The world of Luke's gospel story is not only one of space—heaven, earth, Hades—but also one of time. In principle, all of time is divided into "this age" and "the age to come" (18:30). The event marking the end of this age and the beginning of the age to come is the final judgment (11:31-32). In scope, this age extends from creation and Adam to the Parousia of the exalted Jesus.[23] Luke, however, makes much of Abraham as the father of the Jews,[24] of the fulfillment of the scriptures, and of God's intention to save first Israel and then the gentiles (Acts 13:46-47). Luke's special concern, therefore, is to divide this age into two epochs, the "time of prophecy" and the "time of fulfillment."[25] For its part, the time of fulfillment is the "time of salvation." It encompasses the "time of Jesus," which is the focus of Luke's Gospel, and the "time of the church," which is the focus of Acts. Within the time of Jesus, one also encounters the respective ministries to Israel of John, of Jesus, of the twelve, and of the seventy-two. Among these ministries, that of Jesus is central, for John precedes Jesus' ministry, and the ministries of the twelve and of the seventy-two are an extension of it. Temporally, therefore, the figure of Jesus is pivotal to the whole of Luke's understanding of salvation history.

SETTINGS

Another prominent feature of the gospel story Luke tells is the settings he fashions. A "setting" is the place, time, or social circumstances in which action occurs.[26] Settings may be general, the backdrop for an entire work, or particular, relating to a single episode or scene.

General Setting

The general setting for Luke's gospel story is the land of the Jews. This is true of Mark's story as well. But whereas Mark depicts Jesus as traveling in the gentile regions of Tyre, Sidon, and the Decapolis and places Peter's confession of Jesus near Caesarea Philippi,[27] Luke makes no mention either of such a journey or of Caesarea Philippi. As Jesus makes his way to Jerusalem, Luke does picture him as being in Samaria (9:52-56; 17:11). The Samaritans, however, refuse to receive him (9:53), so that Jesus' ministry continues to be to Israel. This, in fact, is quite in line with the larger story Luke narrates, for successful preaching among the Samaritans has its rightful place in Acts and in the time of the church (Acts 1:8; 8:1-8). Aside from Samaria, only once does Jesus ever set foot in an area populated by gentiles, and then only briefly (8:26-39). By narrowly restricting Jesus to the land of the Jews, Luke deftly places geography in the service of the overall motif of his gospel story: to portray Jesus as proffering salvation to Israel.

Temporal Settings

Within his gospel story, Luke makes ample use of all three kinds of settings, the temporal, local, and social. Whereas some of these settings possess only minimal significance, others are of enormous significance.

For the most part, Luke uses temporal settings to link scenes or episodes with one another and thus create a sense of movement in his gospel story. Temporal settings of this type function as connectives. Minimally, they can be as spare as the word "and" or the expressions "and when" or "and behold."[28] More frequently, they will take the form of a temporal participle (e.g., "*After* the messengers of John *had gone*, he began to speak to the crowds . . ." [7:24]) or a construction with the infinitive (e.g., "*While he was speaking*, a Pharisee asked him . . ." [11:37]). Particularly characteristic of

Luke, however, is his use as a connective of the Semitic expression "Now [And] it happened that . . ." (or "Now [And] it happened when . . .").[29]

Beyond this, Luke's gospel story is also rich in temporal indicators of weighty significance. For example, unlike Mark and Matthew, Luke situates the life of Jesus within the broader context of both Roman and Palestinian history (2:1; 3:1-2a), thus linking Jesus to world history. To signal the beginning of the prophetic ministry of John the Baptist, Luke echoes the call God extends to Jeremiah in the Old Testament (Jer. 1:1; LXX): "The word of God came to John the son of Zechariah in the desert" (3:2b). To attest to Jesus' coming as having inaugurated a new epoch in the history of salvation, whereby the kingdom of God is a present reality, Luke has Jesus declare: "For behold, the kingdom of God is in the midst of you!" (17:21; 11:20). Last, to show that salvation has become a present gift in the "time of Jesus," Luke makes conspicuous use of the adverb "today," as when Jesus exclaims to Zacchaeus: "Today salvation has come to this house" (19:9).

Local Settings

Locally, Luke's gospel story is replete with settings having special meaning. "Galilee"[30] is the place where God has ordained that Jesus should "begin" his ministry of salvation to Israel (Acts 10:36-39).[31] From Galilee, Jesus reaches out to all Israel (4:44). To Galilee, people from every part of Israel and beyond come to Jesus (6:17). In Galilee, Jesus presents himself to Israel as God's Messiah (4:18-21). In discharging his powerful ministry of word and deed, Jesus is not to be misconstrued as instigating sedition against Rome; on the contrary, he goes about doing good and healing those oppressed by the devil.[32] Also in Galilee, Jesus both selects the twelve apostles (6:13-16), those who are to be his witnesses "from the beginning,"[33] and gathers others who will accompany him to Jerusalem, such as women disciples.[34] Galilee, then, is where Jesus begins the ministry that must end in Jerusalem.

The "desert" is a place of end-time renewal and of isolation. As a place of isolation, it is also a place of preparation, of testing, and of miraculous provision. In preparation for his prophetic ministry, John the Baptist lives in the desert until called by God (1:80). Thereafter John goes about the desert region of the Jordan Valley preaching a baptism of repentance for the forgiveness of sins (3:2-3; 7:24). As an isolated and uninhabited area, the desert is, variously, the abode of

Satan and demons (where Jesus is put to the test [4:1]), a place of prayer and communion with God (5:16), and the setting in which Jesus miraculously feeds the five thousand (9:12).

The "lake" is a place of both plenitude and terror.[35] On the one hand, Simon, at Jesus' command, lets down his nets into the water and catches so many fish that neither the nets nor two boats can contain them (5:4-7). On the other hand, the disciples, encountering a squall out on the water, lose trust and cry out to Jesus in fear that the waves engulfing their boat will also engulf their lives (8:22-25).

The "synagogue" is a place in which the scribes and the Pharisees are "at home."[36] It is also a place where Jesus reaches out to Israel,[37] suffers repudiation (4:16-30), and engages in fierce controversy.[38] For the disciples, the synagogue will be a place where they endure persecution because they follow Jesus.[39]

The "mountain" is a place connoting security but also punishment, height and the giving of divine revelation, and fertility; it is the place where heaven touches earth.[40] In nearness to God, Jesus customarily prays atop a mountain, especially the Mount of Olives.[41] Once while Jesus is at prayer atop a mountain, he becomes transfigured and Peter, John, and James become the recipients of divine revelation (9:29-36). In allusion to the mountain as a fertile place, Luke at one point describes a large herd of swine as grazing there (8:32). And at the end of his ministry, Jesus, envisaging the destruction of Jerusalem, counsels both flight to the mountains for refuge (21:21) and prayer that, mercifully, the mountains might fall on the inhabitants and save them from their horrid fate (22:30).

Without question, the most important setting in Luke's gospel story is "Jerusalem" and, in conjunction with it, the "temple" and Jesus' "journey" there.[42] Jerusalem, as the city in which God has chosen to dwell,[43] constitutes the center of Israel. The temple, as the house of God[44] and the place of God's presence,[45] constitutes the center of Jerusalem. Ideally, the temple is a place for prayer,[46] praise of God,[47] instruction,[48] and the exercise of true piety (21:1-4).[49] As Luke begins his gospel story, it is mainly in the temple at Jerusalem— at the very center of Israel—that God, in remembrance of his promises and in continuity with past actions, initiates a new phase in the history of salvation. To mark this, the angel Gabriel, appearing in the temple to Zechariah, announces the birth of his son, John, the one through whom God will effect spiritual renewal in Israel (1:11-22). At the presentation of the infant Jesus in the temple, Simeon, taking him into his arms, extols him as God's gift of "salvation" and Israel's "glory" (2:22-32). In similar fashion, the prophetess Anna, a continual worshiper in the temple, recognizes in Jesus the "redemption" of Jerusalem and speaks to others of him (2:36-38). And as a twelve-year-old, Jesus himself visits the temple and manifests his awareness that, in attending to the things of God, he, the Son and Servant of God, does the will of God (2:41-52).

In Luke's gospel story, Jerusalem is not only the place where God inaugurates the time of salvation; it also becomes symbolic of Israel's repudiation of Jesus. On this score, the religious authorities bear the greatest burden of guilt. Thus, as early in the story as the temptation, Satan puts Jesus to the test in Jerusalem (4:9-13), and this, in turn, foreshadows the final, deadly onslaught in Jerusalem that both Satan and the authorities mount against Jesus (22:3, 53). Later, at Jesus' transfiguration, Luke tells of the sudden appearance of Moses and Elijah, who converse with Jesus about the "exodus" he will soon accomplish at Jerusalem (9:30-31). This "exodus" refers, among other things, to the suffering and death Jesus must endure there. Shortly after the transfiguration, Luke solemnly reports that Jesus begins his long journey to Jerusalem (9:51—19:46). Repeatedly during this journey, Luke himself or Jesus reminds the reader that Jesus' goal is in fact Jerusalem and that awaiting him there are, again, suffering and death.[50] Once he arrives in Jerusalem, Jesus takes possession of the temple and teaches the people but also clashes with the religious authorities and their confederates (19:45—20:40). Hostile in tone, these controversies prepare the way for the events surrounding Jesus' passion, the tearing of the temple curtain, and Jesus' death (22:1—23:49). Not uncharacteristically, in the last scene in Luke's gospel story in which the religious authorities appear, they mock the crucified Jesus and thus attest graphically to Jerusalem's repudiation of him (23:35).

At the close of Luke's gospel story, Jerusalem suddenly sheds its negative image and becomes, from the vantage point of the "time of the church," the place from which the apostolic proclamation concerning repentance and salvation will go out to the nations. In programmatic fashion, Luke twice sounds this theme (24:47; Acts 1:8). In one of the last scenes of the gospel story, the risen Jesus himself, in a word to the disciples, puts it this way: "Thus it is written . . . that repentance for the forgiveness of sins should be proclaimed to all nations, beginning from Jerusalem" (24:46-47).

Social Settings

Far more extensively than either Mark or Matthew, Luke makes use of social circumstances to create settings for episodes in the life of Jesus. "Jesus at meal," for example, is a characteristic feature of Luke's gospel story. And although "Jesus at prayer" does not in itself constitute a setting, in several instances it serves as the backdrop against which subsequent action takes place.

Five times for certain Luke fashions "type-scenes" in which "Jesus is at meal."[51] These five type-scenes, in turn, can be divided into two groups of two and three scenes each. Typical of each group is the same set of features. In the one group,[52] Jesus is at meal with toll collectors and sinners; provoked by this, the Pharisees and the scribes grumble against him; in response, Jesus silences them with a retort or with parables. In the other group,[53] Jesus is at meal in the home of some Pharisee who is his host; either before or during the meal, something occurs that sparks controversy; turning the controversy to advantage, Jesus criticizes the attitudes or behavior of either the host or all the invited Pharisees and lawyers. As is apparent, one purpose for which Luke uses the social setting of "Jesus at meal" is to describe the ongoing conflict in which Jesus becomes embroiled with the Pharisees and the scribes (lawyers).

The quasi-social setting of "Jesus at prayer"[54] is also a characteristic feature of Luke's gospel story. As God's supreme agent, Jesus is sustained and directed by none but God. So as to commune with God, Jesus, immediately prior to (or during) crucial events, prays to God: before he receives the Spirit at his baptism (3:21); before his first series of controversies with the religious authorities (5:16); before he chooses the twelve apostles (6:12); before Peter confesses him to be God's Messiah (9:18); at his transfiguration (9:29); before he teaches the disciples the Lord's Prayer (11:1); atop the Mount of Olives before his passion (22:41); as he hangs on the cross (23:34); and immediately before he dies (23:46).[55] The upshot is that the picture of "Jesus at prayer" calls attention to both God and Jesus: to God, because in guiding the course of Jesus' ministry God guides the history of salvation; and to Jesus, because in submitting to God's guidance, he attests to his utter dependence upon God and perfect obedience to him.[56] In relation to the disciples, Jesus, the master who prays, becomes both the teacher who instructs them in prayer and the exemplar they are to emulate (11:1-13). As a quasi-social setting, therefore, "Jesus at prayer" connotes that God is actively at work in Jesus (and his followers) to achieve his salvation-historical purposes.

CHARACTERS

A third prominent feature of Luke's gospel story is the persons or groups of persons who inhabit the story world. Characterization is the art of bringing these persons or groups to life.[57] Alternative methods for bringing them to life are "showing" and "telling." In "showing," the author simply presents these persons as acting or talking; this leaves it to the reader to infer the traits that constitute their character. In "telling," the narrator (or one of the characters) describes these persons; this usually results in the explicit identification of certain of their character traits (e.g., Luke pointedly states that Zechariah and Elizabeth are both "righteous" [1:6]). In Luke's gospel story, both methods are used, but "showing" is preferred to "telling."

Luke's gospel story is rich in characters. The major characters are Jesus, the religious authorities, the apostles and disciples, and the crowds, or the people. Minor characters of importance are the righteous and devout in the infancy narrative, those living on the margins of society to whom Jesus ministers and who exhibit faith in him, and those during the passion who do not distance themselves from Jesus but serve or acclaim him. Still other characters who stand out are John the Baptist, Pilate, and Herod Antipas, but discussion of them can await the next chapter, where we take up Luke's story of Jesus. Finally, one also encounters transcendent beings in Luke's gospel story, such as God, angels, Satan, and demons, and the figure of the narrator. Strictly speaking, neither God nor the narrator can be said to be characters, and while Satan is alluded and referred to, in only one episode (the temptation) does he assume the more normal role of a character. Still, because of the enormous influence that the narrator, God, and Satan have on Luke's gospel story, we shall discuss them in this section without, strictly speaking, attempting to do a character study of them. Arbitrarily perhaps, the "humans" in Luke's gospel story are the ones we shall be concerned to characterize.

The Narrator

Most scholars believe that the real author of Luke-Acts was an anonymous Christian living toward the end of the first century A.D.[58] To all intents and purposes, this real author is not known to us except through the documents he or she has written. The real author as inferred from Luke-Acts, therefore, may be called the implied author. The narrator, in turn, is the voice telling the reader or hearer the story of Luke-Acts. Since this voice never misleads the reader or hearer, the narrator can be described as reliable.[59] Also, because the narrator is, in effect, merely the reliable voice of the implied author, we may, with few exceptions, refer to both "reliable voice" and "implied author" simply as Luke.

The "place" where the implied author and narrator situate themselves within the story world of Luke-Acts is beyond the end of Acts in the time between Paul's ministry in Rome and the Parousia of the exalted Jesus (1:1-4). From this "place of narration," the implied author looks back over the history of the early church and of Jesus and has the narrator tell the story of Jesus in past time (e.g., "Now it happened when all the people had been baptized and when Jesus had been baptized and was praying, the heaven was opened and the Spirit descended" [3:21-22]). As the narrator tells Jesus' story, he shows himself to be "omniscient," "intrusive," and, because he is reliable, "authoritative." Thus, the narrator is omniscient, for he

> knows everything that needs to be known about the agents and events; . . . he is free to move as he will in time and place, and to shift from character to character, reporting (or concealing) what he chooses of their speech and actions; and . . . he has privileged access to a character's thoughts and feelings and motives, as well as to his overt speech and actions.[60]

And the narrator is intrusive, for he not only reports on characters but also passes judgment on them, evaluating their actions and motives.[61]

Of particular importance is the relationship that Luke as implied author establishes between the narrator, the voice telling the story, and Jesus, the protagonist. A good gauge of this relationship is the way the narrator himself makes use of the name "Jesus" and the title "Lord." Although the name "Jesus" occurs approximately eighty-eight times in Luke's gospel story, only eight times is it uttered by any being or character other than the narrator himself.[62] By thus reserving the use of Jesus' name for himself, the narrator effectively aligns himself with Jesus. This alignment is at once temporal and spatial and ideological, or theological. By continually using Jesus' name, the narrator sees to it that Jesus remains the focus of attention throughout the story. By continually casting Jesus in a favorable light, the narrator effectively insinuates that Jesus is always to be thought of as virtuous, truthful, and right.

A glance at the narrator's peculiar use of the title "Lord" leads to similar conclusions. Fourteen times the narrator, as opposed to any character within the gospel story, speaks of God as "Lord," but never after 5:17.[63] Similarly, the narrator refers fourteen times to Jesus as "the Lord," but only following chapter 5.[64] Consequently, by first stressing at the beginning of his story that "God is Lord" and then subsequently calling Jesus "the Lord," the narrator shows that he himself looks upon Jesus as that unique individual through whom God exercises his divine authority. In Luke's gospel story, then, the narrator, who is authoritative, also views Jesus as authoritative. This, too, indicates that in Luke, as in Mark and Matthew as well, the narrator invites the reader to regard him as firmly aligned with Jesus.

God

Although the world of Luke's gospel story encompasses heaven, earth, and Hades, earth is the place where Luke's story of Jesus unfolds. Because the reader is given glimpses but no vision of heaven, the abode of God, God himself does not come into view. Narratively, therefore, God is not to be counted as one of the characters of Luke's gospel story.

From another perspective, however, God is the chief "actor" throughout the whole of Luke's double work. The very name "God" (*theos*) occurs far more frequently than even the name "Jesus," approximately 122 times in Luke and 166 times in Acts. As the creator of the universe and the ruler of nations,[65] God guides the history of Israel, of Jesus, and of the church. Although God himself may be hidden from view, Luke's entire story is suffused with signs of his presence and guidance. It is these signs and their meaning that we shall now consider.

Luke never tires of stressing in the Gospel and Acts that the life of Jesus and the history of the church do not unfold haphazardly but in line with God's plan of salvation as set forth in the scriptures (e.g., 24:44-45). Indeed, both "objectively" and "subjectively" Luke drives this conviction home. Objectively, Luke has the narrator or characters attest directly to God's guidance of events: by speaking of God's "purpose"[66] or "will,"[67] or of the things God "determines"[68] or "predestines,"[69] or of the persons God "appoints"[70] or "chooses beforehand."[71] Such direct testimony to God's plan of salvation is captured well by Peter's declaration at Pentecost: "This Jesus, delivered up according to the definite plan and foreknowledge of God, you crucified . . . but God raised" (Acts 2:23-24).

Subjectively, Luke underscores the conviction that the way of Jesus and the church has been ordained of God by showing that Jesus, for example, is fully aware of being guided by God. In this connection, Luke's use of the Greek verbs *dei* ("it is necessary") and *apostellein* ("to send") is revealing. The expression "it is necessary" refers to "divine necessity." It occurs eighteen times in Luke's Gospel alone, and fifteen times in the mouth of Jesus. Twelve times Jesus uses it to express his recognition that a divine plan governs his life and destiny. Similarly, Jesus five times uses the verb "send" in some such expression as "I have been sent" or "he has sent me."[72] In each case, Jesus' intent is to affirm his personal awareness that he discharges his ministry as the unique agent of God serving the purposes of God.

In Luke's gospel story, the signs that God is present and at work to carry out his plan of salvation revolve around Jesus. Understandably, they also occur in conjunction with events relating to John the Baptist and the disciples, for John is Jesus' precursor and the disciples are intimately associated with him. Be that as it may, the signs of God's activity or presence in Luke's gospel story abound: Angels from heaven suddenly appear;[73] Zechariah and the women are the recipients of visions;[74] the Spirit of prophecy fills Elizabeth, Zechariah, and Simeon;[75] the neighbors and relatives of Zechariah recognize that the "hand of the Lord" is with John (1:57-66); the word of God impels John to begin his ministry (3:2); heaven opens and the Spirit descends in bodily form upon Jesus (3:21-22); twice God's voice sounds from above (3:22; 9:35); Jesus is led by the Spirit in the desert and into Galilee (4:1, 14); Jesus announces his anointment with God's Spirit (4:18); Jesus teaches with divine authority (4:32); with divine authority Jesus heals (5:17), exorcises demons (4:36), raises the dead (7:16), rebukes wind and wave (8:24-25), and multiplies loaves and fishes (9:16-17); individuals or the crowd sense God's presence in Jesus' mighty acts and praise or glorify God;[76] Jesus is transfigured and Moses and Elijah appear with him in splendor (9:29-31); the disciples preach and heal and demons are subject to them (10:17); darkness and the tearing of the temple curtain attend Jesus' death (23:44-45); Jesus' death incites the centurion to glorify God (23:47); the women enter Jesus' tomb but find it empty and are told God has raised him (24:3, 7); and Jesus' resurrection appearances and ascension into heaven are themselves numinous events (24:13-53).

Why should Luke wish to surround Jesus with such a plethora of signs pointing heavenward to God? Luke's aim is to show that

Jesus himself is the "sign" of God par excellence (11:30).[77] To know God, one must see Jesus. It is as Jesus himself declares: "All things have been delivered to me by my Father; and no one knows . . . who the Father is except the Son and any one to whom the Son chooses to reveal him" (10:22). In Jesus, God is in the midst of Israel proffering peace and salvation (2:30-32).

This brings us to yet another point that is crucial for understanding Luke's gospel story. The authoritative narrator, we said, regards Jesus as authoritative and aligns himself with him. For his part, Jesus is the "sign" of God. In Jesus, God himself is at work to accomplish his plan of salvation. According to Luke's conception of reality, therefore, God is viewed as the supreme arbiter of what is good or bad, right or wrong, true or false. Correlatively, since God makes himself present in Jesus, Jesus becomes the measuring rod against which all other characters are to be judged. Those who align themselves with Jesus "serve the purposes of God" (16:15; Acts 13:36). Those who refuse to align themselves with Jesus "reject the purposes of God" (7:30) and "serve the purposes of humans" (Acts 5:38-39). Consequently, whether one "serves the purposes of God or of humans" becomes the norm in Luke's story for evaluating character.

Satan

Although Satan[78] is, like God, a transcendent being, unlike God he does not remain beyond narrative sight but functions in part as one of the characters within Luke's story (4:1-13). On Luke's view, Satan (or "the devil," or "Beelzebul") is the cosmic personification of evil. He is Jesus' arch-adversary, the Enemy (10:19). Like Jesus, Satan, too, exercises authority, for he has a kingdom (11:18) and demons and magicians who do his bidding.[79] As the enemy of humans, one of the most visible ways in which Satan oppresses people is by afflicting them with sickness and disease.[80] From the standpoint of faith in Christ, all people, both Jews and gentiles, who do not know Jesus as Lord can be said to live under the power of Satan (Acts 26:15-18).

As the arch-adversary of Jesus, Satan confronts Jesus and puts him to the test before he has even begun his ministry (4:1-13). Satan's aim is to frustrate God's plan of salvation at the outset by enticing Jesus to break faith with God.[81] Jesus, however, withstands Satan (4:13), and though he must struggle with evil his entire ministry (22:28), he nonetheless plunders Satan's kingdom by healing and casting out demons.[82] In his final assault against Jesus during the passion, Satan allies himself with the religious authorities (22:53) and takes possession of Judas, leading him to betray Jesus (22:3-6). Satan also wants to take control of Simon Peter (and the other disciples), but Jesus, by petitioning God on Simon's behalf, thwarts this (22:31-32). Indeed, Jesus exhorts all the apostles to pray in order that they may not fall into Satan's clutches (22:40, 46). Satan is a constant threat, for if he were to have his way, the word of God would be heard by no one and no one would come to faith and be saved (8:12). Still, for all his power Satan is no match for Jesus, and even the disciples, when acting in his name and on his authority, are stronger than Satan (10:17-19; 11:20-23).

Jesus

Jesus is the protagonist in Luke's gospel story. Although conceived by the Holy Spirit, he is not presented as a demigod but as a human being. Unswervingly, Jesus "serves the purposes not of humans, but of God." The upshot is that he views reality—what is good or bad, right or wrong, true or false—the way God does. Jesus' judgments, therefore, constitute the "norms of approval": Whatever Jesus favors or disfavors, the reader is invited to favor or disfavor. Because Jesus is the supreme agent of God,[83] he is the one who influences most the course of events in Luke's gospel story.

At various stages of Jesus' life and career, Luke shows that he exhibits a profound awareness of the unique role he will play in the history of salvation. Already as a twelve-year-old visitor to the temple, Jesus reveals that he understands God to be his Father, himself to be the Son and Servant of God, and his life's path to be governed by divine necessity (2:43, 49). And at the beginning and end of his ministry, Jesus publicly points to himself, respectively, as Messiah (4:18) and Son of God (20:13).

Notwithstanding these incidents, Jesus is understood by characters in Luke's gospel story in vastly different ways. Before he is born, the angel Gabriel announces to Mary that he will be David's scion and Israel's King, God's royal Son (1:32-35). Elizabeth and Zechariah, filled with the Holy Spirit, attest to the unborn Jesus as being "my Lord" (1:43) or David's greater Son (1:69). The angel of the Lord, appearing to shepherds, extols the newborn Jesus as the "Savior," who is "Messiah" and "Lord" (2:11). The narrator reports that Simeon recognizes the infant Jesus to be God's "Messiah" (2:26) and that Anna sees in him Jerusalem's liberator (2:38). As an adult, John the Baptist refers to Jesus as the "Coming, mightier One" (3:16;

7:19). Twice during Jesus' ministry, God speaks from above to acclaim Jesus as "my Son" (3:22; 9:35). The devil, too, knows Jesus to be the "Son of God" (4:3, 9). The worshipers in the synagogue at Nazareth, anticipating an answer in the affirmative, ask if Jesus is not the "son of Joseph" (4:22). Like the devil, demons, too, know Jesus to be the "Son of God" (4:41; 8:28). The crowd, or public, thinks of Jesus as a "prophet": John the Baptist, Elijah, or one of the ancient prophets (7:16; 9:18-19). Some of the crowd, however, consider Jesus to be the agent of Beelzebul, or Satan (11:14-15). On behalf of the disciples, Peter confesses Jesus to be the "Messiah of God" (9:20). Wishing to have his sight restored, the blind beggar near Jericho calls upon Jesus as the "Son of David" (18:38-39). At Jesus' entry into Jerusalem, the multitude of Jesus' disciples hail him as "King" (19:38). Before Pilate and at the cross, the religious leaders reveal that they hold Jesus to be a false messiah, or king (23:2, 35). The repentant criminal on the cross appeals to Jesus in true faith as King (23:42). Discussing the events surrounding Jesus' death, the two disciples on the road to Emmaus speak of Jesus as a "prophet" mighty in deed and word (24:19). And the eleven apostles and those about them, comprehending at last that Jesus has in fact been raised, refer to the risen Jesus as "the Lord" (24:34).

Bewildering at first glance, this remarkable assemblage of views regarding Jesus' identity is not without pattern and purpose. If one examines these views, several things about the Lukan Jesus become clear. For example, those humans in the beginning of Luke's story to whom Jesus' identity or mission is revealed—Mary, Elizabeth, Zechariah, the shepherds, Simeon, and Anna—are all exemplary persons, to wit: They are all righteous or lowly, and they receive Jesus with joy and heartfelt gratitude toward God. As such, the purpose they serve is to allow Luke to inform the reader of who Jesus is, what he will accomplish, and how God would have humans receive him.

Once the middle of Luke's gospel story begins with John and Jesus as adults (3:1-2), the situation changes appreciably. Except for Mary, who in any event keeps "all these things" stored in her heart (2:19, 51), these exemplary persons and the divine revelation they receive disappear from the story. In the way Jesus' identity is henceforth understood, Luke distinguishes sharply between supernatural beings and humans. On the one hand, supernatural beings, such as God, Satan, and demons, know as a matter of course that Jesus is the Son of God. On the other hand, humans exhibit a wide variety of perceptions of Jesus. These perceptions range from

Peter's confession that Jesus is "God's Messiah" to the claim of the religious authorities that Jesus is a "false messiah." Accordingly, despite Jesus' public presentation of himself in Nazareth as the Messiah, his identity and therefore also his mission are by no means apparent to persons in Israel. However extraordinary Jesus is, humans confront him as a controversial figure who impels them to decision: Is he or is he not the Messiah in whom God proffers salvation? For humans, Jesus creates division, just as Simeon prophesied: "Behold, this child is set for the fall and rising of many in Israel!" (2:34).

The character traits Jesus exhibits in Luke's gospel story come to light through what he himself says or does or through what the narrator or others say of him. Although these traits are numerous, Luke, like Mark and Matthew, derives them all from a single root trait: that Jesus is "uniquely related" to God. Apart from Jesus' unique relationship with God, neither his identity nor his destiny is, finally, comprehensible. Thus, Jesus is Messiah, Son of God, Lord, and Savior. As the one conceived by a creative act of God's Spirit, anointed with God's Spirit, and entrusted by God with end-time rule, Jesus is the Messiah, the Son of God.[84] As the Messiah Son of God through whom God exercises his rule and proffers Israel salvation, Jesus is also Lord and Savior. As Messiah, Son of God, Lord, and Savior, Jesus is God's supreme agent in the history of salvation, the one in whom God accomplishes salvation. Jesus' identity and destiny are grounded in his unique relationship with God.

Luke as narrator does not specify Jesus' character traits so much as leave the reader to infer them. Nevertheless, as the one "uniquely related" to God, Jesus exhibits such traits as the following: (a) In terms of his ministry, Jesus is "authoritative" in word and deed.[85] Empowered by the Spirit and impelled by divine necessity (God's plan of salvation), Jesus resists Satan, presents himself to Israel as God's Messiah, teaches, preaches, heals, exorcises demons, calls disciples, ministers to the socially disadvantaged, journeys to Jerusalem, clashes with his opponents, suffers and dies, is raised, appears to his disciples, and ascends to heaven. In Jesus, God reaches out to Israel and accomplishes universal salvation. (b) Toward God, Jesus is "obedient." Full of the Spirit and of one will with God, Jesus loves God more than self (4:3-4), worldly power and glory (4:5-9), or even his own life (23:46-47). Jesus is the quintessential "Servant" of God and "Righteous One."[86] (c) Within himself, Jesus is "whole," or "sound." Just as a "tree is known by its fruit," so Jesus is a model of integrity, and no discrepancy exists between what he says and what he does. Jesus teaches the disciples to pray, forgive, renounce possessions, and take up their cross, and he himself prays, forgives, surrenders his possessions, and endures the cross.[87] (d) Toward the disciples, Jesus is "enabling," "exemplary," and "faithful." Jesus is "enabling," for he commissions disciples to ministry (5:1-11), summons them to come after him,[88] gathers them into community,[89] and empowers them for ministry first in Israel[90] and then among all nations (24:44-49).[91] Jesus is also "exemplary," for he holds himself up as the one the disciples are to emulate (6:40). And Jesus is "faithful," for following his resurrection he renews table fellowship with the disciples (24:28-31), guides the apostles and other disciples to spiritual maturity by enlightening them about God's plan of salvation in him (24:25-27, 44-47), and commissions the disciples, as his witnesses, to a ministry proclaiming repentance and forgiveness to all the nations (24:44-49). (e) Toward persons living on the margins of society, Jesus is "compassionate." Jesus pronounces blessings on disciples who are poor, hungry, sorrowful, and excluded (6:20-23). Jesus has table fellowship with toll collectors and sinners, in this way gracing them with his presence and granting them the forgiveness of sins (5:29-32). Jesus forgives, heals, or raises to life, respectively, the sinful woman (7:36-50), the woman with a hemorrhage (8:42-48), the stooped woman (13:10-17), and the widow's dead son (7:11-17). Jesus grants the centurion, a gentile, the plea he makes through intermediaries that his slave be healed (7:2-10). Jesus overrides the objections of the disciples and receives the infants brought to him for touching, or blessing (18:15-17). And Jesus opens paradise to the repentant criminal who is crucified with him (23:40-43). (f) Toward the Jewish people, or crowd, Jesus is "solicitous" and "compassionate" but also "confrontational." On the one hand, Jesus is "solicitous" and "compassionate," for he welcomes the people as they come to him (9:11), permits them to gather round him and follow him,[92] teaches them,[93] tells them parables,[94] heals their sick and possessed,[95] feeds them (9:12-17), and above all summons them to become his disciples.[96] On the other hand, Jesus is "confrontational," for he would summon the people to repentance.[97] In line with this, he chastises some or all of them as an evil generation,[98] as falsely attributing his authority to Satan (11:15), as sign-seeking (11:16), as hypocritical (12:54-56), and, sadly, as those who will be overtaken by the "wrath" of Jerusalem's destruction (21:23; 23:27-31). (g) Toward the religious authorities, Jesus is "open," sharply "confrontational," and "forgiving." Jesus is "open" toward the authorities, for he remains in conversation with them throughout his public ministry, accepts invitations from individual Pharisees to dine at their home,[99] befriends certain elders on one occasion (7:3-6a), and, on another, is warned by Pharisees about Herod Antipas's desire to kill him (13:31). In the main, however, Jesus is "confrontational" in dealing with the authorities. Throughout his ministry, he clashes with them, for they do not understand that in him a new time has dawned and God is reaching out to summon Israel to repentance and salvation. Still, in one of his last acts before dying, Jesus is "forgiving" toward the authorities. In the first of three final utterances, Jesus calls on God to release his opponents from the guilt they have incurred in bringing him to the cross (23:34). (h) And with regard to his death, Jesus stands out as one who "serves." As God's supreme agent of salvation, Jesus knows that death is his destiny and that, in shedding his blood, he will establish a new covenant in which he will preside in the power of the Spirit over the reconstituted people of God who will bear witness of him to Israel and the nations.[100]

Disciples

Though a group, the disciples play a consistent, identifiable role throughout Luke's gospel story and hence may be treated as a single character. Unlike Jesus, who perfectly "serves the purposes of God," the disciples exhibit conflicting traits. While they do not fall away from Jesus as in Mark and Matthew, they nonetheless falter at times and "serve the purposes not of God, but of humans." As followers of Jesus, the disciples exert little influence on the story's plot, or flow of events. In the unfolding of their story line, Luke's predilection is for the twelve even though he also refers to larger or smaller groups of disciples or to individual disciples.[101] This is evident from two observations: First, Luke shows at times that, in using the broader term "disciples," he envisages specifically the twelve.[102] And second, Luke identifies the twelve as "the apostles" (6:13). As the apostles, the twelve constitute a "bridge" to Acts and comprise the leadership of the Christian community that forms in Jerusalem following Jesus' ascension and Pentecost (Acts 1:13, 21-26).

Jesus, himself recognized by his speech as a "Galilean" (23:6), gathers his disciples in Galilee so that they, too, are colloquially referred to as "Galileans."[103] Because the disciples follow Jesus, the character traits they exhibit come to light primarily through their interaction with him. Only on occasion, in fact, do they interact with other characters. In principle, the disciples exhibit two chief traits: On the one hand, they are "loyal," for they hold to Jesus throughout his ministry and not even during his passion do they forsake him. On the other hand, they are "spiritually immature," for they do not comprehend the plan of salvation God accomplishes in him. In particular, they demonstrate no ability whatever to grasp the divine necessity of his suffering and death (9:44-45; 18:31-34).

The disciples first appear in Luke's gospel story in the long middle section (3:1—21:38). Throughout this section, the picture the reader gets of them, in terms of the features that both appeal and repel, is relatively uniform. Fundamentally, Luke portrays the disciples as, again, "loyal" to Jesus: In leaving behind everything to follow him, they pledge to him their allegiance and enter on a new "way."[104] As those loyal to Jesus, the disciples are furthermore "observant," "called to mission," "authoritative," "safeguarded," "enlightened," "obedient," "supportive," and "vulnerable."

Thus, the disciples are "observant," for they are eye- and ear-witnesses of Jesus' words and deeds and summoned to let their lives be shaped by what they see and hear.[105] The disciples are "called to mission" (5:10), "authoritative," and "safeguarded," for Jesus empowers them, dispatches them on missions to Israel, and assures them of divine protection.[106] The disciples are "enlightened," for they are the recipients of divine revelation (10:21-24) and the mysteries of the kingdom (8:10). The disciples are "obedient," for when Jesus commands, they comply.[107] The disciples are "supportive," for on occasions of controversy they stand at Jesus' side. By the same token, the disciples are also "vulnerable," for by being Jesus' followers they, too, incur the displeasure of his opponents.[108]

Though fundamentally loyal to Jesus, the disciples are prone to "spiritual immaturity," for they do not comprehend the divine plan God fulfills in Jesus. Accordingly, not all the traits they exhibit in the middle of Luke's gospel story are flattering. On the contrary, the disciples—whether one or some or all—prove themselves on occasion to be "fearful," "impertinent," inexplicably "perplexed," "dull," "ineffectual" at healing, "status-conscious," "exclusive," "vindictive," given to expressions of "misplaced joy," and "anxious about the future." Without question, however, the gravest failing of the disciples is that they are "without understanding" relative to Jesus' passion.

To illustrate, although Jesus repeatedly tells the disciples about his passion, his predictions are nonetheless hid from them and they receive them "without understanding" (9:44-45; 18:31-34). Caught in a storm out on the lake, the disciples do not persevere in faith but instead lose courage and become "fearful" (8:22-25). Unaware that a woman in the crowd has touched Jesus' garment and been healed, Peter becomes "impertinent" and chides Jesus for asking who touched him (8:42-48). Upon returning from a mission in Israel having just been endowed with power and authority (9:1-10), the disciples become inexplicably "perplexed" at Jesus' challenge that they feed the crowd in the desert (9:12-13). Made "dull" by heavy sleep, Peter, John, and James experience only part of the revelation atop the mount of transfiguration and Peter talks nonsense (9:32-33). When Jesus and the three descend from the mountain and join the nine disciples below, Jesus discovers that the nine, by not availing themselves of the power given them, were "ineffectual" at trying to heal a boy possessed by a demon (9:37-43). Twice, in arguing over which of them would be greatest and in refusing children access to Jesus, the disciples show themselves to be "status-conscious" (9:46-48; 18:15-17). When John tells Jesus that the disciples tried to prevent a "friendly exorcist" from casting out demons in Jesus' name, Jesus reprimands the disciples for wanting to be "exclusive" in their dealings with the man (9:49-50). As James and John ask Jesus for permission to call down fire from heaven to consume the Samaritans who refuse Jesus entry into their village, Jesus rebukes the two disciples for being "vindictive" (9:51-56). As the seventy-two rejoice over their power to subdue demons, Jesus cautions them that such joy is "misplaced" and that they ought rather rejoice because their names are written in the book of life (10:17-20). And in reminding Jesus that they have left all to follow him, Peter in effect expresses the disciples' desire that Jesus assuage their "anxiety about the future" by telling them what is in store for them (18:28-30).

As one moves from the middle to the end of Luke's gospel story (chaps. 22–24), the consequences of the disciples' spiritual immaturity and inability to comprehend God's divine plan become more grievous. True, except for Judas the disciples remain with Jesus "in his trials" (22:28-30). And they are also not without other positive qualities, to wit: The disciples continue to be "obedient" (22:7-13), and when Jesus announces that one who is at table with him will betray him (22:21-23), they all appear to be genuinely "distressed."

In other respects, however, the behavior of the disciples is dismal. Falling under the control of Satan, Judas turns his back on Jesus and becomes "disloyal," hiring himself out to the religious authorities to betray him (22:3-5, 47-48). During Jesus' farewell address, the disciples show yet again how "status-conscious" they are, for they fall to quarreling over who among them is greatest (22:24-27). Above all, however, the disciples demonstrate that they are completely "imperceptive" of the true nature of the events in which they are caught up. In a grand gesture of false confidence, Peter stoutly declares that he is ready to accompany Jesus to prison and even death (22:33). When told by Jesus that the time is now ripe for them to equip themselves with purse, knapsack, and sword—symbols that they themselves, like him, must henceforth be prepared to endure persecution—the disciples misunderstand the intent of Jesus' words and suddenly brandish two swords to show that they are ready for battle (22:35-38). At the place of prayer on the Mount of Olives, the disciples "sleep for grief," a sign that underneath they are "cowardly" instead of courageous (22:45-46).[109] And at Jesus' arrest, the two disciples with the swords only attest further to the incomprehension of all as they ask Jesus whether they should strike with their swords, and one of them, with a swing, severs the right ear of the high priest's slave (22:49-51).

The end result of the disciples' spiritual immaturity and attendant incomprehension is that Judas betrays Jesus (thereby becoming "apostate" and meeting with a sudden death [22:47-48; Acts 1:18]), Peter turns "deceitful" and denies him (22:54-62), and they all watch Jesus' crucifixion in safety "from afar" (23:49). Also, come Easter Sunday the apostles and the disciples with them greet with deaf ears and closed minds the news that Jesus lives. When the women disciples report that Jesus has been raised, the apostles dismiss their words as nonsense (24:1-11). And when Jesus appears in the midst of the apostles and other disciples, the latter still "disbelieve for joy" and think they see a ghost (24:36-43). Indeed, not until the risen Jesus himself enlightens the disciples about the plan of salvation God has accomplished in him do they finally attain to spiritual maturity (24:25-27, 44-46, 50-53).

Religious Authorities

The antagonists in Luke's gospel story are the religious authorities. They, together with the people, constitute Israel. On the human level, the authorities are second only to Jesus as the ones who influence most the plot of the story. Those comprising the authorities are the Pharisees, scribes (lawyers, teachers of the law), chief priests, captains (officers) of the temple,[110] elders, rulers, and Sadducees. Historically, these groups were not homogeneous but highly diverse, and the lines dividing them were hereditary, political, economic, religious, or professional in nature.[111] Still, within Luke's story world these several groups, like the disciples, also stand out as a group character. This is apparent from two observations: First, Luke clearly distinguishes these groups from the Jewish people on the one hand and from Jesus, the disciples, and other minor characters on the other. And second, the role Luke attributes to them in his gospel story is distinct: They are the stereotypical opponents of Jesus, those with whom he becomes locked in controversy and who see to it that he is put to death.

Until Jesus arrives in Jerusalem, he has to do mainly with the Pharisees, but also with scribes (teachers of the law, lawyers), elders, and two rulers of a synagogue. In Jerusalem, Jesus has to do mainly with the chief priests, but also with scribes, elders, rulers, Sadducees, and the temple officers. Although the Pharisees tend to fade from view once Jesus arrives in Jerusalem and hence are not explicitly named as having a hand in bringing him to the cross, it is erroneous to think that Luke is thereby exculpating them from guilt for Jesus' death or picturing them as less opposed to him than the other groups.[112] Against this notion stand several considerations. In the first place, one must not overlook the obvious, namely, that Luke does associate Pharisees with Jerusalem: On the occasion of Jesus' first encounter with the religious authorities in Galilee, Luke remarks that Pharisees have come also from Jerusalem to hear Jesus teach (5:17); and as Jesus is about to enter Jerusalem toward the end of his ministry and his disciples hail him as King, Luke notes that it is the Pharisees who take exception to this and call upon Jesus to silence his disciples (19:39). Second and more importantly, by making the scribes the major partners of the Pharisees[113] on the one hand and of the chief priests[114] on the other, Luke utilizes the device of "guilt by association" to show that the Pharisees are no different in kind than the chief priests. Third, three times Luke indicates that he regards scribes as Pharisaic in orientation (5:30; Acts 5:34; 23:9). This means that Pharisaic hostility against Jesus is not absent during the passion but comes to expression through the actions of the scribes. And last, Luke makes it clear in Acts that all the leaders of the Jews, and consequently also the Pharisees, are understood by him to have made themselves guilty of the death of Jesus (Acts 3:17; 13:27).

Since the religious authorities are the antagonists and Jesus is the protagonist, the primary way the authorities disclose the character traits they possess is through their interaction with Jesus. Secondarily, the reader also learns to know them by observing how they interact with other characters, such as the disciples and the people, and by attending to the comments that Luke as narrator makes about them. Except for the teachers with whom the twelve-year-old Jesus converses in the temple (2:46), the authorities do not make their appearance in the gospel story until the middle section (3:1—21:38). Within the story, they are Israel's "leaders,"[115] the custodians of law, traditional values, and temple cult. Because Luke's characterization of them is on the whole polemical, the reader, apart from certain notable exceptions, is invited to distance himself or herself from them. In contrast to Jesus, who always "serves the purposes of God," the authorities are disposed to "serve the purposes of humans." Indeed, most of the traits they exhibit seem to be manifestations of one chief trait, to wit: They are "self-righteous."[116]

To ascertain Luke's notion of self-righteousness, the place to begin is with his narrative comment at 7:30: Looking back upon the ministry of John, Luke declares with an eye to the Pharisees and the scribes (lawyers) that because they refused to submit to John's baptism, they "rejected the purpose of God for themselves." By refusing John's baptism, the religious authorities affirmed in effect that they had no need of repentance and forgiveness (15:7). The reason they had no such need is that, as they see themselves, they are already righteous (5:32; 18:9). Still, because John discharged his ministry on the authority of God, to reject John's baptism was to reject God. Ironically, therefore, the authorities, although they believe that they stand in a right relationship with God, in reality stand in a wrong relationship with him. In a word, therefore, to be self-righteous is to stand in a wrong relationship with God (18:9-14).

The ultimate consequences of being self-righteous are fatal. In Luke's story world, to stand in a wrong relationship with God is to be a servant of Satan and incapable of perceiving reality from God's point of view. In the temptation episode, Satan shows Jesus all the kingdoms of the world and says to him: "To you I will give all this authority and their glory . . . if you will worship me" (4:5-7). The force of this particular scene is that Satan entices Jesus to break faith with God and to become his servant by offering Jesus the greatest gift of "mammon" imaginable: control over the substance of the entire world. At 16:13-14, Luke juxtaposes his own remark that the Pharisees are "lovers of money" to Jesus' remark that one "cannot serve God and mammon." As Luke sees it, therefore, the Pharisees, as lovers of money, are servants of mammon, and this, in turn, is tantamount to being servants of Satan. Necessarily, those who serve Satan are incapable of perceiving reality from God's point of view. On the contrary, they perceive reality from a human point of view (16:15). Still, to perceive reality in this mode is, finally, to be lost, for one is then found to be "opposing God" (Acts 5:38-39).

Related ways of describing the self-righteous are to say that they are "without love of God" and "without true knowledge" of God.[117] In their relationship with God, the Pharisees, for example, have lost sight of what counts most: While they busy themselves tithing the minutest of garden herbs, they neglect ("bypass") the love they are to show God (11:42). In addition, the religious authorities are among the "others" who do not comprehend the secrets of God's kingdom (8:10). The lawyers, for instance, possess the key of knowledge, yet they have not used it to unlock the treasures of God's scriptures (11:52). Similarly, the Pharisees do not understand what it means to lead God-pleasing lives: As "fools," they think that inner wickedness can be masked by outer cleanliness (11:39-40). Worst of all, the authorities do not grasp that, in Jesus, God visits Israel, holding out the gift of peace (19:42, 44; 23:34).

At the beginning, in the middle, and at the end of his gospel story, Luke directs attention to three individuals who function as foils ("contrasts") for the religious authorities: Zechariah, who is a priest (1:5); Jairus, who is a leader of a synagogue (8:41); and Joseph of Arimathea, who is a member of the Sanhedrin but who opposed that body's resolve to have Jesus put to death (23:50-51).[118] These three are foils for the authorities in that the character traits they exhibit are the opposite of the principal trait ascribed to the authorities: Whereas the authorities are "self-righteous," Zechariah is "righteous and blameless" (1:6), Jairus is a man of great "faith" (8:41, 50), and Joseph is "good and righteous" (23:50). In other words, in Zechariah, Jairus, and Joseph, the reader encounters "exemplary authorities," the kind of persons all the religious authorities could have been expected to be but are not. With the coming of Pentecost following Jesus' ascension, Luke shows that Israel will be given a "second chance"[119] to respond to God's offer of salvation and repent. Accordingly, Zechariah, Jairus, and Joseph are the precursors of those authorities in Acts, including the Pharisee Paul, who will accept this offer and become disciples of Jesus (Acts 6:7; 15:5; 26:5).

Thus far, we have focused on the vertical dimension of the authorities' self-righteousness, that it places them in a wrong relationship with God. Beyond this, Luke also stresses that it places them in a wrong relationship with others. Luke himself underscores this point when he remarks prior to Jesus' narration of the parable of the Pharisee and the publican, "He [Jesus] also told this parable to some who trusted in themselves that they were righteous and despised others" (18:9). Toward others, the authorities are "hypocritical" (12:1), and in this connection "avaricious" and "self-important" (16:15), and "unloving" (18:9).

To illustrate, the religious authorities demonstrate that they are elitist and hence "unloving" toward any whom they do not regard as their equals (14:12-14). Simon, the Pharisee, because he does not recognize that he himself is in need of the love of forgiveness, shows love neither toward the sinful woman nor even toward Jesus, his guest (7:36-50). In point of fact, the Pharisees look with contempt on all those living on the margins of society, such as extortioners, the unjust, adulterers, toll collectors, sinners, and the poor.[120] In principle, they elevate rigid adherence to law above human need (6:1-5, 6-11). And by the same token, the lawyers lay heavy burdens of regulations on the people without at the same time teaching them how to cope with these regulations (11:46).

The authorities are also "hypocritical," "avaricious," and "self-important." The Pharisees and the scribes are hypocritical, for their outward appearance does not reflect their inner disposition. In an attack on the Pharisees, Jesus puts it this way: "You are those who justify yourselves before humans, but God knows your hearts" (16:15).[121] Also, part and parcel of Pharisaic hypocrisy is the avarice it breeds. While scrupulously pure on the outside, the Pharisees, Jesus contends, are inwardly full of plunder, or greed (11:39). And the scribes and Pharisees are self-important, for they lay claim to honor that is not their due, exalting themselves over others (11:43; 20:46). Denouncing this, Jesus declares categorically: "For what is exalted among humans is an abomination in the sight of God" (16:15).

As those who are self-righteous and view reality from a human perspective, the religious authorities stand at odds with Jesus, the disciples, and also the people. Prior to the passion, the authorities are for the most part "perplexed" by Jesus.[122] Once he enters Jerusalem and the temple, however, their antipathies harden and they become "inimical" toward him (19:47—21:38). Generally speaking, the authorities' perplexity expresses itself in a dual attitude toward Jesus: They are both "respectful" of him, desiring throughout his public ministry to remain in dialogue with him, and "antagonistic" toward him.

On the one hand, the religious authorities are "respectful" of Jesus and afford him the honor due a "teacher," which is the term by which they address him.[123] Thus, Pharisees and teachers of the law are attracted to Jesus, coming from all over to hear him teach (5:17), and his miraculous power astounds them (5:26). Jewish elders and Jairus, a ruler of a synagogue, appeal to Jesus to heal a centurion's slave or the daughter who has just died (7:3-4; 8:41-42). Pharisees befriend Jesus, warning him of Herod Antipas's intent to kill him (13:31), and show him hospitality by inviting him to their homes to dine.[124] Pharisees and a ruler solicit Jesus' teaching, the former about the coming of God's kingdom (17:20) and the latter on what one must do to inherit eternal life (18:18). And even after Jesus has arrived in Jerusalem and the authorities are looking for a way to destroy him, the Sanhedrist spies are compelled to marvel at the words with which he silences them (20:26) and some of the scribes express their approval of the answer by which he confounds the Sadducees in debate (20:39).

On the other hand, the religious authorities, though respectful of Jesus, nonetheless take offense at him and become "antagonistic" toward him. While Jesus is in Galilee, Pharisees, supported by the scribes, evince their antagonism toward him in numerous ways: They charge Jesus, in forgiving sins, with speaking blasphemies against God (5:21); demand to know why the disciples violate custom and do not fast (5:33-39); watch him closely to see if he will heal on the Sabbath so as to bring charges against him (6:6-10); become filled with fury when he does heal and deliberate on what they might do to him (6:11); and impugn his integrity when he permits a woman known to be a sinner to touch him (7:39).

As Jesus journeys toward Jerusalem, these same authorities or individuals representing them behave toward Jesus much as before: They attempt to put him to the test (10:25); marvel in dismay because he does not first wash before dinner (11:38); begin to resent him terribly, to watch his utterances closely, and to plot so as to catch him in something he might say (11:53-54); become angry because he heals on the Sabbath (13:14); watch him closely to see, again, if he will heal on the Sabbath (14:1-3); grumble against him because he welcomes toll collectors and sinners and eats with them (15:1-2); and ridicule him because of his teaching (16:13-14). Furthermore, twice, first in Galilee and then upon Jesus' entry into Jerusalem, Pharisees contest the way others construe Jesus' identity: They object to both the people's view that Jesus is a "prophet" (7:16, 39) and the disciples' view that he is "King" (19:37-39).

Once Jesus begins his ministry in Jerusalem (19:47—21:38), the antagonism the religious authorities harbor toward him deepens so that they become "inimical" toward him. Here Jesus faces the chief priests in particular, supported by the scribes and other members of the Sanhedrin or ruling class. More intensely than before, the authorities become "conspiratorial," "contentious," "hostile," and "deceitful." Thus, they seek from the outset to destroy him (19:47); engage him in controversy and demand to know on what authority he teaches and preaches in the temple (20:1-8); become so hostile following Jesus' narration of the parable of the vineyard that they want to seize him on the spot and hold back only for fear of the people (20:9-19); endeavor to snare him by deceit, sending spies to catch him in a political misstatement about paying taxes to Caesar (20:20-25); and attempt to get the best of him in controversy concerning resurrection life (20:27-38). Unfortunately for the authorities, Jesus answers his various opponents so well that, at the end, he reduces them all to silence (20:40).

With the onset of the passion (chaps. 22–23), the authorities' antagonism and enmity toward Jesus express themselves in their single-minded desire to kill him (20:40; 22:2). In bringing Jesus to the cross, the authorities show themselves to be "unjust" and, in this connection, "deceitful" and "deluded." The acts of injustice and deceit the authorities perpetrate are such as the following: They resort to betrayal as the means by which to obtain custody of Jesus (22:3-6); ally themselves with Satan (22:53); falsely charge Jesus before both Pilate and Herod Antipas with being a revolutionary (23:2, 5, 10); and call for the release of the insurrectionist and murderer Barabbas and the crucifixion of the innocent Jesus (23:18-25). And the delusion beclouding the authorities' perception of reality leads them both to deny that Jesus is the Messiah, the Son of God (22:66-71), and to mock him as Messiah (23:35; also 22:63-65).

We noted above that the self-righteousness of the religious authorities places them at odds not only with Jesus but also with the disciples and the people. Comparatively, however, Luke focuses so singularly on the authorities' interaction with Jesus that only infrequently does he show them interacting with either the disciples or the people.

Because the disciples are the followers of Jesus, it is scarcely surprising to discover that the authorities relate to them in much the same way as they relate to Jesus, to wit: The authorities are "contentious," accusing the disciples of breaking both law and custom.[125] They are also "guileful," for they take advantage of Judas's offer to betray Jesus (22:4-6). And in the future, they will be "hostile" and subject the disciples to persecution (12:11; 21:12).

Although together the religious authorities and the people make up Israel, Luke is little concerned in his gospel story to provide a sustained narration of how the authorities relate to the people. Nonetheless, Luke does provide the reader with some insight into this relationship, primarily through sayings or parables of Jesus. Fundamentally, Luke depicts the authorities as leaders who are "oppressive": Instead of dispensing justice, they strive to uphold the status quo (5:39; 11:42). As leaders who oppress their people, the authorities exhibit numerous traits, most of which we noted earlier, to wit: They are elitist and "unloving,"[126] "hypocritical,"[127] "avaricious,"[128] and "self-important."[129] Moreover, remiss as leaders, the authorities are "fearful" of the people: During Jesus' ministry in Jerusalem, they are afraid to arrest and kill him owing to his great popularity (20:19; 22:2). On balance, because the authorities have so completely failed as Israel's leaders, the Jewish people will, following Jesus' ascension, be offered new leadership in the persons of the apostles (22:29-30; Acts).

Overall, then, Luke's characterization of the religious authorities in his gospel story tends to be negative and polemical. Chiefly, the authorities are "self-righteous": Although in their own eyes they see themselves as standing in a right relationship with God, in reality they stand in a wrong relationship with both God and neighbor. As persons who are self-righteous, the authorities "serve the purposes not of God, but of humans." In their interaction with Jesus, they are to be sure "respectful," but they also take offense at him, and the dominant tone of their relationship with him is one of "antagonism." Once Jesus begins his ministry in Jerusalem, the authorities conspire to destroy him, and during the passion, they succeed. Toward the disciples and the people, the authorities are, respectively, "hostile" and "oppressive." In the end, the self-righteousness of the authorities and their opposition to Jesus will cost them their place as Israel's leaders and bring punishment upon the nation.

The People

In Luke's gospel story, the Jewish people, too, constitute a group character. As has been noted, they, along with the religious authorities, make up Israel. In the way they relate to Jesus, the people contrast noticeably with both the disciples and the authorities.

In contrast to the authorities, the people do not become Jesus' enemies until his trial before Pilate, and then only briefly (23:[4], 13-25).
In contrast to the disciples, who pledge to Jesus their loyalty and
become his followers, the people make no such commitment to him.

In referring to the Jewish people in his gospel story, Luke
makes copious use of two terms: "crowd" (*ochlos*) and "people" (*laos*).
At times, Luke apparently uses the two terms interchangeably.[130] For
the most part, however, "crowd" is a more vague and general word
and simply denotes a large number of persons. "People," in turn,
possesses a religious coloration and refers to Israel as God's chosen
nation.[131] Where either word refers to the Jewish masses or to Israel,
we shall henceforth simplify matters and speak of the "people."

On the whole, the reader becomes acquainted with the character traits of the people either by observing them interact with Jesus
or by attending to Luke's narrative commentary on them. Episodes
in which the people interact with a character other than Jesus—or
also John—are exceptional (e.g., 1:21-22; 23:13-25). Both before and
after Jesus' trial, Luke urges the reader to look kindly upon the people or indeed to approve of them. In some few places, however,
Luke also pictures John or Jesus as rebuking them, in which case the
reader is invited to distance himself or herself from them. As in
Mark and Matthew, the people in Luke fundamentally exhibit two
contrasting character traits: While they are "well-disposed" toward
Jesus, they are also "without faith" in him.

On the one hand, the people, who were previously well-
disposed toward John,[132] are also "well-disposed" toward Jesus. As
Jesus commences his ministry, his fame spreads far and wide.[133] People flock to him from all over: from Galilee, Judea, Jerusalem, and
even the gentile regions of Tyre and Sidon.[134] As they reach Jesus,
they gather round him,[135] accompany him,[136] and at times press in on
him.[137] So popular is Jesus that he can be in a deserted place and the
people will still search him out (4:42). Once when Jesus travels into
gentile regions, the people wait for him and welcome him back (8:40).
As Jesus tries to withdraw with the apostles to Bethsaida, the people
learn of this and follow him (9:10-11). On occasion, however, Jesus
does manage to escape the people, retiring to some deserted area to
pray (5:16).

What attracts the people to Jesus is his ministry of word and
deed. Having been spiritually renewed through John's ministry,[138]
the people come to Jesus both to hear his message and to be healed
(5:15; 6:18). Accordingly, Jesus teaches the people,[139] preaches his
message of the kingdom,[140] and tells them parables;[141] they, in turn,

are amazed at his words and hang on them.[142] In similar fashion, Jesus heals the sick,[143] exorcises demons,[144] feeds the five thousand (9:12-17), and raises the dead;[145] in response, the people strive to touch him, are astounded at his deeds, and glorify God.[146] Repeatedly, Jesus also summons the people to become his disciples (9:23; 14:25-33).

In being well-disposed toward Jesus, the people stand in stark contrast to their leaders. While this is clear throughout Luke's gospel story, in certain passages, including one that touches on John the Baptist, Luke stresses this point by juxtaposing some attitude the people take toward Jesus with a contrary attitude their leaders take toward him. For example, Luke himself remarks that whereas the Pharisees and the lawyers refuse John's baptism, the people see it as divinely authorized (7:29-30). Similarly, Luke reports that in reaction to Jesus' healing of the woman who was stooped, all the people rejoice, whereas Jesus' opponents are put to shame (13:17). In Jerusalem, at the same time as the chief priests, the scribes, and the principal men conspire to destroy Jesus, all the people are said to hang on his words (19:47-48; 21:38—22:2). And as Jesus is on the cross, the silent "watching" of the people is mentioned side by side with the "ridicule" the leaders shout (23:34-35).

In less striking ways, too, the contrast between the people and their leaders in their attitudes toward Jesus is apparent. Whereas the people think of Jesus as a prophet (9:18-19), the leaders charge him with being a false messiah, or revolutionary (23:2). In fact, until Judas enters the picture, the leaders remain frustrated in their conspiracy to destroy Jesus out of fear of the people.[147] To be sure, at Jesus' trial before Pilate the people do join with their leaders and call for Jesus' crucifixion (23:4, 13-25); and for this they, too, will suffer punishment in the destruction of Jerusalem (23:27-32). Apart from this brief episode, however, the actions of the people before, during, and after Jesus' crucifixion differ noticeably from those of their leaders. Before Jesus' crucifixion, the people follow Jesus in the company of the women who bewail and lament him (23:27). During the crucifixion, they watch the proceedings but do not mock him (23:34). And after Jesus has died, they beat their breasts (23:48), which foreshadows the repentance of large numbers of the people come Pentecost. Perhaps the last passage in the gospel story in which reference is made to the people captures in a nutshell the contrast Luke draws between them and their leaders: In conversing with the risen Jesus before they have recognized who he is, the Emmaus disciples recount that whereas the people looked upon Jesus as a prophet mighty in deed and word, the leaders delivered him up to be condemned to death and crucified (24:19-20).

Well-disposed though the people may be toward Jesus, they are nonetheless "without faith" in him. John prepared the people to receive God's salvation in Jesus, but the villagers of Nazareth reject Jesus' proclamation of himself as Israel's Messiah and attempt to kill him (4:16-30). When Jesus reclines at meal with Zacchaeus, a chief toll collector, it is the people who grumble (19:3, 7). And Jesus, on more than one occasion during his ministry, has words with the people, warning or even censuring them.

For example, as Jesus speaks to the people about John, he cautions them not to become like "those of this generation" who repudiate both John and himself (7:31-35). After an exorcism, Jesus rebukes some of the people for charging that he expels demons on the authority of Satan (11:15) and others of them for putting him to the test by demanding that he prove that God sanctions his actions (11:16). Indeed, this demand for a sign incites Jesus to tell the people that theirs is an "evil generation" that must repent if it is to escape final condemnation (11:29-32). In equally acerbic terms, Jesus calls the people "hypocrites" who know how to read sky and wind to predict the weather but cannot discern that his very presence in Israel qualifies the present as a time of decision for them (12:54-56). Indeed, unless they all repent, Jesus declares, they will perish (13:3, 5). Consequently, Jesus, like John before him (3:6-9), does not hesitate at times to reproach the people because he, too, would impel them to repent. By the same token, Jesus also, as we noted, invites the people to become his disciples (9:23; 14:25-35).

In brief, then, the people in Luke's gospel story exhibit the conflicting traits of being "well-disposed" toward Jesus but also "without faith" in him. Unlike their leaders, they are not the antagonists of Jesus who become his implacable enemies. Unlike the disciples, neither are they the committed followers of Jesus. In Luke's gospel story, Jesus struggles with the people to win their allegiance. Although he loses in this struggle before Pilate, in Acts Luke tells of thousands of the people who repent, believe, and become his followers.

Minor Characters

Besides such major characters as Jesus, the disciples, the religious authorities, and the people, the world of Luke's gospel story is also populated with a large cast of minor characters. Some play highly significant roles and assume the characteristics of real persons. Examples of these are John the Baptist, Mary (Jesus' mother), Herod Antipas, and Pilate. Others, like the child whom Jesus places beside him (9:47) or the poor widow he notices (21:2), appear only briefly and then vanish. Certain of these characters bear names: Mary, Martha, Simon (the Pharisee), and Jairus, for instance. Most, however, do not and are known simply as Simon's "mother-in-law" (4:38), a "centurion" (7:2), a "widow" (7:13), a "certain man casting out demons" (9:49), or even as a "man" (9:38) or a "woman" (11:27). Some of the most memorable figures in Luke's gospel story exist, not as characters in his story world, but as characters in Jesus' parables. Cases in point are the good Samaritan (10:30-37), the rich fool (12:16-21), the prodigal son (15:11-32), the unjust steward (16:1-9), and the poor man Lazarus (16:19-31). In this section, our aim is to call attention to three particular groups of minor characters. Although the role each group plays is significant, it nonetheless needs to be highlighted if it is not to go unnoticed.

The first of these groups of minor characters comprises those figures who are prominent in the infancy narrative: Zechariah, Elizabeth, Mary, Simeon, and Anna (chaps. 1–2). In the best sense of the words, these persons are "pious" and "lowly." As a group, they are significant because they serve as foils ("contrasts") for the religious authorities and the Israelite people whom the reader encounters throughout the rest of Luke's gospel story. As foils for the people, these persons represent the way the former should be but are not. For example, whereas John assails the people coming out to him as being evil ("brood of vipers" [3:7]), these persons are all made out to be "righteous."[148] Whereas the people fail to discern the new time of salvation that God inaugurates in Jesus (12:54-56), these persons indicate in word and deed that they see God at work in Jesus' fulfilling of God's age-old promises to Israel. Whereas the people think of Jesus as at best a prophet and otherwise charge him with being a false messiah, these persons correctly perceive that Jesus is Israel's Messiah-King, Lord and Son of God.[149] And whereas the people respond to Jesus' coming by ultimately putting him to death, these persons hail his coming by joyfully giving praise and thanks to God. In short, these persons are indicators of how the people should relate to Jesus but do not do so.

The significance of the second of these groups is that the characters involved exemplify the "excluded" of Luke's story world, those persons who live on the margins of society.[150] Jesus' ministry to such persons is one of the major themes of Luke's gospel story. In a series of "quest stories,"[151] Luke shows how Jesus effects a reversal of fortunes, or conditions, for a cross section of these persons. They for their part tend to be individuals who are also models of "faith," or "trust," in Jesus' power to forgive, heal, or save.

To illustrate, men of faith bring a paralytic to Jesus, and Jesus both forgives the paralytic his sins and restores him to health (5:17-26). A centurion, who knows that Jews regard contact with gentiles as rendering them unclean, appeals to Jesus through other Jews for the healing of his slave, and Jesus both grants his request and marvels at the greatness of his faith (7:2-10). A woman, who is known as a sinner, expresses her awareness of having received forgiveness by weeping and anointing Jesus' feet, and Jesus openly confirms that her sins have been forgiven and commends her for her faith (7:36-50). A Samaritan, who is a "foreigner," is the only one of ten lepers cleansed by Jesus to return to give him thanks, and Jesus acknowledges both his act and his faith (17:12-19). A rich ruler, because he prefers to cling to earthly treasures, forgoes the inheritance of eternal life and thus becomes a negative example of Jesus' power to effect the reversal of conditions (18:18-23). Zacchaeus, a chief toll collector who is led by Jesus to repent and promises to divest himself of his ill-gotten wealth, receives from Jesus the incalculably more precious gift of salvation (19:1-10). And during the crucifixion, one of the two criminals calls upon Jesus in repentance and faith to remember him, and Jesus grants him the gift of life in paradise (23:39-43).

The third of these groups of minor characters we wish to highlight is made up of three individuals appearing in the passion narrative: Simon of Cyrene, the centurion beneath the cross, and Joseph of Arimathea. The significance of these three is that they demonstrate what it is to "serve." In Luke's gospel story the disciples do not, as we observed, abandon Jesus during his passion. Nevertheless, Judas betrays him, Peter denies him, and all the disciples watch the crucifixion only "from afar" (23:49). In contrast, Simon, the centurion, and Joseph, through the service they render Jesus, do what the disciples should have done but do not do.[152] Twice during his ministry, Jesus defined discipleship as bearing one's cross and coming "after him" (9:23; 14:27). As Jesus walks toward death during his passion, Simon, who is not a disciple, is the one seen bearing his cross and coming "after him" (23:26). Similarly, although Peter confessed Jesus to be God's Messiah and the multitude of disciples hailed him as King, the one who glorifies God and affirms Jesus' righteousness as he dies in humiliation on the cross is not a disciple but the Roman centurion (23:47). And although it is disciples who pledged loyalty to their master, Joseph, a righteous Sanhedrist who dissented from the decision and action of his colleagues, is the one who goes to Pilate, requests the body of Jesus, and gives him an honorable burial (23:50-53). So again, these three individuals function as foils, or contrasts, for the disciples.

Luke's story, then, is rich in minor characters. The traits they exhibit and the roles they play vary enormously. Important ways in which Luke uses minor characters are as foils for other characters, or as exemplars possessing positive or negative traits such as "faith," "righteousness," or "love of riches," or as a vehicle for highlighting some significant aspect of Jesus' ministry, such as his mission to those living on the margins of society.

PLOT

In an address delivered in 1950, a prominent New Testament scholar asserted that Luke's Gospel is the first "life of Jesus" ever written.[153] Since then, scholars have given much thought to the genre of Luke-Acts. It has been suggested, for instance, that Luke-Acts is best construed as an example of the ancient novel[154] or of ancient biography[155] or historiography.[156] The specific word in terms of which Luke himself seems to have thought of his work is "narrative" (1:1). In narrative, Luke found a suitable vehicle for telling the story of the salvation God accomplished in Jesus (8:39).

Luke's story of the life and ministry of Jesus possesses a clearly defined plot. The plot of a story[157] has to do with the way in which the author arranges the events. In Luke's gospel story, the events unfold in an orderly sequence governed by time, topic, and causality. This sequence reaches an overall climax at the end of Jesus' story, and the whole of the sequence is intended to elicit from the reader a specific response as defined in the prologue (1:1-4).

In broad terms, the plot of Luke's gospel story may be said to have a beginning, a middle in three phases, and an end: In the beginning, John and Jesus are presented to the reader (1:5—2:52). In the middle, Jesus reaches out to Israel from Galilee (3:1—9:50), journeys to Jerusalem (9:51—19:46),[158] and discharges his ministry there (19:47—21:38). And in the end, Jesus suffers, dies, is raised, and ascends to heaven (chaps. 22–24). At the heart of this gospel plot is the element of conflict. The fundamental resolution of the conflict comes with Jesus' death, resurrection, and ascension. At the same time, Jesus' ascension does not mark the end of Luke's story, for it continues in Acts. Nevertheless, at Jesus' Parousia the story of both the Gospel and Acts will come to final resolution. The principal response Luke's story is calculated to elicit from the reader is "certainty," or "assurance," that God has in fact been at work in Jesus to fulfill his promises and accomplish salvation for both Jew and gentile. Addressing Theophilus, Luke himself says this about the purpose of his story: "It seemed good to me . . . to write, most excellent Theophilus, that you may know the truth [certainty] concerning the things about which you have been instructed" (1:3-4).

As the protagonist, Jesus is the one around whom the conflict of Luke's gospel story revolves. On the human level, the conflict Jesus encounters is with Israel on the one hand and with the disciples on the other. In the main, Jesus' conflict with the disciples is to bring them to spiritual maturity by enlightening them about the plan of salvation God accomplishes in him on behalf of Israel and the nations. Of special importance in this regard is that Jesus enable the disciples to comprehend that God ordained from of old that he should enter his glory through suffering and death. Having once become mature followers, the disciples also become proper "witnesses" to Jesus and form the nucleus, under the leadership of the apostles, of the reconstituted people of God. Although Jesus does not guide the disciples to spiritual maturity until after the resurrection, his conflict with them nonetheless concludes on a harmonious note.

Jesus' conflict with Israel (the religious authorities and the people) is to bring the nation to receive him as God's supreme agent of salvation, the one in whom God's scriptural promises to Israel attain to their fulfillment. Virtually from the outset of his ministry, Jesus causes division in Israel: Whereas he encounters opposition especially from the authorities but also from the people, he nonetheless gathers a crowd of disciples. Throughout his public ministry, Jesus remains popular with the people and in dialogue with the authorities; through word and deed, he summons both groups to repentance. Upon his entry into Jerusalem, however, the authorities conspire to kill him, and, with the aid of Judas, Satan, Pilate, and the people, they finally succeed. In the eyes of the authorities, Jesus is a false messiah who "perverts our nation," that is to say, threatens to undermine the status quo, especially the authority by which they rule Israel, and to steal from them the allegiance of the people.

The irony of Luke's gospel story is that Jesus, despite seemingly being stripped of all authority by being put to death, nevertheless triumphs in his conflict with Israel. In Jesus' ministry, suffering, and death, God is at work to accomplish his plan of universal salvation. The religious authorities desire Jesus' death because they are his opponents. But God and Jesus also will Jesus' death. Jesus wills his death because he is God's Son and Servant, the Righteous One who is obedient to God. God wills the death of Jesus because through it he establishes a new covenant in which Jesus will preside in the power of the Spirit over all Jews and gentiles who believe on his name and thus form the reconstituted people of God. In validation of the perfect righteousness with which Jesus leads his life, discharges his ministry, and endures suffering, God raises him to life, thereby putting him in the right in his conflict with Israel. Also, to show that he henceforth rules church and world through the risen Jesus, God exalts Jesus to universal authority by his ascension. Finally, to evince his enduring mercy, God grants Israel a "second chance" on Pentecost to repent of its repudiation ("ignorance") of Jesus and to believe on his name and be saved. Still, at the end of time God has also appointed a final day of reckoning: Jesus will return in splendor to usher in God's consummated kingdom and hence deliver his own and serve as Judge of the living and the dead.

This brief sketch of the conflict Luke depicts in his gospel story reveals that intertwined in this story are three primary story lines and one secondary story line. The secondary story line is that of the people, which we shall deal with only as it touches on the other story lines. The primary story lines are those of Jesus, the religious authorities, and the disciples. It is these that will concern us in the chapters that follow.

2 THE STORY OF JESUS

Because Jesus is the protagonist in Luke's gospel story, the focus of attention is on him. Only rarely does any character other than Jesus occupy the spotlight. Still, one character on whom the spotlight does shine in select episodes is John the Baptist.

In the beginning of his gospel story, Luke presents John and Jesus to the reader (1:5—2:52). In the middle (3:1—21:38), Luke tells of Jesus' outreach to Israel as he travels primarily within Galilee (3:1—9:50), of his journey to Jerusalem (9:51—19:46), and of his ministry there (19:47—21:38). And in the end of his story (22:1—24:53), Luke tells of Jesus' suffering, death, resurrection, and ascension.

THE PRESENTATION OF JOHN AND JESUS

Luke begins his story of the life of Jesus by introducing the reader to John and Jesus (1:5—2:52).[1] Through a carefully arranged sequence of episodes, Luke both parallels John with Jesus and yet underscores the superiority of Jesus. The episodes comprising this sequence are the following: (a) the annunciation of the birth of John (1:5-25); (b) the annunciation of the birth of Jesus (1:26-38); (c) Mary's visit to Elizabeth (1:39-56); (d) the birth, circumcision, and naming of John (1:57-80); (e) the birth, circumcision, and naming of Jesus (2:1-21); (f) the presentation of Jesus in the temple (2:22-40); and (g) the boy Jesus in the temple (2:41-52).

Luke is at pains in his infancy narrative to depict God as undertaking a new action in the history of salvation. The narrative as such is steeped in the atmosphere of the Old Testament, and most of the events take place at the heart of Israel, in and around Jerusalem and in the temple. In these events, God inaugurates the new time of salvation by raising up John and Jesus as those who will serve not human purposes, but God's purposes. To attest to himself as the one guiding events, God sends angels and pours out his Spirit, to wit: The angel Gabriel appears to Zechariah and Mary; an angel, accompanied by a whole army of heaven's angels, appears to the shepherds; and the Holy Spirit comes upon Elizabeth, Zechariah, and Simeon and inspires prophetic utterance.

As those who serve the purposes of God, both John and Jesus stand out in Luke's infancy narrative as unique agents of God. To emphasize their uniqueness, Luke shows how they resemble each other. To highlight such resemblance, Luke narrates the annunciation of the birth of both in terms of the same pattern, attributes to both some of the same personal qualities, and describes the same events associated with the infancy of both.

To take the last point first, Luke establishes resemblance between John and Jesus by narrating the same sequence of events in their early lives. In parallel order, Luke tells of the annunciation of the birth of each, of the birth itself and the circumcision and naming, of the canticle each birth evokes (the Benedictus [1:67-79] and the Nunc Dimittis [2:28-32]),[2] and of the growth and maturing of each in childhood (1:80; 2:40).

Luke also fosters the notion of resemblance between John and Jesus by following the same pattern in narrating the two annunciation episodes and by ascribing to both the personal qualities of greatness and endowment with the Spirit. In terms of form, vocabulary, and content, the two annunciation episodes are remarkably similar.[3] In both, the angel Gabriel appears to one of the parents of John and of Jesus, Zechariah and Mary. In reaction to Gabriel's sudden appearance, Zechariah and Mary are both startled. To reassure both, Gabriel addresses them by name and tells them not to fear. To explain his coming, Gabriel next delivers to each his message: He promises the birth of a son, stipulates the child's name, declares that he will be "great," and sketches briefly what he will accomplish. In reply to Gabriel, both Zechariah and Mary point out that the realization of his message is beyond human capability. In response to Zechariah and Mary, Gabriel reaffirms the truth of his message and announces a sign that betokens its truth. Last, both episodes contain some statement in their closing scenes designed to inform the reader whether Gabriel's words elicit acceptance or doubt in the heart of Zechariah or Mary.

Clearly, then, John and Jesus resemble each other. At the same time, they contrast with each other, for Jesus is manifestly superior to

John.[4] For example, whereas the beginning episode of the infancy narrative features the announcement in the temple regarding the birth of John (1:13), the concluding episode features the boy Jesus sitting in the temple as in his Father's house (2:49). Whereas the miracle of John's conception is that his parents are aged (1:18), the miracle of Jesus' conception is that it is virginal and occurs by a creative act of God's Holy Spirit (1:34-35). Whereas John is endowed with the Spirit from his mother's womb (1:15), Jesus is endowed with the Spirit "from conception" (1:35). Whereas Mary defers to Elizabeth, journeying to her and greeting her, Elizabeth and John show much greater deference to Mary and Jesus: Elizabeth, by calling Mary the "mother of my Lord"; and John, by leaping with exultation in Elizabeth's womb at the sound of Mary's voice (1:39-45). Whereas John's birth is hailed by neighbors and relatives (1:58), Jesus' birth is hailed by a multitude of angels praising God and announcing peace (2:13-14). Whereas John is "great" as a unique "prophet of God" (1:15, 76), Jesus is "great" as the unique "Son of God" (1:32-33, 69). Whereas John is received by his father, Zechariah, as one whose mission is to bring about repentance and the forgiveness of sins (1:16-17, 77), Jesus is received by Mary and by Simeon and Anna in far more exalted terms: In the Magnificat, Mary lauds God because in Jesus he will effect the "reversal of fortunes," putting down the mighty and exalting the lowly (1:46-55);[5] and in the temple, Jesus is received by Simeon as the Savior of Israel and the nations (2:25-32) and by Anna as Israel's Redeemer (2:36-38). And whereas the effect of John's ministry will be to prepare a people ready to meet its Lord (1:17), the effect of Jesus' ministry will be to cause division in Israel (2:34-35).

Overall, therefore, Luke pursues a double purpose in his infancy narrative: On the one hand, he stresses that John is like Jesus; on the other hand, he stresses that Jesus is incomparably superior to John. The point of the first emphasis is to depict John and Jesus as unique agents of God who stand united in their ministries to Israel.[6] The point of the second emphasis is to indicate that the purpose of John and his ministry is to serve the purpose of Jesus and his ministry.

The infancy narrative concludes with the narrator's spotlight resting on Jesus (2:41-52). Before Jesus was born, Gabriel announced to Mary that Jesus would be God's Son entrusted by God with dominion (1:31-33). Now as a twelve-year-old sitting among Israel's teachers in the temple, Jesus shows that he is already aware of being God's Son and Servant sent to carry out God's mission (2:46-49). As a prelude to the public ministry he will begin when thirty years old, the words Jesus utters already elicit amazement on the part of those who hear them (2:47-48).

THE PUBLIC MINISTRY OF JESUS IN ISRAEL

Chapter 3 marks the first major turning point in Luke's gospel story: The reader moves from the beginning (1:5—2:52) to the first phase of the middle (3:1—9:50). John and Jesus are now adults, about to embark on their public ministries. To attest to the magnitude of the new salvation-historical initiative God undertakes, Luke describes the ministries of John and Jesus against the massive backdrop of Roman, Palestinian, and Jewish history (3:1-2), to wit: Tiberius is emperor of Rome (A.D. 14–37); Pontius Pilate is prefect of Judea and Samaria (A.D. 26–36); Herod Antipas is tetrarch of Galilee and Perea (4 B.C. to A.D. 39); his brother Philip is tetrarch of Northern Transjordan (4 B.C. to A.D. 34); Lysanias is tetrarch of Abilene to the northwest of Damascus; and the high-priesthood of Annas (A.D. 6–15) has given way to the high-priesthood of Caiaphas (A.D. 18–36). At the divinely appointed time, God sends first John and then Jesus to Israel.

The Ministry of John

Luke describes the sending of John after the manner of the prophets of old. In solemn tones, Luke recounts that "the word of God came to John the son of Zechariah in the desert."[7] With this announcement, John commences his ministry.

In Luke's gospel story as in Matthew's, John is a "prophet" (1:76) but also "more than a prophet" (7:26). In Matthew, John is "more than a prophet" because he fulfills the end-time expectations associated with Elijah.[8] In Luke, John, though viewed as exercising the same sort of power as Elijah (1:17), does not assume the end-time role of Elijah. Instead, John is "more than a prophet" because he fulfills Old Testament promises. In so doing, John proves to be an end-time figure whom God has chosen to play a special role in the history of salvation.[9] As end-time figure and agent of God, John is portrayed, variously, as the precursor of God[10] and of Jesus.[11] In Acts, John's role is more stereotypically described as that of being the precursor of Jesus.[12]

The mission God entrusts to John is "proclaiming a baptism of repentance for the forgiveness of sins" (3:3). This summary sketch of John's ministry contains several elements. The key element, however, is that of "repentance": In Luke's view, those who "repent" (i.e., "turn to God and undergo a moral change of heart and mind") are the ones who submit to John's baptism and receive forgiveness (1:16-17, 77).

As he discharges his ministry, John greets the people coming out to him with scathing words: He calls them a brood of vipers, thus castigating them as evil; and he summons them to display in their lives the fruits of repentance and not to think that they can depend on descent from Abraham or on Abraham's merits to rescue them from condemnation in the final judgment (3:7-9). Smitten by John's words, the crowds, the toll collectors, and the Jewish soldiers serving Herod Antipas ask him what they should do (3:10-14). John's answers are ethical in nature and specify concrete ways in which persons can evince the fruits of repentance: Share your goods with the needy; don't cheat in collecting taxes; and don't use your police powers to extort money.

Beyond such specifics, the larger purpose of John's ministry is to effect spiritual renewal in Israel so that Israel will receive, or "believe in," Jesus. In words of Old Testament promise, the goal of John's ministry is to prepare the way so that "all flesh shall see the salvation of God" (3:4-6). In Acts, Paul defines this goal more pointedly when he says: "John baptized with the baptism of repentance, telling the people to believe in the one who was to come after him, that is, Jesus" (Acts 19:4).

So profound is the impact of John's ministry that it causes the people to wonder whether he himself is not the Messiah (3:15). Addressing this question, John turns the people's attention to the Coming, mightier One about to appear.[13] So much greater will he be than John that John is not worthy to perform for him even the most menial task one can ask of a gentile slave: to unloose the thong of the master's sandals (3:16). The Coming, mightier One, John asserts, will be both Savior and Judge. As Savior, he will baptize with the Holy Spirit and fire, that is to say, he will pour out the Spirit, which cleanses and refines its recipients (3:16).[14] Apparently, Luke himself identifies the fulfillment of this aspect of John's proclamation with Pentecost.[15] As Judge, the Coming One will, at the end of the age, carry out the final judgment to salvation and damnation.[16] Significantly, John's understanding of the Coming One, or Messiah, makes little allowance for the earthly ministry of word and deed that Jesus will shortly undertake. Later in the gospel story, Jesus will be compelled to adjust John's understanding of the Messiah (7:18-23).

In contrast to both Mark and Matthew, Luke intimates that Jesus is baptized by John, but he does not depict this.[17] Indeed,

Luke mentions Jesus' baptism only in retrospect, after first telling of John's imprisonment by Herod Antipas, the "wicked" ruler of Galilea and Perea (3:19-20, 21). The upshot is that Luke draws a sharp line between the end of John's ministry and the beginning of Jesus' ministry. What is more, he foreshadows future events: Antipas is the same King Herod with whom Jesus will have to do.

The Ministry of Jesus

Jesus in Galilee

With John removed from the scene, Luke henceforth concentrates on Jesus. Here in the first phase of the middle of his gospel story (3:1—9:50), Luke's primary focus is on Jesus' ministry in Galilee. As we recall, Galilee is the place where God's divine plan calls for Jesus to begin his ministry.[18] Still, Jesus' activity in public (4:14) must await his baptism and testing (3:21—4:13).

The purpose of the baptismal episode is to depict God as empowering Jesus with the Spirit and himself announcing who Jesus is (3:21-22). Hereafter, God's view of Jesus becomes—terminological differences notwithstanding—normative for judging the way others view Jesus. To set the scene for Jesus' empowerment and God's announcement, Luke notes that all the people and Jesus have been baptized and that Jesus is now at prayer (3:21). This reference to "Jesus at prayer" prepares the reader for the revelatory events about to take place.

Luke reports that the Spirit descends upon Jesus in bodily form as a dove, empowering him (3:22a). Also, God's voice affirms from heaven, "You are my beloved Son, in you I take delight!" (3:22b). As in Mark 1:11, these words are a composite quotation derived from Psalm 2:7, Isaiah 42:1, and Genesis 22:2.[19] In Isaiah 42:1, the servant in whom God delights is one whom God has "chosen" for ministry. In Genesis 22:2, Abraham's beloved son Isaac is his "only" son. And in Psalm 2, God is described as solemnly addressing the words "My son are you" to his "anointed" ("messiah") from the royal house of David. Within the context of Luke's story, God's baptismal affirmation essentially reiterates the declaration the angel Gabriel made to Mary when announcing Jesus' birth (1:32-33, 35). In both instances, Jesus is presented as the Messiah-King from the house of David, God's only, or unique, Son whom God has chosen to be the bearer of his end-time rule.

In Luke's gospel story, Jesus' genealogy[20] is an appendage of the baptismal episode (3:23-38). By citing the names of Jesus' fore-bears, the genealogy functions as "historical documentation" for God's baptismal affirmation (3:22). By tracing the line of Jesus in ascending order back to God himself (3:38), it raises the claim that God has guided the whole of human history so that it might culminate in the coming of Jesus. By citing Adam in the list of names, the genealogy affirms that Jesus is of decisive significance for all humankind (3:38). In naming the patriarchs Abraham, Isaac, and Jacob, it affirms that Jesus is of decisive significance for Israel (3:34). Although the genealogical list does not follow a branch of David's line that includes Solomon and his sons, it does make prominent mention of David himself, thus pointing to Jesus' royal pedigree (3:31). In noting at the outset that Jesus is thirty years old, the genealogy stresses that he has now reached the acknowledged age of maturity and can begin his work (3:23).[21] Also, because Mary was a virgin when Jesus was conceived, the genealogy aptly reports that Jesus is the son of Joseph only as "people supposed" (3:23). Finally, by stipulating in the closing link that Jesus is the Son of God (3:38), the genealogy functions as a "bridge" between the baptismal episode, in which God declares Jesus to be his Son, and the story of the temptation, where Jesus is put to the test as God's Son. Viewed overall, the genealogy underscores the truth that God is authoritatively and decisively at work in Jesus to save.

Following the baptismal episode, the Spirit, with whom Jesus Son of God has been permanently endowed, leads him into confrontation with Satan,[22] or the devil, Jesus' arch-adversary (4:1-13). For forty days Jesus wanders in a desert region without food as the Spirit guides him and the devil puts him to the test. At the end of this time, the devil's testing of Jesus comes to a head in three confrontations. In these confrontations, the devil adopts God's understanding of Jesus as his Son and endeavors to get Jesus to sacrifice commitment to God on the altar of self-concern. At stake is the integrity of Jesus' obedience and his unique relationship with God. Entice Jesus to sever this relationship and his mission suffers ruin.

As God's Son, Jesus loves God perfectly, with heart, soul, strength, and mind (10:27). In each confrontation, the devil puts some aspect of Jesus' absolute love of God to the test, and Jesus, in turn, withstands the test. Thus, the devil invites Jesus to perform a miracle to alleviate his hunger (4:3). Jesus refuses, however, for were he to do so he would be cultivating self-interest at the expense of giving thought to God's interests (4:4). Again, the devil invites Jesus to worship him on promise of receiving in return power and glory (4:5-7). Jesus refuses, however, for were he to do so he would be rendering to the devil the homage and service due God alone (4:8). Last, the devil invites Jesus to cast himself down from the pinnacle of the temple so that God might make good on his promise to protect him from harm (4:9-11). Jesus refuses, however, for were he to do so he would make himself guilty of putting God to the test and attempting to coerce him into proving that he is faithful and can be trusted to keep his promises (4:12). Following this final test, which takes place in Jerusalem, the devil leaves Jesus "until an opportune time" (4:13). Although Jesus will continue to struggle with the devil throughout his ministry (11:14-22),[23] the "opportune time" alluded to is the passion. During the passion, the devil will mount his final assault on Jesus, also in Jerusalem (22:3, 53).

JESUS' OUTREACH TO ISRAEL. Victorious in resisting the devil's challenges, Jesus follows the promptings of the Spirit and travels to Galilee to begin his public ministry.[24] As word of him spreads throughout the region, he teaches in the synagogues to the acclaim of all (4:15).

Jesus' public ministry in Luke's gospel story is one of "word" and "deed" (24:19; Acts 1:1).[25] To alert the reader to this at the outset of Jesus' ministry, Luke highlights the message Jesus proclaims in Nazareth (4:16-30) and the miracles he performs in Capernaum (4:31-44).

Within Luke's story, Jesus' visit to the synagogue of Nazareth is of programmatic significance. Here Jesus publicly presents himself to Israel as God's Messiah and announces the nature of his ministry. Invited by the leader of the synagogue to read from scripture, Jesus stands, is handed a scroll that he unrolls to the intended passage, reads the passage, rolls the scroll up again, hands it back to the attendant, and sits down to speak while all eyes remain fixed on him (4:16-21).[26]

So as to announce both who he is and what he is about, Jesus reads the greater part of Isaiah 61:1-2 (LXX) combined with one phrase taken from Isaiah 58:6 ("to set at liberty those who are oppressed" [4:18]). The first words Jesus utters, "The Spirit of the Lord [God] is upon me because he has anointed me" (4:18), assert who he is. In the baptismal episode, Luke told how God anointed Jesus with the Spirit and declared him to be his Son (3:22). Consequently, as Jesus now describes himself as "anointed" with God's

Spirit, the reader recognizes the allusion to the baptismal episode. In addition, the verb "to anoint" alludes to the noun "Messiah," which means "Anointed One."[27] In Luke's story, then, the Messiah is the Son whom God anoints with his Spirit, and at Nazareth Jesus boldly lays claim to messiahship.

As Messiah, the Son of God, Jesus is the supreme agent of God. To affirm that he "serves the purposes not of humans, but of God," Jesus proclaims at Nazareth that "[the Lord] has sent me" (4:18). To describe the substance of his ministry, Jesus draws on four purpose-clauses: God has sent him (a) "to preach good news to the poor," (b) "to proclaim release to the captives and sight to the blind," (c) "to set at liberty those who are oppressed," and (d) "to proclaim the acceptable year of the Lord" (4:18-19).

The clause having the position of stress in this series is the final one: "to proclaim the acceptable year of the Lord" (4:19). The "acceptable year" to which Jesus refers is the year of Jubilee commanded by Moses (Lev. 25:10).[28] At Jubilee, which occurred once every fifty years, two key provisions were to be put into effect: Any property Israelites had been forced to sell was to be returned to the original owner or his family; and Israelites who had indentured themselves because of financial hardship were to be released (Lev. 25:8-12).[29] In other words, at the heart of Jubilee was the "cancellation of debts," or the notion of forgiveness. Hence, as Jesus refers to Jubilee in his reading of Isaiah, he uses it as a metaphor connoting forgiveness[30] in the sense of "salvation." Jesus' assertion, then, is that he is the Messiah through whom God proffers salvation to Israel. As he says elsewhere, he "has come to seek and to save the lost" (19:10).

Jesus designates the lost whom he has come to save as the "poor," the "captives," the "blind," and the "oppressed" (4:18). The term "poor" in Luke's story is global in scope, encompassing many sorts of persons who are outcast, disabled, or needy, to wit: the economically disadvantaged, the hungry, those who weep, the persecuted, the blind, the lame, the deaf, the crippled, those who are lepers, and even those suffering death.[31] In turn, the "captives" and the "oppressed" are all those whom Satan holds in bondage because of sin, disease, or demon possession.[32] And the "blind" are not only those who are physically without sight but also those who are spiritually benighted and in need of divine enlightenment.[33] To all such as these Jesus brings salvation by calling them to repentance and granting them forgiveness (5:32), or by healing them (7:22), or by summoning them to live even now in the sphere of

God's end-time rule (4:43), or by promising them the "reversal of their fortunes" at the coming of God's glorious kingdom at the end of time (6:20-23).

Jesus concludes his proclamation to the people of Nazareth with a homiletical pronouncement: "Today," he declares, "this scripture has been fulfilled in your ears!" (4:21). With this pronouncement, Jesus emphatically invites the people to accept him as Israel's Messiah and to receive the salvation he has announced.

The reaction of the people to Jesus is one of "pleasure and puzzlement."[34] On the one hand, they speak well of him and marvel at the inspired words he has spoken (4:22).[35] On the other hand, they are puzzled that Jesus, whom they have known from youth (4:16), should advance such weighty claims on his own behalf. Indeed, the question they pose to one another attests to their puzzlement: "Isn't this the son of Joseph?" (4:22).[36] As the reader knows, the people should have responded by exclaiming, "This is the Messiah, the Son of God!"[37]

Jesus' reaction to the people is swift and sharp. "Doubtless," he remarks, "you will quote to me this proverb, 'Physician, heal yourself,' [and say,] 'What we have heard you did at Capernaum, do here also in your own country'" (4:23). The point of both the proverb Jesus quotes and the rest of his remark is perhaps easier understood if the proverb is changed to read, "Physician, heal *us!*" As Luke pictures Jesus, Jesus is aware that the people of Nazareth have already heard news of miracles he has performed in Capernaum. Consequently, in citing the proverb, Jesus in effect takes the people to task. He warns them against putting him to the test, assuming that he is somehow obligated to demonstrate the truth of his proclamation by performing miracles for the benefit of his own people here in Nazareth.[38] Indeed, Jesus goes one step further and applies to himself yet another maxim expressing his rejection by the people: "No prophet," he tells them, "is [ever] acceptable in his own country" (4:24).

As is apparent, therefore, Jesus performs no miracles in Nazareth. Instead, he continues his address to the people and compares his situation to the time of Elijah and Elisha: Just as Elijah and Elisha on particular occasions benefited not Israelites but gentiles, so he, too, will benefit not the Nazarenes, who want miracles on demand, but others (4:25-27). In the gospel story, these "others" whom Jesus will benefit are Jews; in Acts, they are the gentiles to whom the word of salvation is proclaimed because Jews have first repudiated it. Be that as it may, the people of

Nazareth, enraged by Jesus' comparisons, suddenly rise up and haul him out of the city to throw him to his death (4:28-29). Still, because their attempt to kill Jesus is not yet the divinely appointed "hour of darkness" (22:53), Jesus passes untouched through their midst (4:30).

Rejected at Nazareth, Jesus goes to Capernaum (4:31-41). On the Sabbath, he again visits the synagogue. After astonishing the people with the authority of his teaching (4:31-32), he does what he refused to do in Nazareth, perform miracles.

The first two miracles Jesus performs in Capernaum are "parallel miracles" (4:33-39): In the synagogue, Jesus heals a "man" possessed of a demon; at Peter's house, he heals a "woman" (Peter's mother-in-law) suffering from a fever. In the one case, Jesus "rebukes" the demon so that it "goes out" of the man. In the other, he "rebukes" the fever so that it "leaves" Peter's mother-in-law. By the power of his word, Jesus has in both cases "proclaimed release to the captives" and "set at liberty those who are oppressed." Later, with the onset of evening and the Sabbath past, Jesus heals by touch all the sick brought to him and frees many from the clutches of demons (4:40-41). Although next morning he departs Capernaum, the people, impressed by his mighty acts, search him out and attempt to keep him from leaving them (4:42). Jesus, however, has already begun the "way" that is his ministry. Divine necessity impels him to proclaim his message of salvation elsewhere (4:43). Hence, he leaves the region of Capernaum and proclaims the kingdom in synagogues thoughout the whole land of the Jews (4:44).

Through his ministry of word and deed, therefore, Jesus reaches out to Israel from Galilee, the place where God ordained he should begin his work, and proffers Israel salvation. As part and parcel of his outreach, Jesus calls disciples and teaches, preaches, heals, and exorcises demons. His fame spreads,[39] so that people from all Judea, Jerusalem, and the seacoast of Tyre and Sidon throng to him (6:17). Even Pharisees and scribes from every village of Galilee and Judea and from Jerusalem come to observe him (5:17). Whereas the people tend to be favorably disposed toward him and many of them become his disciples,[40] controversy erupts between him and the religious authorities (5:17—6:11). The result is that Jesus causes division in Israel. Toward the close of this first phase of his ministry, Jesus commissions the twelve to a mission in Israel. Modeled after his ministry, their mission is also one of word and deed (9:1-2).

THE ENIGMA OF JESUS' IDENTITY.   In Nazareth, Jesus publicly presented himself as God's Messiah (Anointed), but the people did not accept him as such. In this failure to grasp Jesus' identity, the Nazarenes become typical of other humans in Luke's gospel story. Despite Jesus' travels, fame, and outreach to Israel, human beings, unlike supernatural beings such as God, Satan, and demons, do not know who Jesus is. As humans encounter Jesus, he continually perplexes them. The upshot is that they wonder about his identity, or assert who they think he is, or even dispute the opinion of others. Although this motif of wonderment and assertion concerning Jesus' identity is also prominent in Mark and Matthew,[41] it is not so extensively developed in them as in Luke.

To elaborate, throughout the entire Galilean phase of Jesus' public ministry Luke punctuates his story with questions and statements uttered by human beings or supernatural beings that touch on Jesus' identity. The long series begins already in the pericope on the ministry of John the Baptist (3:1-20). Aware that the people ponder whether he is not "the Messiah," John redirects their ruminations by pointing them to the Coming, mightier One (3:15-17).[42] In so doing, John effectively becomes the instrument by which Luke leads the reader to anticipate that humans in his gospel story will also wonder and speculate about Jesus' identity.

As the immediate backdrop for human query concerning Jesus' identity, Luke informs the reader how supernatural beings and himself as narrator view Jesus' identity. In the baptismal episode, God himself declares, as we have seen, that Jesus is "my Son" (3:21-22). In the genealogy (3:23-38), Luke as narrator provides the reader with a "historical record" of Jesus' pedigree: Jesus is the "son of Joseph" only in the sense that people suppose him to be such (3:23); in other respects, he is the "Son of David" (3:31) and the "Son of God" (3:38). In the temptation (4:1-13), Satan appropriates God's understanding of Jesus and approaches Jesus as "Son of God," even if only to entice him to break faith with God. And to round things out, Luke informs the reader a bit later that like God and Satan, demons, too, know Jesus to be the "Son of God" (4:41). Indeed, demons shout aloud Jesus' identity (4:34, 41). Still, so quickly does Jesus muzzle them that their knowledge does not get out (4:35, 41).

Following baptism, genealogy, and temptation, Jesus, we know, embarks on his public ministry in Israel (4:14-15). From this point on, it is principally humans who wonder or declare their beliefs about Jesus' identity. These questions and statements commence with the villagers of Nazareth and do not end until Peter declares how the disciples view Jesus and God declares for a second time, in the presence of three disciples at the transfiguration, his understanding of Jesus' identity. Thus, at 4:22 the villagers of Nazareth, though they marvel at Jesus' reading of Isaiah and his pronouncement of the fulfillment of this reading in their hearing, nonetheless ask themselves, "Is not this the son of Joseph?" At 4:36, the people in the synagogue of Capernaum, after having witnessed Jesus expel a demon, query one another about his identity by asking about the authority of his speech: "What is this word?" they shout aloud, "For with authority and power he commands the unclean spirits, and they come out!" At 5:21, the scribes and Pharisees, taking offense at Jesus for having forgiven the paralytic his sins, question in their hearts, "Who is this that speaks blasphemies? Who can forgive sins but God only?" At 7:16, the people, after having seen Jesus raise the young man of Nain from the dead, exclaim in awe as they glorify God, "A great prophet has arisen among us! God has visited his people!" At 7:19, John the Baptist, who wrongly believed that the Coming, mightier One would, upon his appearance, usher in the final judgment (3:16-17), inquires of Jesus through two disciples, "Are you the Coming One, or shall we look for another?" At 7:39, Simon the Pharisee, observing that Jesus has permitted himself to be touched by a sinful woman and aware that Jesus has been publicly acclaimed by the crowd as a prophet,[43] denies Jesus such public acclamation as he mutters to himself, "If this man were a prophet, he would have known who and what sort of woman this is who is touching him, for she is a sinner." At 7:49, the guests of Simon the Pharisee, having heard Jesus forgive the wayward woman her sins, take offense at this and wonder to one another, "Who is this, who even forgives sins?" At 8:25, the disciples, for whom Jesus has just calmed wind and wave, ask one another in fear and astonishment, "Who then is this, that he commands even wind and water, and they obey him?" At 9:7-9, a perplexed Herod Antipas, having heard of the happenings surrounding Jesus' ministry and noting that the people surmise that Jesus is a prophet of some note, wonders in his own mind, "Who is this about whom I hear such things?" At 9:18-20, Jesus himself, after first asking the twelve who the people think he is, pointedly asks them who they think he is; in reply to Jesus' question, Peter declares on behalf of all, "You are the Messiah of God!" And at 9:35, God announces from a cloud to Peter, John, and James atop the mount of transfiguration that Jesus "is my chosen Son" and enjoins them to "hear him!"

Plainly, then, as Jesus travels about Galilee discharging his ministry, humans ask continually about his identity or state who they believe he is or is not. Because Peter's declaration, though followed by God's announcement at the transfiguration, is nonetheless the last human pronouncement in this chain, it occupies a position of stress and therefore invites closer scrutiny.

At the outset of this episode featuring Peter's declaration (9:18-22), Luke again pictures Jesus at prayer (9:18). By invoking this picture, Luke prompts the reader to understand that divine revelation is the source of the insight into Jesus' identity the disciples will shortly express. Against the background of public perplexity and speculation about Jesus' identity, Jesus asks the twelve disciples two related, yet contrasting, questions. In the first one, Jesus asks, "Who do the crowds say that I am?" (9:18). In reply, the disciples repeat the news that has also reached Herod Antipas (9:7-8): "[Some say] John the Baptist; and others, Elijah; and others, that one of the ancient prophets has risen" (9:19). Disregarding this answer, Jesus immediately puts a second question to the disciples: "And you, who do you say that I am?" (9:20). In response, Peter confesses as spokesperson for the disciples, "You are the Messiah of God!" (9:20). In reaction to Peter's confession, Jesus first charges the disciples to tell this to no one (9:21) and then solemnly announces, "The Son of man must suffer many things, and be rejected by the elders and chief priests and scribes, and be killed, and on the third day be raised" (9:22).

The crux of this episode is how to assess the merits of the two answers Jesus receives from the disciples. In this connection, it should be noted that the three views of the crowds, or Jewish public—that Jesus is John, Elijah, or one of the ancient prophets— are at bottom variants of the single perception that Jesus is some prophet of great stature who has returned from the other world.[44] Since these three public views prove to be variants of a single notion, the key question becomes this: How does the notion in 9:19 that Jesus is a "prophet" (John, Elijah, or one of the ancient prophets) relate to Peter's declaration in 9:20 that Jesus is the "Messiah" of God?

For several reasons, it seems certain that Luke would have the reader adjudge the views of the crowds to be wrong and Peter's declaration to be right. Formally, the sharp juxtaposition of the two questions and answers in 9:18-20 and the emphasis on "you [disciples]" as a group contrasting with "the crowds" suggest that the two answers are antithetic. Narratively, it is apparent from even the briefest reading of Luke's gospel story that Jesus cannot be John the Baptist come back to life; on the contrary, Luke has presented John as a distinct character in his own right. But if Jesus is most assuredly not John the Baptist come back to life, neither is he Elijah who has reappeared or one of the ancient prophets who has arisen. Twice the reader learns that Jesus is perceived by segments of the Jewish public as being one of these three figures (9:7-8, 19). Each time the three are mentioned, it is as persons who are placed in "parallel position" on the same plane. What this means rhetorically is that if the reader knows for certain that Jesus is not to be identified with one of these figures (e.g., "John"), then he or she can infer with equal certainty that neither is Jesus to be identified with the other figures ("Elijah" or "one of the ancient prophets").

Another reason for believing that the views of the crowds are false and Peter's declaration is correct is based on application of the principle of "point of view." In the infancy narrative Luke, as we have observed, introduces John and Jesus to the reader. To convey God's understanding of John and of Jesus (God's "point of view" regarding their identity), Luke makes use of angels and persons inspired of the Holy Spirit. Noteworthy is that whereas these angels or persons explictly announce that Jesus is the Davidic Messiah and Son of God (Lord and Savior),[45] they make no such announcements to the effect that Jesus is either a "prophet" or "the Prophet." Conversely, it is equally striking that the one whom God does declare through intermediaries to be not merely a "prophet" but even a "great prophet" is precisely John the Baptist. When the angel Gabriel appears to Zechariah and announces John's birth, he predicts that John will be "great" (1:15); and when Zechariah is suddenly filled with the Spirit and prophesies, he designates John as the "prophet of the Highest" (1:76). Accordingly, "prophet," or indeed "great prophet," is a designation that God ascribes not to Jesus but to John and, as such, is the normative understanding of John in Luke's gospel story.

This insight, in turn, opens the way to a proper understanding of the key passage, 7:16. At 7:16, the crowd witnesses Jesus raise the young man of Nain and extols him as a "great prophet": "A great prophet has been raised up among us! God has visited his people!" Without question, the crowd rightly perceives that Jesus has performed this miracle as an agent of God and that in it God is acting graciously toward his people. Still, in that the crowd extols Jesus as a "great prophet," the reader recognizes that the crowd's perception of Jesus is exactly the same as Luke's characterization of John the Baptist. For his part, the "great prophet" John is without question a unique agent of God (3:3-6; 7:27-28a). This notwithstanding, Luke leaves no doubt that John and his work are simply preliminary to Jesus "Messiah" and his work. In Luke's perspective, therefore, to the same degree as Jesus is immeasurably superior to John, being "Messiah" is immeasurably superior to being "prophet." From this angle, too, one can see that Luke invites the reader to construe the crowds' views of Jesus in the episode containing Peter's confession as false and Peter's declaration as true.

This brings us to the passage in Luke's gospel story that is perhaps most revealing for discerning Luke's understanding of "prophet" in relation to "Messiah" and hence for perceiving the incorrectness of the crowds' views of Jesus and the correctness of Peter's declaration, namely, 3:15-17. This passage, we remember, introduces the long series of questions and statements concerning Jesus' identity that can be found throughout 3:1—9:50, and it does this by leading the reader to anticipate that just as John is asked about his identity, so Jesus will be asked about his. Significantly, a comparison of 3:15-17 with the episode featuring Peter's declaration (9:18-20) indicates that the two passages are virtually the converse of each other. In 3:15-17, John is asked by the people whether he is the "Messiah," and he effectively replies in the negative by describing himself as being "incomparably less" than the Messiah. In 9:18-20, Jesus is told that people think of him as a "prophet," and he elicits from Peter the declaration that, in reality, he is "incomparably greater" than a prophet because he is the Messiah.

Now Luke's normative understanding of John, we have learned, is that he is a "great prophet." Consequently, in that John, the "great prophet," denies in 3:15-17 that he is the Messiah and compares himself with that Coming, mightier One, so Luke has John himself apprise the reader of the "absolute difference" that exists between himself as "prophet" and the Coming One as "Messiah." John describes this absolute difference along three lines. First, the Coming One is so much mightier than he that he is not even worthy to loose the thong of his sandals, that is, to perform for the Coming One the most menial task that can fall to a gentile slave (3:16). Second, whereas he baptizes with water, the Coming One will baptize with the Holy Spirit and with fire (3:16). As we pointed out, these words of John come true in Luke's narrative on Pentecost, when the exalted Jesus pours out the Spirit upon the disciples.[46] And third, the Coming One will utterly surpass anything that he, John, has done in his ministry because he is destined to carry out the final judgment (3:17).[47] Accordingly, as Luke attests through the witness of the "great prophet" John, the difference that exists between "prophet" and "Messiah" is as absolute as the difference that exists between the one whom God has sent to baptize with water and the one whom God has destined to be exalted to heaven and to come at the end of time as Judge of all. To Luke's way of thinking, to look upon Jesus as "prophet" is not to perceive who he is, for in being "Messiah," he is infinitely more than "prophet." To reiterate, the views of the crowds, or Jewish public, that Jesus is some prophet returned from the other world (9:18-19) are incorrect, whereas Peter's declaration that he is the Messiah (9:20) is correct.

In identity, then, Jesus is neither a "prophet" nor even "the Prophet" but the "Messiah," the Son of God. This is the one side of the coin, and Luke places great store by it because it highlights the absolute "uniqeness" of Jesus. The other side of the coin, which is of equal significance to Luke, highlights the element of "salvation-historical continuity," to wit: Exactly as the Messiah Son of God, Jesus stands in the line of the prophets, especially Moses and Elijah.[48] Thus, "Moses said" that God would raise up a "prophet like him," and in fulfillment of Moses' prophecy God has raised up "Jesus Messiah."[49] Also, the pattern to which the life and ministry of Jesus Messiah conforms is that typifying the life and ministry of the prophets:[50] Like the prophets, Jesus Messiah is mighty in word and deed (24:19; Acts 7:22). Like the prophets, he suffers rejection,[51] condemnation (Acts 13:27), and death (13:33-34). And like Moses and Elijah in Old Testament and Jewish traditions, he also ascends to heaven (9:30-31). On balance, therefore, if Jesus stands out in Luke's story as "the Messiah," he can in truth be said to be a "prophetic Messiah."[52]

Before we leave this pericope on Peter's confession, one further question calls for comment: If Peter's confession that Jesus is God's Messiah is correct, how is one to explain that Jesus immediately commands the twelve disciples to silence (9:21)? The answer is that although the disciples know who Jesus is, they do not as yet know that his destiny is suffering and death. Until they comprehend the latter, they are in no position to proclaim the former. Directly following his command to silence, Jesus tells the disciples for the first time that he is constrained by divine necessity to suffer, die, and be raised (9:22). Without informing the reader how the disciples react to Jesus' first passion-prediction, Luke pictures Jesus as turning toward the people ("all") and summoning them to discipleship (9:23-27).

Eight days (i.e., a week) after Peter's confession, the transfiguration takes place (9:28-36). Accompanied by Peter, John, and James, Jesus ascends a mountain to pray (9:28). The twin settings of "Jesus on the mountain" and "Jesus at prayer" suggest that divine revelation is about to occur. While Jesus is at prayer, the appearance of his face suddenly changes, his garments become dazzling white, and Moses and Elijah appear in glory speaking with him about the "exodus" he will accomplish in Jerusalem (9:29-30). Heavy with sleep, Peter and the other two disciples awake to see the glory of the three figures (9:32). As Moses and Elijah begin to depart, Peter, not knowing what to say, foolishly chatters about building shelters in which the three heavenly figures may dwell (9:33). Before he can finish, however, the cloud of God's presence overshadows the disciples and a voice announces, "This is my chosen Son, hear him!" (9:34-35).[53] After the voice has sounded, Moses and Elijah disappear and Jesus is found alone (9:36).

Within the context of Luke's gospel story, the transfiguration constitutes the culmination of earlier events and points forward to Jesus' passion. As the culmination of earlier events, the transfiguration calls attention, again, to the question of Jesus' identity. In retrospect, Jesus has been declared to be God's Son (baptism; 3:22), God's Messiah (Nazareth; 4:18), God's Messiah (Peter's confession; 9:20), and God's Son (transfiguration; 9:35). If one considers now the disposition of the events just alluded to, one sees that "baptism and Nazareth" on the one hand and "Peter's confession and the transfiguration" on the other form brackets around the entire first phase of Jesus' ministry (3:21—9:51). Also, if one views these events in conjunction with one another, one recognizes that Jesus' identity has been proclaimed, respectively, by God, Jesus, Peter, and God in terms of a chiastic order: Jesus is God's Son, God's Messiah, God's Messiah, and God's Son. Add to these observations the fact that "Son of God" and "Messiah" are complementary titles in Luke's gospel story (4:41), and one key function of God's announcement at the transfiguration becomes apparent: It apprises the reader not only that Peter's confession was fully valid but also that it constitutes the correct way to view Jesus relative to all the questions and statements concerning Jesus' identity that humans posed or made throughout this first phase of Jesus' ministry.

The transfiguration likewise points forward to Jesus' passion. Atop the mount, God describes Jesus as his "chosen one" and enjoins the disciples to "hear him" (9:35). God calls Jesus "chosen" because Jesus is God's Servant and Jesus' ministry is guided by divine purpose (Isa. 42:1). And God enjoins the three disciples to "hear Jesus" because Jesus speaks for God (10:22) and would teach them about his passion (9:22). Jesus' passion, in fact, was the topic of his conversation with Moses and Elijah (9:31). Specifically, Moses and Elijah spoke with Jesus about his "exodus" (i.e., his suffering, death, resurrection, and ascension), which is to take place in Jerusalem. In that the transfiguration directs attention to Jesus' passion, it prepares the reader for the journey that will take Jesus to Jerusalem.

Shortly after Jesus and the three have rejoined the other nine disciples, Jesus delivers his second passion prediction (9:44). To impress upon the disciples the seriousness of what he is about to say, Jesus exhorts them to "let these words sink into your ears." Regardless, the disciples do not understand Jesus' talk about suffering, for two reasons: First, they are afraid to ask him what his prediction means (9:45). And second, God withholds such understanding from them (9:45). In other words, as far as the disciples are concerned, the thought that Jesus must suffer, and this in line with God's plan of salvation, is inconceivable (9:22, 44).

The Journey of Jesus to Jerusalem

At 9:51, the reader moves from the first phase of the middle of Luke's gospel story (3:1—9:50) to the second phase (9:51—19:46): Jesus' journey to Jerusalem. Luke signals this change with a dramatic narrative comment: "When the days drew near for his assumption, he set his face to go to Jerusalem" (9:51). The term "assumption" refers to the rest of Jesus' ministry: his going up to Jerusalem, and his suffering, death, resurrection, and ascension. The clause "he set his face to go to Jerusalem" expresses Jesus' unconditional resolve to travel to the "city of his destiny."[54] The oft-repeated theme in 9:51—19:46 of "Jesus on the way to Jerualem" serves as a constant reminder that he is unwavering in his resolve (9:53; 13:22; 17:11; 18:31; 19:11, 28).

The ministry Jesus discharges on his journey to Jerusalem is not fundamentally different from the ministry he previously discharged mainly within Galilee. As Jesus embarks on his journey, for example, events occur that are strongly reminiscent of earlier events. Earlier, God sent John as a messenger before Jesus;[55] Jesus was rejected by the villagers of Nazareth (4:16-30); Jesus called certain individuals to become his disciples;[56] and Jesus sent out the twelve to proclaim the kingdom of God and to heal (9:1-2). Correspondingly, as Jesus now sets out for Jerusalem, he sends disciples as messengers before him (9:52); he is rejected by the villagers of a Samaritan town (9:52-56); he apprises certain individuals of the costs of discipleship

(9:57-62); and he sends out the seventy-two to proclaim the kingdom of God and to heal (10:9). Parallel events such as these point up the similarity between these first two phases of Jesus' public ministry.

On the way toward Jerusalem (9:57), Jesus continally engages in dialogue and speaks in parables. His most frequent partners in discussion are the disciples, though he also addresses the religious authorities and the people. Because Jesus interacts somewhat randomly with first the one and then the other of these groups, the narrative pattern that emerges is one of "alternation and contrast."[57] In speaking with the disciples, Jesus instructs them in the life of discipleship.[58] In his encounters with the religious authorities, he tends to be unsparing in his criticism of them.[59] And in his words to the people, he endeavors to win them to his side.[60] Far from flattering the people, however, Jesus often mints his message in harsh terms, calling them to repentance through reproach. Still, he also summons them to discipleship (e.g., 14:25-26), and he is not without success. Previously, in the Galilean phase of his ministry, Jesus had already gathered about him a "great crowd" of disciples (6:17). At the time he finally enters Jerusalem, the number of his disciples will have grown to become a "multitude" (19:37). By attracting large numbers of disciples, Jesus continues to effect division in Israel.

The penultimate episode in Jesus' journey places him in sight of Jerusalem and about to enter both city and temple (19:28-44). Without question, the two most dramatic incidents in this episode are Jesus' reception as King and his lament over the city. These two incidents, in turn, recall Jesus' earlier lament of Jerusalem (13:34-35) and an episode near Jericho in which a blind man appealed to him as Son of David (18:34-35). Because these various episodes are interrelated, they call for comment.

Jesus utters his first lament over Jerusalem following a warning given him that he should leave Galilee because Herod Antipas is out to kill him (13:31). Vowing not to deviate from his course, Jesus likens himself to a prophet divinely appointed to die in Jerusalem (13:32-33). Envisaging the sweep of history, Jesus laments Jerusalem for killing the prophets and stoning God's emissaries (13:34). Like a mother hen, he himself has tried to gather its people,[61] but to no avail. As a result, Jerusalem's house (i.e., the "temple" or the "city" itself)[62] stands abandoned by God, which is to say that it is ripe for judgment (13:35).[63]

Jesus ends his lament over Jerusalem with the following declaration: "And I say to you, you [Jerusalem] will not see me until the time comes when you say, 'Blessed is he who comes in the name of the Lord!'" (13:35). The participle translated in this saying as "he who comes" may also be translated as "the Coming One." Within Luke's gospel story, Jesus is depicted as the "Coming One" in two senses: In the view of John the Baptist, Jesus is the "Coming One" in the sense that his appearance will mark the arrival of the final day of judgment.[64] In the view of Luke as narrator, Jesus is the "Coming One" in the sense that he is the King whose earthly journey will bring him to Jerusalem (19:38). Against the background of these two connotations of the "Coming One," one can see that Jesus' declaration constitutes both a hope and a threat. The hope Jesus expresses is that when he later completes his journey and arrives in Jerusalem, the people will receive him as the "Coming One" who is their God-sent King. The threat he expresses is that should the people choose to repudiate him as King, they will nonetheless not have finished with him. On the contrary, they will still face him at the end of time as the "Coming One" who returns as Judge of all.[65] As Luke soon reports, when Jesus approaches Jerusalem, the people do not hail him as King (19:37-38). Unwittingly, therefore, they themselves dash the hope inherent in Jesus' lament and reduce it to a threat. Even at this, however, God will give the Jerusalemites yet another chance to receive Jesus as King: At Pentecost, when the apostles proclaim to them the word of salvation.

We just saw that one of the connotations of "Coming One" is King (19:38). As Jesus draws near to Jericho (18:35-43), a blind beggar twice cries aloud to him as "Son of David," appealing to him in faith to restore his sight. Jesus hears the beggar's plea and grants him his request, whereupon the beggar glorifies, and the people praise, God.

This episode is striking on two counts. First, the blind beggar's appeal to Jesus as "Son of David" is the first time in Jesus' ministry that any human has publicly acknowledged him to be Israel's Davidic Messiah-King. True, Peter has already confessed Jesus to be God's Messiah, but this took place in private and Jesus immediately commanded the twelve to silence (9:18-21). Shortly, Jesus will enter Jerusalem (19:28-46). Apropos of this, this episode depicts a "blind beggar," one of the "poor" in Israel, as "seeing" and "confessing" what Israel thus far has refused to "see" and "confess": that Jesus is Israel's Davidic King. Ironically, therefore, this blind beggar indicts Israel for its obduracy. Nor does the people's praise of God mitigate this harsh judgment (18:43). In itself, their praise does not mean that they share the beggar's faith and insight into

Jesus' identity. Recall the episode at Nazareth. There the people approved of Jesus and marveled at the words of grace coming from his mouth. Regardless, they did not accept him as God's Messiah but saw in him only the son of Joseph (4:22).

Because Luke makes much of the Davidic lineage of Jesus,[66] it is obvious that the beggar's understanding of him as the Son of David is correct. At the same time, Luke is also concerned to assert that Jesus is not merely the "son of David." To emphasize this point, Luke later has Jesus put a question of antinomy to the scribes: How can the Messiah simultaneously be both the son and the lord of David (20:41-44)? The reason this question is antinomous is that it contains within it two, ostensibly contradictory, views about the Messiah: If one says that the Messiah is the son (descendant) of David, one makes him out to be less than David. If one says that the Messiah is the lord of David, one makes him out to be greater than David. The problem of antinomy, then, is this: How can the Messiah at the same time be both "less" than David and "greater" than David? Although Jesus does not himself resolve this problem, the reader has no difficulty doing so: The Messiah is the "son of David" because he is from the house of David (1:32-33). The Messiah is also "greater" than David because he is, as the heavenly voice declared at the baptism and transfiguration, the Son of God.[67]

As Jesus begins the last leg of his journey to Jerusalem, he, the "Coming One" (13:35), appropriately places himself at the head of his entourage (19:28). Nearing Bethphage and Bethany, Jesus arrives at the Mount of Olives opposite the city (19:29). In line with the royal prerogative of kings,[68] he sends two disciples to requisition a colt[69] for his use (19:29-34). Mounted on the colt, Jesus rides toward the city while the disciples, paying him the honor befitting a king, spread their garments before him (19:36; 2 Kings 9:13). As Jesus reaches the descent of the Mount of Olives leading to Jerusalem, the "whole multitude of the disciples," inspired by all the miracles they have seen him perform, suddenly burst forth in praise of God and hail both Jesus and heaven itself: Him they hail as the "Coming One" who is Israel's "King." Heaven they hail as the realm where salvation already reigns (19:37-38).[70]

This is the triumphant aspect of Jesus' entry into Jerusalem. The tragic aspect is that although Jerusalem has now "seen" Jesus as the "Coming One" and "King," neither the people nor their leaders have joined the disciples in "blessing" Jesus and receiving him as such (13:35). On the contrary, they remain "blind" to Jesus' kingship, and some of the Pharisees attest to this by calling upon Jesus to rebuke the disciples for acclaiming him as King (19:39). After all, they reason, to acclaim one as king who is no king is to jeopardize Jerusalem's peace by inviting Roman reprisal. In quick reply to the Pharisees, Jesus not only does not rebuke the disciples but defends them (19:40). Moreover, as he beholds Jerusalem, he is moved to tears and laments it a second time (19:41-44). In words of great pathos, he bewails the ignorance and blindness that prevent Jerusalem from recognizing that he is the "horn of salvation" in whom the Lord God of Israel would "visit" his people to grant them peace and well-being (1:68-69). To repudiate him is to repudiate the peace God would bestow.[71] Not peace, therefore, but terrible destruction will one day befall Jerusalem (19:43-44).

The climactic event of Jesus' entry into Jerusalem is his cleansing of the temple (19:45-46).[72] Once in Jerusalem itself, Jesus proceeds directly to the temple. Here he challenges the rule of the religious authorities (20:1). Quoting from the prophets, Jesus charges that although the temple is to be a place of worship (Isa. 56:7), they have turned in into their own haunt (Jer. 7:11). In Luke's eyes, this apparently means that the authorities have made themselves liable for the desecration of the temple by sanctioning crass commercialism.[73] To purge the temple, Jesus expels the traders. Indeed, he effectively takes possession of the temple and makes it the site for his ministry of teaching in Jerusalem (19:47-48; 21:37-38). By thus shaming[74] the authorities and undermining their leadership, Jesus himself sets the stage for the fierce controversies he will shortly have with them.

Jesus in Jerusalem

The third phase of the middle of Luke's gospel story focuses on Jesus' ministry in Jerusalem (19:47—21:38). As one moved from the Galilean phase of Jesus' ministry (4:14—9:50) to his journey to Jerusalem (9:51—19:46), one could observe that the conflict between him and the religious authorities intensified only marginally. To be sure, this conflict was not without acrimony. This notwithstanding, the truly surprising factor is that the authorities remained in dialogue with Jesus and did not plot to have him killed. Once Jesus enters Jerusalem and cleanses the temple, however, all this changes: Henceforth the authorities, led by the chief priests and the scribes, actively conspire to destroy Jesus. The corollary to this is that the controversies between Jesus and the authorities become more hostile. This third phase of the middle of Luke's story plainly paves the way for the end of the story (22:1—24:53), which tells of Jesus' passion.

The ministry Jesus conducts in the temple in Jerusalem is one of teaching the people (19:47-48). Apparently, it lasts for several days (19:47). Whereas all the people "hang on Jesus' words," the chief priests, scribes, and prominent men (elders) actively search for a way to destroy him. Accordingly, at the same time as Jesus attracts the people, he stirs fear in the hearts of the authorities. For the present, therefore, Jesus becomes a source of division between people and leaders.

Provoked by Jesus' teaching and preaching in the temple, the chief priests, the scribes, and the elders (=the membership of the Sanhedrin) approach him one day and demand to know on whose authority he does "these things" (20:1-8). While "these things" refer primarily to Jesus' teaching, they also include his cleansing of the temple.[75] In answer to the authorities' question, Jesus cleverly poses a counterquestion: When baptizing, did John act on divine, or merely human, authority? In a stroke, the authorities see themselves trapped. Because they refused to submit to John's baptism, the only answer they can give Jesus would be to insist that John acted on human authority. Still, for them to say publicly that John acted on his own without divine authorization would be for them to incite the people to stone them, for the people honor John as a prophet. Fearful of answering Jesus' question, the authorities prudently remain silent. As a result, neither does Jesus answer their question about the authority on which he acts.

This, however, is not the end of the matter. Having momentarily silenced the authorities, Jesus himself seizes the initiative and narrates the parable of the vineyard (20:9-19). Though he addresses it to the people, he nonetheless aims it at the authorities (20:9, 19). In this parable, Jesus identifies God with the owner of the vineyard, himself with the owner's son, and the authorities with the wicked tenant farmers who kill the owner's son. In the way Jesus makes these identifications, he advances two claims: that he is, in God's own eyes, the beloved Son whom God has sent Israel (20:13); and that they, Israel's leaders, will be the ones who put him, God's Son, to death (20:14-15). In advancing these claims, Jesus' pursues a dual objective. On the one hand, through the vehicle of parabolic speech he has willingly done the very thing he earlier refused to do, answer the question the authorities put to him. On whose authority does he teach and act? As the beloved Son whom God has sent, he acts on the authority of God. On the other hand, Jesus also issues a stern warning to the authorities: By willfully closing their eyes to his divine sonship and authority and by becoming his mortal enemies, they oppose not simply him but, in fact, God. Because the authorities, though they grasp the message of Jesus' parable, nevertheless reject it out of hand, they want to lay hold of him immediately. Out of fear of the people, however, they restrain themselves (20:19).

Following the narration of his parable, Jesus clashes twice more with opponents: with spies, whom the members of the Sanhedrin send to discredit him in the eyes of the people (20:26); and with some of the Sadducees, who attempt to make both Jesus and belief in resurrection-life appear foolish by serving up a question calculated to stump Jesus (20:27-39). Jesus, however, answers both sets of opponents so adroitly that even the spies and the scribes have to admire him (20:26, 39).

Following Jesus' controversy with the Sadducees, all debate between him and the religious authorities suddenly ends. As Luke remarks, "For they no longer dared to ask him any question" (20:41). To be sure, although the authorities fall silent, Jesus does not. As he brings his ministry in Jerusalem to a close, he continues teaching in the temple, and early each morning the people throng to him to hear him (21:37-38). In contrast to this genial picture, the termination of the many controversies the authorities have had with Jesus means that the slim thread of their "remaining in dialogue with him" has now been severed. The struggle of words gives way to a struggle to the death.

THE PASSION, RESURRECTION, AND ASCENSION OF JESUS

The suffering, death, resurrection, and ascension of Jesus constitute the end and culmination of Luke's gospel story (22:1—24:53). At the beginning of the end, the gospel story takes a second major turn. In retrospect, the first major turn occurred when John began his public ministry (3:1-2).

The end of Luke's gospel story is the place where Jesus' conflict with the religious authorities comes to fundamental, though not final, resolution. The final resolution of this conflict must await Jesus' Parousia at the end of time. Retrospectively, we recall that Jesus' conflict with the religious authorities has twice intensified noticeably: Content at first to debate Jesus (5:17—19:46), the authorities next coupled debate with the more sinister goal of seeking Jesus' death (19:47—21:38). Here at the beginning of the end of the story (22:1—24:53), the conflict between Jesus and the authorities becomes still more intense: The authorities, having been reduced by Jesus to silence, forgo further attempts to debate him and concentrate all their attention on how to kill him (22:2).

Jesus before the Sanhedrin

Luke sets the stage for the end of his gospel story by noting that the Passover, which he equates with the feast of Unleavened Bread, is close at hand (22:1).[76] To indicate that events are rapidly moving toward their climax, Luke draws together important threads of his story. At earlier junctures, the reader learned that Jesus would accomplish his "exodus" in Jerusalem (9:31); that the religious authorities would kill him (9:22); that Judas would betray him (6:16); and that Satan, who left Jesus at the end of the temptation, would return at the "opportune time" (4:13).

Already in Jerusalem, Jesus at last embarks on his "exodus" of suffering, dying, rising, and ascending to the Father. Because the "opportune time" for Satan's final assault against him has now arrived, the "coalition of darkness" forms (22:2-6). Satan, therefore, enters into Judas, and Judas makes common cause with the religious authorities by agreeing to betray Jesus for a price. Thus, Satan, Judas, and the authorities emerge as the chief opponents of Jesus. Because the people are as yet favorably disposed toward him (22:2), when Judas does betray Jesus, he will do so "apart from the crowd" (22:6).

Ever since boyhood, Jesus has known himself to be God's Son and Servant and his life to be guided by God's plan of salvation (2:43, 49). Consequently, he, not his opponents, controls the events of his "exodus." For example, on Thursday, the day before he dies, Jesus dispatches Peter and John with instructions about making preparations for eating the Passover meal, and they, Luke remarks, find everything exactly as he told them (22:7-13). Similarly, when evening comes and Jesus eats the Passover meal with the apostles, he reinterprets the meal[77] within the context of the farewell discourse he delivers (22:14-38):[78] Henceforth, his own body and blood will constitute the signs of a new covenant he will establish in his death (22:15-20). Again, as the Passover meal draws to a close, Jesus predicts that one of the twelve will betray him (22:21-23). Thereafter, he not only readies the disciples for things to come but also foretells that Peter will deny him (22:24-38). Later, as Jesus leaves the upper room that same night, he exhibits his mastery of events even by the route he takes: He holds to his custom of retiring to the Mount of Olives for prayer and there, gaining in strength and courage, he dedicates himself anew to serve the purposes of God by submitting to death (22:39, 42). Later still, as he directly confronts Judas and the members of the Sanhedrin, they do not lay hands on him but he in effect gives them permission to arrest him:[79] "But this is your hour," he says, "and the power of darkness" (22:47-53). And throughout the night, as the underlings of the Sanhedrin mock and blaspheme him, the very silence he keeps shows that he, not they, controls the situation (22:63-65).[80]

Come Friday morning, the day of his death, Jesus is brought before the Jewish Sanhedrin (22:66-71). This is the first phase in a four-part trial,[81] for Jesus will also stand before Pilate (23:1-5), Herod Antipas (23:6-12), and, again, Pilate (23:13-25). Before the Sanhedrin, Jesus is challenged to give testimony concerning his identity (22:66-71). As the reader listens in, he or she remembers that Jesus publicly presented himself at Nazareth as God's "Anointed," or Messiah (4:18-21); that the blind man outside Jericho openly appealed to him as the "Son of David" (18:38-39); that the multitude of his disciples hailed him in the hearing of the Jerusalemites as "King" (19:38); and that in the parable of the vineyard, told in the hearing of the members of the Sanhedrin, he laid claim to being the "Son of God" (20:13). Against the backdrop of these events, the Sanhedrin commands Jesus: "If you are the Messiah, tell us!" (22:67).

In response to this command, Jesus breaks his silence and replies. His reply, however, is also conditioned by previous events, to wit: When Jesus' disciples hailed him as King on Jerusalem's doorstep, the Pharisees "objected" to this (19:39). And when Jesus claimed in the parable of the vineyard to be God's Son, members of the Sanhedrin repudiated this claim and wanted to "seize" him on the spot (20:19). In light of these events, Jesus says to the Sanhedrin: "If I tell you [whether I am the Messiah], you will not believe; and if I ask you [this], you will not answer" (22:67-68).

Nor is this all. In words alluding to Daniel 7:13 and Psalm 110:1, Jesus also renews before the Sanhedrin his parabolic claim to be God's Son: Following my death, he declares in effect, I am "the [particular] man" who will be exalted to universal lordship at the right hand of God (22:69). On hearing Jesus' declaration, the whole Sanhedrin presses him with the question, "So then you are the Son of God?"[82] (22:70). Answering indirectly[83] but in the affirmative, Jesus retorts, "You say that I am!" (22:70). Instantly, the Sanhedrin judges that Jesus stands condemned by his own words: "What further testimony do we need? We have heard it ourselves from his own lips!" (22:71). As earlier, the members of the Sanhedrin, confronted with the truth of Jesus' identity, refuse to "see" and acknowledge who he is. In their minds Jesus, in affirming to be God's Son, has laid false claim to divine authority and majesty. The irony, however, is that in repudiating Jesus' affirmation, the Sanhedrin has once again rejected not only Jesus' understanding of himself but also God's understanding of him (20:13, 17).

Jesus' Crucifixion

After the Jewish phase of Jesus' trial Friday morning, the entire Sanhedrin takes him to Pilate (23:1; 18:32). As the Roman prefect, Pilate is the one who must decide capital cases and authorize executions. In the episodes that now follow—Jesus before Pilate (23:1-5), Jesus before Herod Antipas (23:6-12), Jesus again before Pilate (23:13-25), Jesus underway to crucifixion (23:26-32), and Jesus on the cross (23:33-49)—Luke stresses repeatedly that Jesus is innocent and righteous.

In the second phase of his trial (23:1-5), the religious authorities charge Jesus before Pilate with "perverting [misleading] our nation" (23:2, 14).[84] To clarify this charge, the authorities contend that Jesus is a revolutionary, to wit: He forbids the payment of taxes to Caesar (23:2); he asserts that he himself is Messiah, a king (23:2); and by his teaching he incites the people to rebellion throughout the entire land, from Galilee to Jerusalem (23:5).

The authorities' charge that Jesus is a revolutionary is revealing in two respects. First, it reveals that as they conceive of their conflict with Jesus, it is fundamentally one of authority:[85] Will he, or will they, rule and guide God's people? And second, it reveals that as they make every effort to destroy Jesus, they know full well that their case against him is fraudulent. On the matter of paying taxes to Caesar, the authorities' own spies had asked Jesus about this and he had replied, ". . . render to Caesar the things that are Caesar's" (20:20-26). And as for the charge that Jesus has claimed to be Messiah, a king, the authorities and all Israel have been witnesses to the peculiar character of Jesus' ministry. Far from pursuing the political overthrow of either Herod Antipas or Rome, Jesus' ministry has been one of proclaiming good news to the poor and giving sight to the blind (4:18-19). When publicly appealed to as the "Son of David" outside Jericho, Jesus did not rouse the populace to arms but healed (18:35-43). When hailed as "King" upon his entry into Jerusalem, Jesus received the acclaim, not for any display of military prowess, but because of the miracles he had performed in the sight of all Israel (19:37). In bringing Jesus to the cross, the authorities willfully practice deceit by making him out to be an advocate of political and military revolt.

Upon hearing Jesus accused of being Messiah, a king, Pilate concentrates his inquiry on this. Pointedly, he asks Jesus, "Are you the King of the Jews?" (23:3). In Pilate's mind, the very title "King of the Jews" conjures up images of insurrection. Nevertheless, for a second time Jesus replies indirectly but in the affirmative, "So you say!" (23:3). Still, despite Jesus' affirmation, Pilate is so completely dissuaded that Jesus poses any kind of revolutionary threat that he rules Jesus to be innocent: "I find," he says, "no crime in this man" (23:4). Then, learning that Jesus is a Galilean and knowing that Herod Antipas is presently in Jerusalem for Passover, Pilate seizes the opportunity to rid himself of a troublesome case and sends Jesus to Herod for trial (23:6-7).

Herod Antipas, tetrarch of Galilee and Perea (3:1), has long been wanting to see Jesus (9:9; 23:8). Characterized by Luke as evil (3:19), Antipas is the one who first jailed and then beheaded John the Baptist (3:19-20; 9:9). He is also the one who, in hearing remarkable reports about Jesus, wondered who he is (9:7-9). It is a measure of Antipas's wickedness (3:19) that some Pharisees had warned Jesus, as he traveled toward Jerusalem, that Antipas had designs on his life (13:31). The reason Antipas desires to "see" Jesus is to have him perform some sign, or miracle (23:8). But Jesus does not perform miracles on demand, for their purpose is to summon to repentance (10:13). Because Antipas is spiritually "blind" to the need for repentance,[86] the reader knows not to anticipate that Jesus will satisfy his wish. Then, too, as Antipas attempts to conduct an interrogation of Jesus, Jesus repays his efforts with silence (23:9). Standing by are also the chief priests and the scribes, and they vehemently reiterate their accusations against Jesus (23:10). After a time, Antipas and his soldiers unwittingly fulfill Jesus' own words of prophecy by treating him with contempt and mocking him.[87] Indeed, Antipas caps the mockery by sending Jesus back to Pilate wearing a "white garment." Ironically, this symbol of mockery is also a symbol of innocence (23:11). That same day, as Pilate receives Jesus, he and Antipas set aside their differences and become friends (23:12). In Acts, this newfound mutuality is interpreted by the church for what it is: the gathering together of kings and rulers against the Lord (God) and his Messiah (Acts 4:26-27).

With Jesus back in his custody, Pilate assembles both the members of the Sanhedrin and the people and conducts what amounts to the fourth and final phase of Jesus' trial (23:13-25).[88] At this juncture, therefore, all Israel, people and leaders, stand united in their opposition to Jesus. This is noteworthy, for as Jesus first stood before Pilate earlier that morning, the crowds looked on almost as spectators (23:4). Also, during Jesus' ministry in Jerusalem and even as he embarked on his passion, the people's affinity for him had been a source of anxiety for the religious authorities (20:6, 19; 22:2). Still, despite this newfound unity between people and leaders, Pilate, convinced of Jesus' innocence, does his utmost to persuade them to free Jesus. With this as his goal, Pilate firmly reminds them that he has already found Jesus innocent of the accusations brought against him and, he adds, so has Herod Antipas (23:14-15). To conclude his inquiry, Pilate announces that he will have his soldiers administer a beating to Jesus as a "warning" and then release him (23:16). Indeed, throughout the whole of Jesus' trial, Pilate three times declares his intention to have Jesus beaten and released, just as he also declares three times that Jesus is innocent (23:4, 15-22). But to no avail. At every turn, the people and leaders resist Pilate: Ironically, they demand that Barabbas, who is a known insurrectionist and murderer (23:18-19), be released and that Jesus be crucified (23:21, 23). At length, Pilate acquiesces and orders that Barabbas be freed and that Jesus be "delivered up to their will" (23:24-25). At this, Israel's repudiation of its Messiah-King is complete.

Although Luke does not say so, it is Roman soldiers who lead Jesus out to be crucified (23:26). The tip-off to this comes later, in the scene of soldierly mockery at the cross. Instead of ridiculing Jesus as "the King of Israel," the soldiers use Pilate's designation and ridicule Jesus as "the King of the Jews" (23:3, 36-38). While underway to the crucifixion, the soldiers conscript one Simon of Cyrene and "lay on him the cross, to carry it behind Jesus" (23:26). In this brief scene, Simon concretizes Jesus' own description of the nature of true discipleship (9:23; 14:27).

Along with Jesus, the soldiers lead out two criminals (23:32). Following in Jesus' wake is also a great multitude of the people and of women mourning and lamenting him (23:27). Turning to the women and addressing them as "daughters of Jerusalem," Jesus leaves Jerusalem as he entered it, with a lament—his third—on his lips (23:28-31; 19:41-44; 13:34-35). Predicting anew the coming destruction of Jerusalem,[89] Jesus enjoins the women to weep not for him, but for themselves and their children. The point of the proverb, "For if they do this when the wood is green, what will happen when it is dry?" (23:31), seems to be: What is about to befall me cannot be compared with what will befall the inhabitants of Jerusalem.[90]

When Jesus, the two criminals, the soldiers, and the multitude at last reach the place called "Skull," the soldiers crucify Jesus and the criminals (23:33-49). In the first of three words from the cross, Jesus prays, "Father, forgive them; for they know not what they do" (23:34). This word of Jesus plays a crucial role within Luke's gospel story, for it is the last one he speaks that envisages his opponents. Instead of railing against them, Jesus asks that they be forgiven. He thus keeps the counsel to love the enemy that he himself gave to the disciples (6:35; Acts 7:60). In declaring that his opponents, in bringing about his death, act in "ignorance," Jesus himself sounds the theme that Peter and Paul will proclaim in Acts so as to summon Israel, people and leaders, to repentance (Acts 3:17; 13:27-28). Meanwhile, as Jesus utters his prayer from the cross, the soldiers below gamble for his garments (23:34). In so doing, they strip him of all earthly possessions and the last vestige of human dignity (Ps. 22:18). Farther away the people, who do not, as in Mark and Matthew, subject Jesus to abuse,[91] stand watching (23:35).

As the moment of Jesus' death draws near, four sets of scenes stand out: scenes of mockery (23:35-38); scenes focusing on the two criminals and Jesus (23:39-43); scenes climaxing in Jesus' death (23:44-46); and scenes depicting human reactions to Jesus' death (23:47-49). In the first two sets of scenes, the element of "derision" is prominent. In them, Jesus is derided three times as "Messiah" and "King of the Jews": by the Jewish rulers (23:35); by the Roman soldiers (and Pilate's inscription; 23:36-38); and by the one criminal (23:39). The irony is that in thus deriding Jesus, the rulers, soldiers, and criminal are all unwittingly speaking the truth (1:31-33; 2:11). Also in these scenes, these same persons put Jesus to the test three times to "save himself." Earlier, Satan, too, had put Jesus to the test three times (4:1-13). Just as Jesus remained obedient to God and resisted the challenges of Satan, so now he remains obedient to God and resists the challenges of his opponents. The reason "saving oneself" constitutes a test, or temptation, is that it denies that God is the source of all salvation (1:46-47). Because Jesus' trust for salvation is in God, he resists the test to "save himself." Previously in Luke's story, Jesus himself had said: "For whoever desires to save his life, will lose it" (9:24). In Luke's story, Jesus' life will indeed be saved, but by God through resurrection (20:17; 24:5-6).[92]

In the set of scenes focusing on the two criminals and Jesus (23:39-43), Luke shows what it means for Jesus, whom his opponents have derided as Messiah-King, to be Messiah-King. In these scenes, the first criminal serves as a foil for the second one. Whereas the first criminal is "blind" to the desperate nature of his situation, the second one "sees" things aright and repents. Whereas the first one reviles Jesus as Messiah, the second one accepts him as such. Whereas the first one regards Jesus as being of the same ilk as he and the other criminal, the second one affirms the innocence of Jesus. And whereas the first one puts Jesus to the test by challenging him to "save himself and us," the second one "prays" to Jesus: He utters Jesus' name, which is tantamount to appealing to Jesus as God's agent of salvation ("Jesus" means "God saves"); and he petitions Jesus to remember him whenever Jesus should be exalted to kingly reign. In answer to the second criminal's "prayer," Jesus gives him solemn assurance that upon death he will partake of the gift of salvation: "Truly, I say to you, today you will be with me in Paradise!" (23:43).[93] In Luke's story, Jesus is in fact Messiah-King, not as one who foments revolution against Rome, but as one who mediates salvation to such as this second criminal: to the "poor," the "captives," and the "lost" (4:18-19; 19:10).

The third set of scenes tells of the occurrence of supernatural portents immediately preceding Jesus' death and of the extraordinary manner in which Jesus dies (23:44-46). To signal the arrival of Jesus' death as that of an "exceptional moment" in history,[94] darkness covers the land of the Jews from approximately noon till three o'clock. The miraculous tearing of the temple curtain[95] calls to mind Jesus' laments over Jerusalem and presages the city's destruction for having repudiated him.[96] Finally, the manner in which Jesus dies is one that betokens oneness with God[97] and supreme trust in him: At the moment he himself chooses, Jesus, uttering his third word from the cross, prayerfully and confidently commends his "spirit" to God (Ps. 31:5) and breathes his last (23:46; Acts 7:59).

The final set of scenes attending Jesus' death depicts the reactions various humans register to his death (23:47-49). The most significant of these is the first. The Roman centurion, seeing the manner in which Jesus dies, glorifies God and exclaims, "Truly, this man was righteous!" (23:47). As Luke describes it, the centurion commanding the Roman death squad experiences a "conversion." In the manner in which he sees Jesus die, he senses the presence of God and so glorifies God. Moreover, in declaring Jesus to have been "righteous," the centurion trumpets two prominent themes Luke has highlighted in his gospel story: On the one hand, the centurion—in company with Pilate, Herod Antipas, and the repentant criminal— affirms that Jesus is "innocent" of the charge for which he was made to die (23:3, 38). On the other hand, the centurion prompts the reader to recall that Jesus has, throughout Luke's gospel story, per- sonified "righteousness":[98] As God's Son and Servant, Jesus has con- tinually been guided by divine necessity and has perfectly "served the purposes not of humans, but of God." The upshot is that God establishes in Jesus' death a new covenant in which Jesus will preside in the power of the Spirit over the reconstituted people of God (22:19-20).

Luke describes not only the centurion's reaction to Jesus' death but also that of the people ("crowds"), of Jesus' acquaintances, and of the women disciples. As the people, who have been looking on since Jesus was placed on the cross (23:35), leave the site of his crucifixion, they "beat their breasts" (23:48). "Beating the breast" is a sign of repentance (18:13). Following Jesus' ascension, first three thousand and then five thousand of the people will respond to Peter's proclamation and hence act on their readiness to repent, be- coming believers (Acts 2:38-42; 3:12—4:4). Among the acquain- tances of Jesus who watch his crucifixion are also the apostles (23:49). In contrast to Simon of Cyrene, the centurion, and Joseph of Arimathea, none of them either walks behind Jesus carrying his cross, nor proclaims his righteousness, nor looks after his burial. Still, neither do they abandon Jesus (22:28). Indeed, if they are to be his witnesses in Acts, they must of necessity witness his crucifixion (Acts 1:8). Finally, the women disciples who had followed Jesus from Galilee (8:2-3) likewise take note of the events surrounding his death (23:49). They even follow Joseph of Arimathea and learn the location of Jesus' tomb (23:55). On Easter, they will be the first to hear the good news of Jesus' resurrection (24:5-7).

Jesus' Resurrection and Ascension

Along with his suffering and death, Jesus' resurrection and ascension are also part and parcel of the "exodus" he accomplishes in Jerusalem. By the same token, the death, resurrection, and ascen- sion of Jesus constitute the resolution of Luke's gospel story.

The first to experience the reality of Jesus' resurrection are the women from Galilee (23:56b—24:11). Coming to the tomb at dawn on Easter to wash and anoint Jesus' body,[99] they enter it but find it empty. While still inside, two men (angels) appear to them with a message and an injunction (24:5-7, 23). The message the angels deliver is the Easter announcement: "Why do you seek the living among the dead? He [Jesus] is not here, but has been raised [by God]!" And the injunction they give summons the women to recall the passion-predictions that Jesus made while still in Galilee.[100] Reminded of these predictions, the women hurry off to tell the eleven apostles and other disciples of their encounter with the angels. The apostles, however, do not believe them (24:11). Nevertheless, their report does prompt Peter to run to the tomb and peer in (24:12). But although he, too, finds it empty, he simply goes home wondering what has taken place.

Against the backdrop of these incidents, the rest of chapter 24 focuses on the appearances of the risen Jesus to the apostles and other disciples and on Jesus' ascension. In Jesus' appearances (24:13-49), the key events are these: Jesus renews table fellowship with the disciples (24:30); he "opens their minds" to comprehend the plan of salvation God accomplishes in him and thus leads them to spiritual maturity;[101] and he commissions them to a worldwide ministry (24:47-49).

The final, climactic episode in Luke's gospel story is the ascension (24:50-53).[102] Through ascent to heaven, Jesus completes his "exodus," which he began in 9:51 as he set his face to go to Jerusalem. Just as Bethany figured in the "close" of Jesus' journey to Jerusalem, so now it figures in the "close" of his stay on earth.[103] In taking his departure, Jesus will be exalted to universal lordship at God's right hand (22:69). In blessing the disciples as a priest blesses the people, Jesus commends to God's care those who will form the nucleus of the reconstituted people of God. For their part, the disciples worship the ascending Jesus (24:52). By this act, they attest to the spiritual maturity to which Jesus has led them and the understanding he has given them of God's plan of salvation. By identifying with the disciples at this point, Theophilus and the reader, too, attain to the spiritual maturity, or "certainty," that Luke would convey through the narration of his gospel story, to wit: that Jesus is God's supreme agent in whom God has brought to fulfillment the plan of salvation he long ago announced in the scriptures.

Luke's story of Jesus, we have stressed, is a story of conflict. In the events of Jesus' death, resurrection, and ascension, this conflict comes to fundamental resolution, just as it will come to final resolution at his Parousia. At the human level, Jesus' chief opponents, we remind ourselves, are the religious authorities. In bringing Jesus to the cross, the authorities believe that he is shown to be a fraud and that the victory in their conflict with him is theirs (23:35). The truth of the matter, however, is that Jesus willingly relinquishes his life to accomplish God's plan of salvation. To put Jesus in the right, therefore, God raises him from the dead (24:4-7). Indeed, through the ascension God furthermore exalts him to universal authority (22:69). Thus exalted, Jesus, not the religious authorities, becomes the one who will preside, in the power of the Spirit and through his apostolic agents, over God's reconstituted people. But though God gives Jesus the victory in his conflict with Israel, Jesus is not unmindful of the authorities: Already from the cross he forgives them their "ignorance" (23:34). Also, come Pentecost they, too, will be given a "second chance," as Jesus' followers proclaim anew to Israel the word of salvation.

SUMMARY

Luke's story of Jesus is primarily a story of conflict between Jesus and Israel, made up of the religious authorities and the people. Jesus' conflict with the people is to win their allegiance. Jesus' conflict with the authorities is over "authority" and who will rule God's (reconstituted) people.

In the beginning of his gospel story (1:5—2:52), Luke presents John and Jesus to the reader. John resembles Jesus, for both are end-time agents of God. The crucial distinction between them is that whereas John is a prophet—indeed, a great prophet—Jesus is the Davidic Messiah and Son of God, Lord and Savior. In Jesus, the reader encounters the one who perfectly "serves the purposes not of humans, but of God."

The middle of Luke's gospel story (3:1—21:38) unfolds in three phases. In phase one (3:1—9:50), Luke first tells of John's ministry of summoning Israel to repentance (3:1-20) and then focuses all attention on Jesus (3:21—9:50). The commencement of the public ministries of John and of Jesus marks the first major turning point in Luke's gospel story.

In line with God's plan, Jesus "begins" his ministry in Galilee.[104] After baptism and temptation (3:21—4:13), he visits his hometown of Nazareth. Here he presents himself to Israel as God's Messiah, the one in whom God fulfills his promises and proffers the gift of salvation "today" (4:18-21). The people of Nazareth, however, repudiate Jesus and thus set the tone for his entire ministry: It is one of "outreach and rejection."

To reach out to Israel, Jesus discharges a ministry of word and deed, summoning Israel to repentance and forgiveness (4:14—9:50). He gathers disciples and thus effects division in Israel. Although the people do not believe in him, they are nonetheless well-disposed toward him and hold him to be a prophet (9:7-8). Correctly, Peter confesses on behalf of the disciples that he is God's Messiah (9:18-20). For their part, the religious authorities engage him in fierce controversy (5:17—6:11).

In phase two of the middle of Luke's gospel story (9:51—19:46), Jesus travels to Jerusalem. On his "way," he teaches the disciples, calls both people and religious authorities to repentance, and clashes with the authorities. Arriving at Jerusalem, Jesus proceeds directly to the temple. He cleanses it and thus dares to challenge the rule of the authorities at the very center of their power (19:45-46).

Phase three of the middle of Luke's gospel story features Jesus' activity of teaching in the temple (19:47—21:38). It also prepares for the story's end, because for the first time the religious authorities search for a way to destroy Jesus (19:47). While the people throng to him to hear his teaching (19:48; 21:38), the authorities challenge him in debate (20:1-40). No match for Jesus, he reduces all of them to silence (20:40). Unable to defeat Jesus in debate, the authorities will defeat him by killing him.

Luke's narration of Jesus' suffering, death, resurrection, and ascension (Jesus' "exodus") coincides with the end of his gospel story (22:1—24:53). At the start of the end, Luke's story takes its second major turn. At this juncture, the "coalition of darkness" forms, as Satan enters into Judas and Judas makes common cause with the religious authorities (22:3-6). Delivering himself into the hands of the authorities (22:47-53), Jesus submits to a lengthy trial in four phases. Before Pilate, the authorities charge him with "perverting our nation" and being a revolutionary (23:1-5). Although Pilate three times rules that Jesus is innocent (23:4, 14-15, 22), at the last he accedes to the demand of the authorities and people that Jesus be crucified as a false messiah (23:24-25, 38).

In the hours he hangs on the cross, Jesus invokes God to forgive his enemies (23:34); endures mockery as the Messiah-King who cannot save himself (23:35-39); exercises his authority as Messiah-King by assuring the repentant criminal of salvation "today" (23:43); and voluntarily relinquishes his life, committing himself in trust to God's care (23:46). In witnessing Jesus' death, the Roman centurion suddenly glorifies God and declares that Jesus was "righteous" (23:47). From the standpoint of the reader, the centurion's declaration expresses a dual truth: Within the immediate context, it affirms that Jesus was "innocent" of the political charge for which he was made to die. Within the wider context of Luke's story, it affirms that Jesus had lived all his days in perfect "obedience" to God.

It is in the death, resurrection, and ascension of Jesus that his conflict with Israel comes to fundamental resolution. At his Parousia, it will come to final resolution. As the people see Jesus die, they leave the scene of the crucifixion beating their breasts (23:48). This betokens a readiness to repent. In the eyes of the religious authorities, Jesus' death proves that he was in fact a false messiah and that they have triumphed in their conflict with him. Ironically, what the authorities do not perceive is that God and Jesus, too, will Jesus' death. Jesus wills his death because he wills what God wills (22:42). God wills Jesus' death because he thereby establishes a new covenant in which Jesus will preside in the power of the Spirit over the reconstituted people of God (22:20). In raising Jesus from the dead, God vindicates him in his conflict with Israel (24:6). And in Jesus' ascension, God exalts him to rulership over all (22:69; 24:51). Hence, at the end of Luke's gospel story, the reader, like Theophilus (1:1-4), recognizes in all "certainty" that Jesus is in fact God's supreme agent in whom God fulfills his promises to reach out to Israel (and the nations) so as to proffer the gift of salvation.

EXCURSUS: JESUS' USE OF "THE SON OF MAN"

In Luke's gospel story, as in Mark and Matthew, Jesus refers to himself numerous times as "the Son of man." Fundamentally, Jesus uses "the Son of man" in the same manner in Luke as he does in these other two Gospels.

To see how "the Son of man" functions in Luke's gospel story, perhaps one does best to compare it with the way in which the major messianic titles function. The latter are "Messiah," "Son of God,"[105] "Son of David," and "King [of the Jews]."

In function, "the Son of man" is both "like" and "unlike" these other titles. On the one hand, "the Son of man" is "like" these other titles because it, as they, applies to Jesus in a way in which it can be applied to no other human being. Thus, Jesus alone—except for the two angels who "quote" him (24:6-7)—makes use of "the Son of man" in Luke's gospel story, and when he does, he envisages only himself. Also, the ministry Jesus discharges in Luke is unique, and Jesus closely associates "the Son of man" with the peculiar aspects of his ministry. For example, Jesus declares, respectively, that the Son of man has come to seek and to save the lost (19:10); that the Son of man must suffer, be rejected, and be raised (9:22); that the Son of man will be exalted to the right hand of God (22:69); and that the Son of man will come again to usher in the consummated kingdom of God (21:27, 31). Like the messianic titles, therefore, "the Son of man" marks Jesus out as a singularly significant figure.

On the other hand, "the Son of man" is "unlike" the major messianic titles because it does not divulge, either to the reader or to other characters within Luke's gospel story, the identity of Jesus ("who he is"). As one peruses Luke's gospel story, one discovers numerous questions or (conditional or unconditional) statements featuring messianic titles the purpose of which is to address precisely this central question of Jesus' identity. Examples of such questions or (conditional or unconditional) statements are the following: "He [Jesus] shall be called the Son of the Most High" (1:32); "To you is born a Savior, who is Messiah the Lord" (2:11); "You are my beloved Son" (3:22; [9:35]); "If you are the Son of God, command . . ." (4:3; [4:9]); "You are the Son of God!" (4:41); "So then you are the Son of God?" (22:70); "He is the Messiah!" (4:41); "If you are the Messiah, tell us" (22:67); "How can they say that the Messiah is the Son of David?" (20:41); "Are you the King of the Jews?" (23:3); "This [is] the King of the Jews" (23:38); "If you are the King of the Jews, save yourself" (23:37). Contrariwise, conspicuously absent from Luke's gospel story are similar questions or statements highlighting "the Son of man." Never, for example, does the narrator or any character say, ask, or command: "You are (Are you?) the Son of man"; or "He is (Is he?) the Son of man"; or "If you are the Son of man, tell us."

To observe how remarkable this latter phenomenon is, consider how characters in Luke's gospel story regularly skirt "the Son of man" when dealing with the matter of Jesus' identity. Thus, supernatural beings such as God, angels, the devil, and demons all know who Jesus is. Still, when identifying him, they do not name him "the Son of man," but the "Son of God" or "Savior," "Messiah," and "Lord."[106] In the course of his ministry, Jesus openly designates himself, before both disciples[107] and the people,[108] as "the Son of man." Regardless, when these two groups weigh the question of Jesus' identity, neither one defines its understanding of him in terms of "the Son of man."

On the contrary, the people decide that Jesus is a "prophet" of some stature (9:7-8, 19), and Peter, on behalf of the disciples, confesses Jesus to be the "Messiah of God" (9:20). In similar fashion, although Pharisees, teachers of the law, and the entire Sanhedrin hear Jesus refer to himself as "the Son of man,"[109] the Sanhedrin does not ask him at his hearing whether he is "the Son of man" but whether he is the "Messiah" and the "Son of God" (22:67, 70). When characters in Luke's gospel story concern themselves with the question of Jesus' identity, they do not draw on "the Son of man" to explicate who he is.

Even in the case of Jesus' Parousia-sayings, "the Son of man" does not declare "who he is." In Luke's gospel story, the Jesus who will come again at the end of this age is the exalted Jesus.[110] At his hearing before the Sanhedrin, Jesus speaks of his exaltation in these words: "But from now on the Son of man shall be seated at the right hand of the power of God" (22:69). Of significance is the response Jesus' statement elicits from the Sanhedrin. Although the members of the Sanhedrin have just heard Jesus refer to himself as "the Son of man," the immediate question they pose is whether his statement is not a claim to be "the Son of God" (22:70). By way of reply, Jesus answers them in the affirmative ("So you say that I am" [22:70]). In short, what the reader learns from this exchange is that the exalted Jesus, who will one day come again in splendor (21:27), is, in identity, the Son of God.

If Jesus does not use "the Son of man" in Luke's gospel story to inform others of who he is, what does this self-designation mean? Literally, the Greek term underlying "the Son of man" denotes "the son of the man" or, more simply, "the man" or "the human being." Because this Greek term is always definite in form ("'the' Son of man") and consistently refers to one specific human ("Jesus"), it resists being deflated in meaning so that it becomes the mere equivalent of the pronoun "I" (or "me") or of such indefinite expressions as "a man" (i.e., "a human being") or "one." Nevertheless, for the reader simply to substitute in Luke "the man," or "the human being," each time one encounters "the Son of man" is not always sufficient. The reason is that although "the Son of man" invariably refers to Jesus, the expression "the man," or "the human being," taken by itself, still invites the question of "Which man?" or "Which human being?" Perhaps a glance at a particular passage will illustrate the problem. At 12:8, Jesus says, "And I tell you, everyone who acknowledges me before humans, 'the man' [some man, or human being, other than Jesus?] will also acknowledge him [that person] before the angels of

God." To forestall any possibility of confusion or ambiguity in dealing with "the Son of man," one does well to render it in English as
"this man," or "this human being." The expression "this man," or "this
human being," is a dynamic equivalent of "the Son of man." If sub-
stituted for "the Son of man," it reveals at once that "the Son of man"
does in fact refer directly to Jesus. Consider, for instance, these examples: "Foxes have holes, and birds of the air have nests, but 'this
man' has nowhere to lay his head" (9:58); "Let these words sink into
your ears, for 'this man' is to be delivered into the hands of humans"
(9:44); "And I tell you, everyone who acknowledges me before humans, 'this man' will also acknowledge him before the angels of
God" (12:8); "And then they will see 'this man' coming in a cloud
with power and great glory" (21:27).

Once one recognizes that "the Son of man" in Luke's gospel
story means "the man," or "the human being" (dynamic equivalent:
"this man," or "this human being"), one can easily make sense of the
striking phenomenon we noted above: that Jesus can openly desig-
nate himself as "the Son of man" before the religious authorities, the
people, and the disciples, and yet no one—neither supernatural being nor human being—ever asks him whether, or declares that, he
is "the Son of man." The expression "the Son of man" does not function to explicate the identity of Jesus; it does not tell the reader or
the characters "who Jesus is." In identity, the Jesus of Luke's gospel
story is the Davidic Messiah and Son of God, Lord and Savior.

To turn from Luke's gospel story to Acts, however, there is
one passage that may or may not harmonize with the view of "the
Son of man" just sketched. At Acts 7:56, Stephen exclaims, "Behold,
I see the heavens opened, and the Son of man standing at the right
hand of God." The question this passage raises is whether Stephen,
in designating Jesus as "the Son of man," is not identifying him. If
this is what Stephen is to be understood as doing, then Luke's use
of "the Son of man" in Acts is completely different from that found
in the Gospel. Instead of simply denoting "the man," or "the human
being," "the Son of man" has now been transformed into a name,
or title, explicating "who Jesus is." In this event, a clear development has taken place between the Gospel and Acts as regards the
way in which the term "the Son of man" functions.

It is my firm belief, however, that such a development has not
taken place and that the use of "the Son of man" in Acts tallies with
that found in Luke's Gospel. In Acts 7:56, Stephen, gazing into
heaven, speaks of the exalted Jesus. Indeed, his words are a variation

of the ones Jesus uttered in the Gospel at his hearing before the Sanhedrin: "But from now on," Jesus asserts, "the Son of man shall be seated at the right hand of the power of God" (22:69). In both Acts 7:56 and Luke 22:69, "the Son of man" may be taken to mean "the man," or "the human being." When so understood, it then becomes, in Stephen's saying, an alternate way of referring to "Jesus." Notice, for example, that immediately preceding Acts 7:56, Luke as narrator anticipates Stephen's words but makes mention of "Jesus" instead of "the Son of man": At Acts 7:55 Luke reports, "But he [Stephen] . . . gazed into heaven and saw . . . *Jesus* standing at the right hand of God." By the same token, the subsequent prayer Stephen makes in Acts 7:59 is also offered not to "the Son of man," but to "Jesus": "Lord *Jesus*," Stephen cries out, "receive my spirit!" In sum, the thrust of this argument is that the sense of Stephen's use of "the Son of man" in Acts 7:56 may be captured as follows: "Behold, I see the heavens opened, and 'the man' [i.e., 'Jesus'] standing at the right hand of God." If this is correct, then Acts 7:56 can be seen to stand in a line with the way Paul describes Jesus in a passage like Acts 17:31: ". . . because [God] has fixed a day on which he will judge the world in righteousness by a *man* [i.e., Jesus] whom he has appointed. . . ."

To return to the gospel story of Luke, the evidence here concerning the way "the Son of man" is used is clear. Viewed as a whole, this evidence strongly suggests that "the Son of man" does not function as a christological title but as a technical term. The purpose of a christological title is to set forth in some measure both the identity and the significance of Jesus. For its part, "the Son of man" proves not to be a christological title: Although it points to Jesus as a singularly significant figure, it does not explicate his identity (tell "who he is"). Instead, it refers to Jesus more modestly as "the man," or "the human being" ("this man," or "this human being").

Still, although "the Son of man" is not a christological title, it does stand out as a technical term. It is such because, like other technical terms, it bears a precise meaning within the world of Luke's story (not "I" or "one" or "a human being" but always "the man," or "the human being," referring exclusively to "Jesus"). In the final analysis, therefore, "the Son of man" is of the same nature as such other key terms and expressions in Luke's gospel story as "the kingdom of God," "peace," "salvation," "today," and "it is necessary."

In light of our discussion of "the Son of man," what role does the latter play in Luke's gospel story? The role "the Son of man" plays in Luke is fundamentally the same as the role it plays in Mark and Matthew. In designating himself as "the Son of man," Jesus refers to himself as "the man" who, though acting on divine authority, is repudiated by Israel and gentiles but vindicated and exalted by God (now in the resurrection and ascension; later at his Parousia). In Luke's gospel story, therefore, the designation "the Son of man" emphasizes the twin features of repudiation and vindication.

3 THE STORY OF THE AUTHORITIES

The major conflict in Luke's gospel story pits Jesus against Israel. Israel, we know, is made up of the religious authorities and the people. Still, in their attitudes toward Jesus, Luke draws a sharp distinction, as we have seen, between the people and the authorities. For the most part, Luke's treatment of the people is irenic, to wit: Except for isolated incidents,[1] the people remain well-disposed toward Jesus; until Jesus appears before Pilate, the people take no concerted stand against him (23:4, 13-25); at Jesus' crucifixion, the people watch but do not mock (23:35); and after Jesus has died, the people exhibit a readiness to repent (23:48). Because Jesus tends to be on good terms with the people, his chief antagonists at the human level are the religious authorities. Together with Judas, who becomes Satan's pawn (22:3), they are the ones responsible for Jesus' death. Apart from Jesus himself, they influence most the development of the plot of Luke's gospel story.

The groups Luke identifies as constituting the religious authorities are the Pharisees, scribes (lawyers, teachers of the law),[2] chief priests, captains (officers) of the temple, elders, rulers, and Sadducees. Although historically these groups are all known, scholarly portraits of them tend to be tenuous and conflicting.[3] In Jesus' own lifetime, the Pharisees and Sadducees were politically active and socially rivalrous groups. The Sadducees[4] were from among the governing class, and their base of power was in Jerusalem. Wealthy and conservative, they were concerned with the survival of Israel as a nation in the here and now. As such, they supported the status quo, including cooperation with Rome. They also took a traditionalist approach to the interpretation of scripture, stressing human responsibility for history and repudiating Pharisaic doctrines concerning the near end of this age, the resurrection of the dead, the last judgment, and eternal life. Less privileged than the Sadducees, the Pharisees[5] were nonetheless highly respected leaders who apparently enjoyed considerable influence among the people. Their goal was that Israel should become the righteous nation of the covenant.[6] To this end, they cultivated an approach to scripture and traditions intended to enhance the distinctiveness of Israel among the nations. The stress the Pharisees placed on such matters as tithing, ritual purity, and Sabbath observance was part and parcel of this program.[7]

The factor distinguishing the chief priests, the captains of the temple,[8] the scribes, the elders, and the rulers[9] was either the hereditary office they occupied, or the profession they practiced, or the social position they enjoyed. The elders were members of the governing class,[10] whether in the villages or in Jerusalem, which meant that they wielded considerable political power and tended to be both wealthy and landed. The chief priests,[11] who were also members of the governing class and supposedly descendants of Zadok (priest under David and Solomon),[12] formed a consistory of approximately ten persons entrusted with the supervision of the temple and its sacrificial system. The scribes[13] were the professional people of Jewish society, the bureaucrats and educators. They stood in the service of the governing class, keeping the records and functioning as administrators, teachers, and judges. Those scribes who were especially learned in the law were the theologians and lawyers of the day. Along with the chief priests and elders, scribes, too, were members of the Sanhedrin, or High Council, which had its chambers on the grounds of the temple. Presided over by the high priest, the Sanhedrin numbered seventy-one members. During the rule of the Roman prefects from A.D. 6 to 41, it functioned as the domestic government of Judea (=Idumea, Judea, Samaria); during the rule of the Roman procurators from A.D. 44 to 66, its area of influence encompassed Galilee as well. Although the Sandedrin was ultimately subject to Roman rule (represented in Luke's story of Jesus by Pilate), it nonetheless exercised broad powers of a religious, judicial, and financial nature.

In his polemical portrayal of the religious authorities, Luke highlights not so much the historical differences that characterized the various groups as the solidarity they exhibit in their opposition to Jesus. Indeed, Luke stereotypes the religious authorities, which is the major reason they can be treated as a group character. One exception to the authorities' show of solidarity is the compliment

some scribes pay Jesus after he has silenced the Sadducees in a controversy concerning resurrection-life (20:39). Apparently, Luke
thinks of the scribes as Pharisaic in orientation (5:30; Acts 23:9). As
such, they would approve of Jesus' defense of the notion of resurrection in the face of a Sadducean denial of this (20:27; Acts 23:6-
9). Overall, however, Luke's description of the scribes contributes
significantly to the impression he conveys that the several groups
of religious authorities are, in fact, fundamentally united in their
opposition to Jesus. In Galilee and on the way to Jerusalem, the
scribes support the Pharisees in opposing Jesus. In Jerusalem,
the scribes support the chief priests. The scribes, therefore, serve to
knit together, in a bond of opposition against Jesus, Pharisees and
chief priests.

In Luke's gospel narration, then, the principal opponents
of Jesus, until he reaches Jerusalem, are the Pharisees. Otherwise,
Jesus also has to do with scribes (lawyers, teachers of the law);[14]
elders of the Jews (7:3); rulers of synagogues (8:41; 13:14); a ruler of
the Pharisees (14:1); and a rich ruler (18:18). Once he is in Jerusalem,
Jesus' principal opponents are the chief priests, and they, in turn, are
abetted by the scribes,[15] elders,[16] and temple officers (22:4, 52).

CONFLICT OVER AUTHORITY

In Luke, as in Mark and Matthew,[17] the matter of "authority"
lies at the heart of the conflict between Jesus and the religious
authorities. Indeed, a strong indicator of this is the way Luke characterizes Jesus and the authorities.

Jesus, as we have frequently observed, is the one who perfectly "serves the purposes not of humans, but of God." God in his
end-time rule is present in Jesus as Messiah and Son of God, inau-
gurating the time of salvation. Morally, Jesus stands in a right relationship with both God and humans: Perfectly obedient to God and
guided by his plan of salvation, Jesus has come to seek and to save
the lost (19:10; 23:47).

In stark contrast to Jesus, the religious authorities are stereo-
typed as those who "serve the purposes not of God, but of humans."
The root character trait distinguishing them, we learned in chapter 1,
is self-righteousness.[18] By virtue of their self-righteousness, the authorities stand in a wrong relationship with both God and humans.
They stand in a wrong relationship with God, for they reject John's
baptism of repentance (7:30) and falsely believe that they are already

righteous (5:32; 18:9). Equally, they stand in a wrong relationship with humans. Instead of being leaders who serve others, they are hypocrites who strive for self-exaltation and the preservation of the status quo even while despising and taking advantage of others, especially the "poor."[19] In consequence of their self-righteousness, the authorities are unable to comprehend reality aright: Their perspective tends to be self-centered, human, and this-worldly. In encounter with Jesus, they do not perceive him to be Israel's Messiah-King in whom God's rule is present.[20] Just the opposite, they grow to regard him as a false messiah who perverts Israel by stirring the people to rebellion with his teaching (23:2, 5). Accordingly, their conflict with Jesus is over authority and the critical question of who will rule God's people.[21] To preserve their own authority as Israel's leaders and the survival of Israel as the nation of the covenant, they conclude at last that they must destroy Jesus (19:47; 22:2). Their conflict with him, therefore, is to the death, and it holds unforeseen consequences for them. The purpose of this chapter is to trace both the development and outcome of this conflict.

PRELUDE TO THE CONFLICT

In the beginning of his gospel story, Luke presents John and especially Jesus to the reader (1:5—2:52). As a result, the religious authorities make only the most fleeting of appearances in this part (2:46). Despite this, Luke uses this part to influence in a preliminary way the attitude the reader will take toward the authorities.

The first representatives of the religious establishment the reader encounters are Zechariah, who is a common priest,[22] and the teachers in the temple with whom the twelve-year-old Jesus converses (2:46-47). When compared with the religious authorities the reader later meets, Zechariah is a study in contrast, a foil or antitype.[23] In God's eyes, Zechariah is "righteous," for he does God's will and keeps his law (1:6). Also, Zechariah looks forward in prayer to the time when God will remember his promises and act decisively on behalf of Israel and even himself (1:13-17). Upon the birth of his own son, John, and having heard news of Jesus, Zechariah bursts forth in prophetic utterance, praising God because he will raise up Jesus, Israel's "horn of salvation," and thus visit and redeem his people (1:68-69). Both in the right relationship in which he stands with God and in his ready reception of Jesus as Israel's Davidic Messiah and Savior, Zechariah exemplifies the kind of person that the reader now anticipates all the religious authorities in Israel will be. Regrettably, we already know that this expectation is doomed to disappointment.

Other representatives of the religious establishment the reader meets in the beginning of Luke's gospel story are the teachers in the temple (2:46-47). At the end of his public ministry, Jesus will clash in the temple with religious authorities (19:47—20:40). As a twelve-year-old "boy" who is already aware that he is the "Son" and "Servant" of God (*pais* [2:43]), Jesus converses in the temple with teachers. That his first meeting with members of the religious establishment should take place in the temple is thoroughly fitting, for this is not only the place of God's presence but also the seat of the establishment's power. Accordingly, both Jesus and the teachers are "at home" here. Still, at a future date Jesus will wrest control of the temple from religious authorities (19:45-46). For now, however, the teachers, in their exchange with the boy Jesus, are "amazed" at his understanding and answers (2:47). Even so, "amazement" is an ambiguous response, because it suggests "perplexity."[24] In point of fact, the amazement the teachers exhibit prompts the reader to wonder how Jesus will be received by religious authorities later in the gospel story.

CONFLICT IN GALILEE AND ON THE WAY TO JERUSALEM

The major debut of the religious authorities occurs in the middle of Luke's gospel story (3:1—21:38). The moment Jesus encounters the authorities, conflict erupts (5:17—6:11). Nevertheless, as Jesus goes about Galilee in the first phase of his ministry (3:21—9:50) and travels to Jerusalem in the second (9:51—19:46), the tenor and intensity of his conflict with the authorities remain remarkably the same. Not until Jesus is in Jerusalem (19:47—21:38) does the conflict become perceptibly more acute, leading to his passion (chaps. 22–23). In discussing the conflict Jesus has with the authorities in Galilee and on the way to Jerusalem, we shall begin by exploring some of the features characterizing it.

Characteristic Features of the Conflict

From the standpoint of the reader, Jesus' conflict with the religious authorities in Galilee and on the way to Jerusalem is of the nature of an extended, intermittent "conversation."[25] To be sure, this conversation tends to be heated, fierce, and acrimonious. Also, it gives the impression of being one-sided: Although Jesus never hesitates to face his opponents and speak his mind, they are not disposed to do the same. Still, the many exchanges between Jesus and the authorities do constitute a conversation in the sense that, through them, the reader comes to know the position of both parties on a variety of issues.

The settings in which many of the exchanges take place are typical.[26] At times, the religious authorities find Jesus sitting at table with toll collectors and sinners and become provoked by this.[27] On three occasions a Pharisee invites Jesus to dinner, and either before or during the meal something happens to incite controversy.[28] Twice Jesus is asked the selfsame question, once by a lawyer and once by a ruler: "[Good] Teacher, what shall I do to inherit eternal life?" (10:25-37; 18:18-27). And repeatedly, Jesus heals on the Sabbath, to the dismay or indignation of the authorities watching him.[29]

The issues Jesus and the authorities debate are weighty and go to the heart of what it means to rule God's people. They have to do with matters of authority, tradition and rules of purity, law, and one's relationship to God or neighbor. Jesus addresses these issues from the divine point of view, in light of the end-time rule of God that in him is a present reality in Israel. The authorities address these issues from their human, this-worldly point of view. The upshot is that as these issues are contested, the reader is consistently invited to adjudge Jesus to be right and the authorities wrong.

Despite the fierce nature of the exchanges between Jesus and the religious authorities, neither side severs ties with the other and both see to it that the conversation continues. Jesus remains open to the authorities because he would summon them to repentance. The authorities apparently maintain contact with Jesus because they are perplexed[30] by him: Although he antagonizes them, they are nonetheless attracted to him (5:17). For example, the authorities recognize that Jesus is powerful in word and deed,[31] yet they can conceive neither that he is Israel's Messiah-King (19:38-39) nor even that he is a prophet (7:39). By the same token, they are quite willing to afford him the respect due a teacher[32] and thus deal with him as one who is their social equal.[33] For this reason, they invite him to dine with them,[34] ask him to heal a centurion's slave (7:3-5), warn him against Herod Antipas's desire to kill him (13:31), and solicit his teaching (17:20; 18:18). In one extraordinary episode, Jairus, a ruler of a synagogue, appeals to Jesus in great faith that he come and see after his daughter, and Jesus readily complies (8:41-42, 49-56). Because of his faith, however, Jairus becomes a foil for the other authorities: He exemplifies that attitude of heart with which all the authorities should receive Jesus but do not do so.

One of the most striking features of Jesus' conflict with the religious authorities in Galilee and on the way to Jerusalem is that Luke tends not to permit it to intensify to the point of becoming "acutely confrontational": Save perhaps for three instances (10:25; 11:45, 53), the authorities do not challenge Jesus to his face because of something he himself says or does. To illustrate: (a) When Jesus forgives the paralytic his sins, the scribes and the Pharisees, though they charge Jesus with speaking blasphemies, nevertheless utter their thoughts "in their hearts" (5:21-22). (b) As Jesus and the disciples feast in Levi's house with toll collectors and sinners, the Pharisees and their scribes grumble about this but address their words to the disciples, not Jesus (5:29-30). (c) Disturbed that the disciples do not honor the custom of fasting, the Pharisees and their scribes come to Jesus but complain about the disciples (5:33-35). (d) Offended because the disciples, while walking with Jesus through grain fields, have in their judgment broken the Sabbath rest by unlawfully working, some of the Pharisees and their scribes say nothing to Jesus but take vigorous issue with the disciples (6:1-2). (e) Although the scribes and the Pharisees watch Jesus to see if he will heal on the Sabbath and thus give them reason to charge him with breaking the Sabbath rest, they nevertheless do not confront him when he does heal but instead discuss among themselves what they might do to him (6:6-11). (f) Appalled that Jesus should have allowed a woman known to be a sinner to touch him, Simon the Pharisee voices his objection not to Jesus, but "to himself" (7:39). (g) Despite being shocked that Jesus does not first wash before eating, the Pharisee hosting him does not challenge him but holds his tongue (11:38). (h) In a synagogue, the ruler, angered because Jesus has healed a stooped woman on the Sabbath, vents his indignation not on Jesus, but on the people (13:14). (i) At meal on a Sabbath in the home of a ruler of the Pharisees, Jesus challenges the lawyers and the Pharisees there to debate the legality of healing on the Sabbath; they remain silent, however, for they are at a loss for words (14:1-6). (j) Once, when all the toll collectors and the sinners draw near to Jesus to hear him, the Pharisees and the scribes, though they find this repugnant, nevertheless content themselves with merely grumbling about Jesus (15:1-2). (k) Overhearing Jesus as he teaches the disciples, the Pharisees sneer at him, but apparently among themselves (16:1, 14). (*l*) Finally, when Jesus, about to enter Jerusalem, is hailed by the whole multitude of the disciples as King, some of the Pharisees there are not so bold as to attack Jesus himself for accepting such acclaim but instead call upon him to rebuke the disciples (19:37-39). To repeat, despite the fierce nature of the conflict that occurs between Jesus and the authorities in Galilee and on Jesus' way to Jerusalem, this conflict tends not to become acutely confrontational. Quick though the authorities are to assail the disciples or the people for doing what they believe to be wrong, they are far less inclined to challenge Jesus himself for some action of his.

The Course of the Conflict

In Galilee

In the first phase of the middle of Luke's gospel story (3:1— 9:50), Jesus discharges his public ministry principally in Galilee (4:14—9:50). Despite his rejection by the villagers of Nazareth, news of him circulates and the people gather about him. Against a backdrop of widespread activity and popularity, Luke tells of the first encounter between Jesus and the religious authorities in the persons of the Pharisees and scribes (teachers of the law).

This first encounter between Jesus and the authorities gives rise to sustained conflict: In a cycle of five controversies, Jesus clashes with the authorities over questions of authority, tradition and rules of purity, and law (5:17—6:11). To situate Jesus and the authorities at the same place and to describe both him and them, Luke fashions a brief setting and places it at the head of this cycle (5:17). In this setting, Jesus stands out as the center of attention. He is pictured as teaching and as a figure of extraordinary authority, for the "power of the Lord [is] with him to heal." By the same token, Jesus' presence has attracted a huge throng of Pharisees and teachers of the law who have come from "every village of Galilee and Judea and from Jerusalem" (5:17). These Pharisees and teachers are themselves figures of authority: Not only are they leaders in Israel, but they also "sit" about Jesus, which is itself a posture of authority. Overall, therefore, the purpose for which Luke uses this setting is to describe Jesus' first cycle of controversies with the religious authorities as a clash between "figures of authority": In these controversies Jesus, the supreme agent of the new time of the kingdom, confronts Pharisees and scribes, representatives of the (religious) establishment of the villages of all Israel.

Surrounded by the seated scribes and Pharisees and a standing crowd of people, Jesus himself provokes the first controversy (5:18-26). At issue is the critical question of "authority." When men bring a paralytic to Jesus, he sees their faith and forgives the man his sins. In Luke's story world, forgiving sins can accomplish healing, for sickness can be viewed as symptomatic of sin.[35] As the scribes and the Pharisees witness Jesus forgive sins, they charge him "in their hearts" with speaking blasphemies. To their way of thinking, Jesus has spuriously arrogated to himself a prerogative belonging to none but God (John 10:33).[36] Perceiving their thoughts, Jesus addresses the authorities and repudiates their charge, asserting that he is "the man" who in fact has authority on earth to forgive sins (5:24). As proof of this, Jesus turns to the paralytic and commands him to rise, take up his bed, and go home. When the paralytic does as Jesus commands, all those present—both crowd and authorities—are seized by amazement, glorify God, and, filled with awe, exclaim that they have seen strange things today. In other words, in the healing Jesus performs both the authorities and the people find themselves overwhelmed by a strong sense of God's presence. Still, commendable as this is, it does not mitigate the hard truth that to sense in Jesus God's presence is not yet to receive him in faith, or to hear his call to repentance, or to become his disciple. It may mean that one concludes that he is, at most, a prophet of some sort (9:7-8, 19).

The second controversy revolves around tradition and matters of purity. With the disciples at his side, Jesus triggers it, too, as the guest of Levi, who gives a banquet in his honor (5:29-32). When the Pharisees and their scribes observe a great crowd of toll collectors and sinners reclining with Jesus and the disciples, they approach the disciples grumbling their displeasure and demanding to know why the disciples eat with toll collectors and sinners. Apparently, Pharisees in Jesus' day were concerned to eat meals at home in the same state of ritual purity as was required of priests in the temple.[37] In a special sense, therefore, to be at table was, for them, to be in the presence of God. Correlatively, to share table fellowship with toll collectors and sinners was in their eyes abhorrent. Toll collectors were of the same ilk as thieves, robbers, and extortioners,[38] and sinners were persons who lived in flagrant disregard of God's law or pursued dishonorable vocations.[39] By breaking bread with unclean persons like toll collectors and sinners, Jesus and the disciples make themselves unclean.

In his retort to the outrage of the Pharisees and their scribes, Jesus places the table fellowship he has with toll collectors and sinners squarely within the context of his mission: In granting toll collectors and sinners the gift of his presence, he is seeking out the "lost" to summon them to repentance and to proffer them forgiveness, salvation, and community (5:32; 19:10). Implicit in Jesus' reply is also a thinly veiled warning: Although the Pharisees and their scribes may think that they are righteous with God, in reality they are as lost as the sinners with whom he has table fellowship (5:32).

The third controversy follows the second without change of setting, and once again the focus is on tradition (5:33-39). What sparks this controversy is the behavior of the disciples. The Pharisees and their scribes have noticed that in contrast to their own disciples and the disciples of John, Jesus' disciples not only do not fast as custom dictates but also seem overly eager to feast.[40] This prompts these Pharisees and scribes to approach Jesus and insist on knowing why. By way of reply, Jesus gives two answers, the first of which is cryptic and the second of which is a parable.

In his first answer (5:34-35), Jesus likens himself to a bridegroom, the present time of salvation to a wedding celebration, and his disciples to wedding guests. To the reader, though not to the Pharisees and their scribes, the point Jesus makes is plain: Just as the present time of salvation is tantamount to a time of celebration, so the disciples, like wedding guests, feast because they are joyful and do not fast, as bespeaks sorrow and mourning. Nevertheless, just as the time comes when the wedding celebration ends and it becomes appropriate again for the celebrants to fast, so the time will come when Jesus will be removed from the disciples by death and then they, too, will fast.

In his second, parabolic answer (5:36-39), Jesus makes two points. To score the first one, he draws on maxims telling of a new patch, of a new and an old garment, and of new wine and old wineskins. By means of these maxims, Jesus asserts categorically that the "new" time of salvation is utterly incompatible with the "old" time of Pharisaic tradition (5:36-38).[41] One must beware, therefore, not to "tear," or destroy, the "new" in a futile attempt to preserve the "old." And the second point Jesus makes is this: Just as a person who has drunk old wine shuns new wine because he or she is not accustomed to it, so the Pharisees and their scribes resolutely cling to the "old" ways of their tradition even while resisting the "new" ways of the present time of salvation (5:39). As is obvious, Jesus uses this controversy to describe for his opponents the clash taking place between the "new" time of the kingdom he has inaugurated and the "old" time of the religious establishment they are defending. In this clash, Jesus observes, they have determined that they will preserve the status quo, on the grounds that the "old" is what is good (5:39).

In the fourth controversy, the topic shifts from tradition to law and those inciting conflict are the disciples (6:1-5). One Sabbath, as Jesus makes his way through grainfields, the disciples, hungry, pluck ears of grain, rub them with their hands, and eat. Witnessing this, some of the Pharisees promptly accuse the disciples of unlawfully breaking the Sabbath rest. What disturbs the Pharisees is not that the disciples have plucked ears of grain in a stranger's field, for that is permitted (Deut. 23:25; Lev. 19:9-10). No, the problem is that the disciples have rubbed the ears of grain to separate the kernels from the chaff. To the Pharisees, this is tantamount to "reaping," to putting a sickle to standing grain, and is forbidden on the Sabbath (Exod. 34:21; Deut. 23:25). In defense of the disciples, Jesus rejects the Pharisees' accusation with a double reply. In his initial response (6:3-4), Jesus appeals to scripture. In scripture, he argues, one reads approvingly of what David once did. When he and his companions were hungry, David entered the house of God, took the loaves of presentation, which were reserved by the law for use by the priests alone, and ate from them and gave to his men (1 Sam. 21:1-6). The inference one is to draw from this, Jesus implies, is clear: The act of the hungry disciples enjoys the same kind of scriptural sanction as the act of hungry David;[42] accordingly, the disciples have not violated the Sabbath rest. In his second response (6:5), Jesus effectively exculpates the disciples of any guilt for breaking the Sabbath rest by flatly invoking his own absolute authority: As "the man" who has authority over the Sabbath, he has sanctioned what the disciples have done and they are therefore not to be accused of breaking the Sabbath rest.

The fifth controversy also centers on a matter of the law (6:6-11), but it is Jesus, not the disciples, who touches it off. Teaching in a synagogue on another Sabbath, Jesus encounters a man whose right, or "main," hand is atrophied. So as to turn up something with which they can charge Jesus, the scribes and the Pharisees lurk in the background "watching him." As they see it, for Jesus to heal this man would be for him to violate the Sabbath: Because this man's ailment is in no sense life-threatening, he has no need to be healed on the Sabbath and Jesus could just as easily heal him some other day (13:14). Aware of their thoughts, Jesus challenges the authorities' interpretation of Sabbath law by posing a rhetorical question. By means of this device, he affirms that, in principle, it is always lawful on the Sabbath to do good and to save life. Then, looking around at all the authorities, Jesus restores the man's hand to wholeness. Becoming furious, the authorities react to Jesus' healing by considering what they might do to him (6:11).

On this note, Luke draws the curtain on this first cycle of controversies between Jesus and the religious authorities. The final reaction of the authorities—they become furious with Jesus and discuss among themselves what they might do to him (6:11)—bespeaks the hostility that they will henceforth harbor against him until the time he enters Jerusalem and their antipathy becomes still more intense (19:47—21:38). But again, such hostility on the part of the authorities neither induces them to break off "conversation" with Jesus nor precludes them from making a friendly gesture (13:31). In Mark, by contrast, the comment on which the first cycle of controversies concludes is that the conflict between Jesus and the authorities has already become a struggle to the death (Mark 3:6).

Later during his ministry in Galilee, Jesus again becomes embroiled in conflict. Invited to a banquet by a Pharisee named Simon, Jesus reclines at meal (7:36-50). Upon learning that Jesus is in Simon's house, a woman approaches him and stands back of him at his feet. This woman, known to be a sinner, has nonetheless experienced God's forgiveness.[43] Weeping at having been forgiven, she performs three acts to express her gratitude, to wit: She washes Jesus' feet with her tears and, to dry them, lets down her hair—an immodest act for a woman in public;[44] and she both kisses Jesus' feet and anoints them with expensive perfume. The counterpart to these three acts are three acts of hospitality that, significantly, Simon does not extend to Jesus: Simon neither gives Jesus water to wash his feet, nor does he greet Jesus with a kiss, nor does he provide Jesus with olive oil to groom his head. Indeed, in witnessing the woman's acts, Simon becomes contemptuous of Jesus. Having heard that people look upon Jesus as a prophet (e.g., 7:16), Simon thinks to himself: "If this man were a prophet, he would have known who and what sort of woman this is who is touching him, for she is a sinner" (7:39). To Simon's way of thinking, Jesus has made himself unclean by allowing this woman to touch him.

Perceiving Simon's thoughts, Jesus tells him a parable. The point of this parable is that, given a creditor and two debtors, the debtor to whom the creditor forgives the greater sum is also the debtor who shows the creditor the greater amount of gratitude (7:40-43). Applying this parable to Simon and the sinful woman (7:44-47), Jesus invites the following comparison: The woman, knowing herself to be a sinner and having experienced God's forgiveness, has shown "much" gratitude toward Jesus; Simon, believing himself to be righteous and therefore in need of little forgiveness, has shown Jesus "little" hospitality (7:47). Then, turning directly toward the woman, Jesus confirms that, by virtue of her faith in God, she has indeed been forgiven and saved (7:48, 50). The upshot of this episode is that Jesus, through this altercation, has confronted Simon with the necessary fruits of his own self-righteousness: Wrongly believing that he is right with God and in need of little forgiveness, Simon unwittingly closes himself to God's forgiveness and becomes both exclusive (e.g., toward the sinful woman) and loveless (e.g., toward Jesus).

Jesus' quarrel with Simon marks the end of his conflict with the religious authorities during this first, largely Galilean, phase of his ministry. Still, as he is about to complete this phase, Jesus looks ahead and, envisaging the authorities, utters his most ominous word yet. In delivering his first passion-prediction, he tells the disciples that divine necessity dictates that he "be rejected by the elders and chief priests and scribes, and be killed" (9:22). Clearly, Luke uses Jesus' prediction to prepare the reader far in advance for the passion, the culmination of Jesus' conflict with the authorities.

On the Way to Jerusalem

In phase two of the middle of Luke's gospel story (9:51—19:46), Jesus journeys to Jerusalem to accomplish his "exodus." On the way, Jesus repeatedly clashes with the religious authorities so as to summon them to repentance. As the authorities view these clashes, however, they prove Jesus to be a dangerous adversary. Even so, the authorities still are not moved to terminate their dealings with him. On the contrary , they continue to respect him as a teacher and therefore to accept him as their social equal. As a result, one or more of them invite him to dinner, warn him about Herod Antipas's desire to kill him (13:31), and apparently ask him for instruction about the coming of the kingdom or how to inherit eternal life (17:20; 18:18). But again, none of these overtures should be taken to mean that Jesus has in any sense become their friend.

Because Jesus interacts on his way to Jerusalem not simply with the religious authorities but also with the disciples and the people, his clashes with the authorities occur periodically, almost on a rotating basis. The opponents Jesus faces are primarily the Pharisees and the scribes (lawyers). Thus, in an initial controversy a lawyer stands up to test Jesus' theological acumen by asking him how he might inherit eternal life (10:25-37). At bottom, the lawyer's question is

ethical in nature: How is he to lead his life now so that it will ultimately issue in eternal life? Jesus replies by asking a counterquestion: "What is written in the law?" Reciting from Moses, the lawyer
answers that one is to love God wholly and the neighbor as self.[45] To
this Jesus gives his assent: "You have answered right; do this, and
you will live."

So far, Jesus and the lawyer ostensibly agree. Behind the notion
of "neighbor," however, lies profound disagreement. To the lawyer's
way of thinking, the neighbor he is to love is the Israelite. To Jesus'
way of thinking, the neighbor is also the enemy (6:27-35). Wishing
to assert himself in debate with Jesus, the lawyer presses Jesus to tell
him who his neighbor is (10:29). Replying with the parable of the
good Samaritan, Jesus demolishes the lawyer's notion of neighbor by
leading him to admit that his neighbor is anyone, even a perceived
enemy like a Samaritan, who is in need of his love (10:36-37).[46]

Invited by another Pharisee to dinner, Jesus reclines at table
without having first washed (11:37-38). This shocks the Pharisee,
since it means to him that Jesus dares to begin the meal without
having bothered to cleanse himself ritually. In the Pharisee's eyes,
Jesus' life style constitutes an offense against tradition and the rules
of purity. Addressing first the Pharisees present and then the lawyers
(scribes), Jesus assails the two groups with a litany of three woes
each (11:39-52). In these woes, he castigates both groups because of
their "character" and "life style": As Israel's leaders, Jesus contends,
they have utterly failed.[47]

As a preface to his three woes against the Pharisees, Jesus levels
a programmatic charge against them: In principle, they are hypocrites,[48] for although outwardly they are clean, inwardly they are
full of greed and avarice (11:39). Indeed, if they would become as
clean on the inside as on the outside, they must give away their possessions as alms yet ask nothing from the poor in return (11:41).[49]
Following this programmatic charge, Jesus enunciates specific woes
against the Pharisees. He condemns them for paying diligent attention in the practice of religion to what is peripheral while disregarding what is central: Concerned to tithe the most insignificant of the
garden herbs, they neglect justice and love of God (11:42). Also, they
are self-important, destroying community: They wrongly exalt themselves over others, laying false claim to honor and status by loving
the best seat in the synagogues and salutations in the market places
(11:43).[50] And they are like unmarked graves, unclean to the core, so
that anyone who comes in contact with them is defiled (11:44).[51]

Taking sharp note of Jesus' woes against the Pharisees, a lawyer at the dinner objects that these woes are equally insulting to lawyers (scribes) (11:45). In swift reply, Jesus launches into a series of three woes against the lawyers, charging them, too, with failed leadership. In particular, Jesus denounces the lawyers for reasons such as these: They impose a superabundance of regulations on the people, yet do nothing to help them cope in trying to keep these regulations (11:46). They build impressive tombs for the prophets their fathers slew, yet they take after their fathers, for they, too, will kill the emissaries God sends (11:47-51). And although they have been entrusted with the key to the knowledge of God as revealed in scripture, they have used this key neither to avail themselves of this knowledge nor to enlighten the people (11:52).[52]

After pronouncing these woes, Jesus promptly leaves the dinner. Incensed at him, the scribes and the Pharisees begin to resent him terribly, to watch closely his utterances on many things, and to lie in wait to see if they can't catch him in something he might say (11:53-54). Meanwhile, Jesus, in the company of his disciples and a massive crowd, warns his disciples to beware of the hypocrisy of the Pharisees (12:1). Because outwardly they appear to be one thing but inwardly prove to be something else, at the latter day they will most assuredly be exposed for what they truly are (12:2).

Still underway toward Jerusalem. Jesus incites further conflict when he again performs healings on two different Sabbaths. In the first healing (13:10-17) Jesus, by the power of touch and command, enables a stooped woman to stand erect. Angered by this, the leader of the synagogue reproaches not Jesus, but the crowd of people. Since the woman was not in danger of dying, to heal her on the Sabbath is to engage in "unnecessary work." In point of fact, God has made available six other days each week on which such deeds can be done. Lashing out at the leader and his supporters, Jesus chastises them as "hypocrites" and argues: If it is lawful, as they believe, to release an ox or an ass on the Sabbath to give it water, then certainly it is much more God's will that this woman, who is Abraham's daughter, be released on the Sabbath from the eighteen-year bond in which Satan has held her. Shamed because of their narrow legalism and lovelessness, Jesus' adversaries fall silent. All the crowd, however, rejoices over the glorious things Jesus has done.

The second healing is a doublet of the preceding one (14:1-6). Not untypically, Jesus is a guest at a dinner, this time on a Sabbath at the home of a ruler of the Pharisees. Other Pharisees and lawyers (scribes) are also guests, as are prominent persons from the village. Immediately to the front of Jesus is a man who has dropsy. To see whether Jesus will perform another "unnecessary healing," the Pharisees and lawyers "watch" him. Knowing their thoughts, Jesus does three things: He first asks them whether it is lawful to heal on the Sabbath; next, he heals the man; and third, he asks them if it weren't true that if one of them had a son or ox fall into a well on the Sabbath, that man would go at once and rescue his son or ox. To neither of Jesus' questions can the lawyers and Pharisees muster a reply. They concede by their very silence that their understanding of the law is exclusive and loveless.

Hearing no word from the lawyers and Pharisees, Jesus heals the man with dropsy. Also, making the most of this opportunity, he delivers ethical advice to his host and narrates two parables criticizing the dinner guests. The topic Jesus continues to pursue is that of "life style," as it relates to those like the lawyers and the Pharisees and their friends who comprise the leaders of society and the wealthy. In the parable of the choice of places at the table (14:7-11), Jesus treats the matter of "honor and shame."[53] Paradoxically, one acquires true honor, Jesus asserts, not by exalting oneself over others, but by humbling oneself. How can this be so? Because at the latter day God will reverse human fortunes, exalting the humble and humbling the exalted.[54] In the ethical advice Jesus gives his host (14:12-14), he calls on him to share his largesse, not with social equals who can repay him, but with the "poor," who cannot repay him. Paradoxically, by sharing his blessings with no strings attached, he will in fact be reimbursed, by God at the latter day.[55] And in the parable of the great supper (14:15-24), Jesus warns the ruler's wealthy guests that those who will one day eat bread in the kingdom of God will not be Israel's elite, who will exclude themselves from the banquet, but the "poor" and gentiles.

A brief time later on his journey, Jesus again resorts to parabolic speech to warn the religious authorities about their attitudes toward the "poor" and the unclean. As all the toll collectors and sinners throng to Jesus to hear his word, the Pharisees and the scribes grumble against him for receiving these people and eating with them (15:2). In reply to the Pharisees and the scribes, Jesus narrates three parables, that of the lost sheep (15:3-7), of the lost coin (15:8-10), and of the prodigal son (15:11-32).[56] As the reader hears these parables against the background of the authorities' grumbling, the message they convey is clear: God and the whole host of heaven rejoice when what is "lost" (sheep, coin, son) is "found."[57] Jesus' purpose in receiving toll collectors and sinners and in eating with them is to "find" the "lost," to summon them to repentance and salvation. The Pharisees and the scribes, by believing that they are in no need of repentance (15:7) and by refusing to have anything to do with the "poor" and the unclean (15:30), are in reality alienating themselves from God. In point of fact, they are the "lost" who are in dire need of being "found."

Turning away from the Pharisees and the scribes, Jesus next begins teaching his disciples (16:1). Apparently, however, the Pharisees and the scribes remain in Jesus' company. When, therefore, he completes his instruction to the disciples with the words, "You cannot serve God and mammon," the Pharisees, having heard this saying, sneer at him (16:13-14). What prompts this, Luke explains, is that they are "lovers of money" (16:14). Addressing the Pharisees directly, Jesus once again assails them for their hypocrisy. Although outwardly they project the appearance of being righteous, God knows what they are like in their hearts (16:15). Although in the eyes of humans they are regarded as exalted, God regards them as abominable, as servants of mammon and therefore of Satan (16:13, 15). From the time Jesus has come proclaiming God's kingdom, or rule, the law has not only not been annulled but upheld in all its parts, to the very last serif (16:16-17). Indeed, the presence of God's rule in Jesus means that the law is to be observed even more stringently than before: For example, whereas before there was provision for divorce and remarriage (Deut. 24:1-2), now to divorce and remarry is tantamount to committing adultery (16:18). For their part, the Pharisees will stand or fall in light of the law as Jesus understands it.[58] To date, however, the law and the prophets have done them little good. As lovers of money, they are like the rich man in the parable of the rich man and Lazarus (16:19-31).[59] The rich man, in willful disregard of the severe plight of poor Lazarus, practices conspicuous consumption strictly for his own benefit. At death, however, his fortunes and those of Lazarus are reversed: Whereas he suffers the torment of Hades, Lazarus rests in the bosom of Abraham. The irony of the rich man's ill-starred life is that despite having had Moses and the prophets all along, he did not hear them so as to repent and use his wealth to benefit others.

Moving ever closer to Jerusalem, Jesus twice more takes aim at the self-righteousness of the Pharisees and their love of wealth. While speaking to some (Pharisees) who "trust in themselves that they are righteous and despise others," Jesus tells them the parable of the Pharisee and the toll collector (18:9-14). In this parable, Jesus depicts both Pharisee and toll collector in prayer to God. For his part, the toll collector utters a prayer of repentance ("he beat his breast") and asks God for mercy, or forgiveness. God, in turn, hears his prayer, so that the toll collector goes to his house justified, that is, in right relationship with God. In contrast, the Pharisee indicates no awareness that he is even in need of repentance and forgiveness. The tenor of his prayer is that of giving God thanks because the life he leads is proof that he stands in a right relationship with him.[60] Significantly, however, in the very act of giving thanks to God the Pharisee expresses his contempt for the "poor" and marginal in society: extortioners, the unjust, adulterers, or even "this toll collector." Consequently, the extreme irony of the Pharisee's prayer is that it reveals that his perceived "righteousness" is in fact "self-righteousness": Imagining himself to be in right relationship with God, he in reality stands in a wrong relationship both with God and others. The upshot is that the Pharisee goes to his house "unjustified." Toward the end of his journey, therefore, Jesus uses the most vivid sort of imagery to shock the Pharisees into opening their eyes and seeing that they are in solidarity with the "lost" whom he has come to save. Jesus summons them to awake to their need for the repentance to which he calls and the forgiveness he would grant.

In conversation with a ruler, Jesus touches on one of the most anticommunal manifestations of self-righteousness, love of wealth (18:18-25). This ruler, like the lawyer earlier (10:25), asks Jesus what he must do to inherit eternal life. As before, the question is ethical in nature: The ruler wants to know how he should structure his life now so that it will issue in eternal life. Jesus' answer is to urge the ruler to keep the commandments, and he cites particular ones enjoining love of neighbor. As a rejoinder, the ruler insists that he has kept all these commandments, from the time he legally became an adult. Without contesting the ruler's answer, Jesus asserts that he is yet deficient at one point. If he would demonstrate fully his love of neighbor, he should sell all he has and distribute the proceeds to the poor—an act God will surely reward in heaven—and become Jesus' disciple (18:22). On hearing Jesus' injunctions, the ruler becomes exceedingly sad, for, Luke mentions, "he was very rich." Noting this, Jesus looks at the ruler and wryly observes that wealth can make it more difficult for a rich man to enter God's Kingdom than for a camel to pass through the eye of a needle. In the reader's ears, this observation calls to mind Jesus' previous remark: One cannot serve God and mammon (16:13).

Underlying the whole of Jesus' conflict with the religious authorities, we said above, is the root issue of "authority." Just as at the beginning of Jesus' ministry in Galilee (5:17-26), so now, at the end of his journey to Jerusalem, this issue takes on prominence (19:37-40). As Jesus is about to enter Jerusalem, the whole multitude of his disciples hails him as "King." Vigorously objecting to this, some of the Pharisees demand that Jesus rebuke his disciples. Thus far in Luke's story, the authorities have acknowledged Jesus as teacher but nothing more. That he should be greeted as King and accorded messianic authority is a notion they cannot abide. In a caustic retort, however, Jesus affirms his messianic kingship: If his disciples were not to hail him as King, the rocks themselves would do so!

Upon his entry into Jerusalem Jesus immediately goes to the temple and cleanses it (19:45-46). Thus, he brings his entire journey to Jerusalem to its climax by pitting his authority squarely against that of the religious authorities. God's house is both the place of God's presence and the seat of the authorities' rule. Quoting Old Testament prophecy, Jesus expels from the Court of the Gentiles the merchants who are selling animals and other items associated with sacrifice: God's house, Jesus declares, is to be a house of prayer, not a den of thieves (Isa. 56:7; Jer. 7:11). Apparently, the implication is that the merchants, in their buying and selling, have desecrated the temple.[61] As a twelve-year-old boy, Jesus visited the temple and exchanged questions and answers with the teachers there (2:46). Now he takes control of the temple, and he will be teacher.

CONFLICT IN THE TEMPLE IN JERUSALEM

In the first two phases of the middle of Luke's gospel story, Jesus reached out to Israel (3:1—9:50) and journeyed to Jerusalem (9:51—19:46). Early on, he became embroiled in conflict with the religious authorities, and his chief opponents were the Pharisees, supported by the scribes (lawyers). Throughout these two phases, both the tenor and the intensity of Jesus' conflict with the authorities remained remarkably constant. Though fierce and even acrimonious, this conflict nonetheless assumed the form of an extended, intermittent "conversation." Concerned to summon the authorities to repentance, Jesus willingly associated with them. They, in turn, afforded him the respect due a teacher and accepted him socially as their equal. True, provoked to fury, the authorities discussed what they might do to Jesus (6:11) and began to resent him and lie in wait to catch him in something he might say (11:53-54). Despite such animosity, their conflict with him never became mortal.

Intensification of the Conflict

Here in the third phase of the middle of Luke's gospel story (19:47—21:38), all this abruptly changes. In cleansing the temple upon his entry into Jerusalem and taking possession of it to teach, Jesus has struck at the heart of the religious authorities' power. In response, the chief priests, the scribes, and the leaders of the people now do what their confederates to this point have not done: They plot to destroy Jesus (19:47-48). The result is that the conflict that occurs between Jesus and the authorities in the temple intensifies dramatically.

This dramatic intensification of the conflict reveals itself in noticeable ways. First, the very setting of the temple, the only site where Jesus and the authorities clash during his ministry in Jerusalem, heightens the intensity of their conflict. The reason has already been noted: The temple is both the center of the authorities' rule and the place of God's presence; here the Son of God, too, is "at home" (2:46, 49). Second, the "extended conversation" that Jesus and the authorities have conducted to this point suddenly becomes transmuted into controversy leading ineluctably to death (20:1-40). In Jerusalem, the authorities no longer invite Jesus to dinner, solicit him for healing or honest instruction, or warn him against the murderous intentions of one like Herod Antipas. On the contrary, they themselves become the ones who desire to kill him. To this end, they engage in intrigue: They conspire to ensnare him in a political misstatement (20:20) and to discredit him in the sight of the people (20:26). In a similar vein, Jesus, too, forgoes all social contact with the authorities, except to clash with them in debate. In strong language, he warns not only the disciples but also the people against them (20:9-19, 45-47). Third, conflict between Jesus and the authorities in the temple becomes "acutely confrontational": Each time the authorities clash with Jesus, they challenge him to his face concerning matters that pertain directly to him. For example, members of the Sanhedrin, their spies, or some Sadducees all confront Jesus himself so as to demand that he tell them the source of his authority (20:1-8) or to get the best of him in either political or theological debate (20:20-26, 27-39). Fourth, dominating the conflict between Jesus and the authorities in the temple is the critical issue of "authority." For their part, the chief priests, the scribes, and the elders order Jesus to declare on whose authority he acts (20:1-2). For his part, Jesus lays claim, though in parabolic speech, to being the Son of God acting on the authority of God (20:13). Fifth, the atmosphere in which Jesus and the authorities engage in controversy in the temple is one of unmitigated hostility: Following Jesus' narration of the parable of the vineyard, the scribes and the chief priests want to seize him on the spot and restrain themselves only out of fear of the people (20:19). Last, because Jesus, at the end of the conflict in the temple, reduces all the authorities to silence (20:40), the latter see themselves as able to prevail against him in only one way: They must devise a means by which to kill him (22:2). To reiterate, the conflict that Jesus has with the authorities in the temple in Jerusalem is markedly more intense than earlier conflict.

Conflict in the Temple

Having taken possession of the temple, Jesus teaches the people for several days (19:47, 21:37). Because the people hang on his words, the religious authorities are at a loss how to bring about his death (19:47-48). As a first move, the chief priests, the scribes, and the elders approach Jesus in the temple and demand that he tell them on whose authority he teaches and preaches there (20:1-8).

Jesus answers the authorities by posing a question of his own: "Was the baptism of John from heaven or from humans?" Trapped by Jesus' question, the authorities cannot answer him. If they acknowledge that John acted on divine authority, Jesus can ask them, "Why, then, did you not believe John [and submit to his baptism]?" (7:29-30). If they insist that John acted solely on his own authority, they fear that the people, who hold John to have been a prophet, will stone them. Hence, to avoid exposing their rejection of John, the authorities beg off answering Jesus' question. By the same token, neither does Jesus answer their question.

This is not to say, however, that Jesus simply dodges the question of authority. To the contrary, he deals with it in the parable of the vineyard (20:9-19), which he addresses to the people but which the members of the Sanhedrin overhear (20:9-19). In this parable, Jesus identifies God with the owner of the vineyard, himself with the son of the owner, and the authorities with the wicked tenant farmers. Also, Jesus makes use of Old Testament imagery according to which "stone" can serve as a metaphor for "son."[62] With the aid of this imagery and these identifications, Jesus raises the claim that he is the Son of God who acts on the authority of God (20:13). As the "stone/son" destined to be rejected and killed by Israel's leaders, he will become the head of the corner; that is to say, through resurrection God will vindicate him (20:14-15, 17). Moreover, as a result of their opposition to him, the leaders will call down destruction upon themselves and others will take their place (20:16). On hearing Jesus' parable, the authorities understand only too well the claim he has made to divine authority and the attack he has made on them (20:19). As a result, they want to seize him at once but, fearing the people, decide otherwise (20:19).

In reaction to Jesus' attack, the scribes and the chief priests send spies to trick him into incriminating himself politically (20:20-26). The idea is to entice Jesus to make a statement that the spies can use to deliver him up to the Roman governor for prosecution as a revolutionary. Plying Jesus with flattery for being a highly learned and principled teacher, the spies set their trap: "Is it lawful for us [Jews] to pay tribute [the poll tax] to Caesar, or not?" To the spies' way of thinking, Jesus can answer neither "Yes" nor "No." If he answers "Yes," he will offend Jews, for to pay tribute with coins bearing Caesar's image is to acknowledge Caesar's lordship, and lordship belongs to none but God (Exod. 20:4-5).[63] If Jesus answers "No," he will have done as the spies wish, namely, promote sedition against Rome. Perceiving their trickery and evading their trap by answering neither "Yes" nor "No," Jesus asserts, "So render to Caesar the things that are Caesar's, and to God the things that are God's" (20:25).[64] Jesus denies that paying tribute is automatically elevating Caesar above God. Rendering God his due still leaves room for rendering Caesar his due. Left marveling in silence at Jesus' answer, the spies succeed neither in making him out to be a revolutionary (20:20) nor in discrediting him in the eyes of the people (20:26).

That same day in the temple, some Sadducees step forward to challenge Jesus in debate (20:27-39). Consonant with their denial of the notion of resurrection (Acts 23:8), they concoct a question based on a hypothetical case having to do with levirate marriage. Their intention is both to stump Jesus and to make belief in resurrection seem absurd. In the Old Testament, the law of levirate marriage prescribes that in the event a married man having a brother dies childless, the brother is obliged to take the dead man's wife and sire a child so that the dead man's name might live on (Deut. 25:5-10). The Sadducees' question concerns seven brothers. One woman is the wife of them all, and they all die childless, as does the woman. When the day of resurrection arrives, to which of the seven does the woman belong as wife?

Jesus' reply to the Sadducees is dual. First, the Sadducees wrongly assume, Jesus contends, that resurrection-life is but an extension of earthly life (20:34-36). Quite the opposite, those accounted worthy to attain to resurrection-life become children of God who, like angels, neither die any more nor marry. And second, the Sadducees err in their very denial of resurrection-life (20:37-38). Indeed, Moses already revealed its existence, at the burning bush (Exod. 3:6). There he called the Lord "the God of Abraham and the God of Isaac and the God of Jacob" (20:37). Now God is not the God of the dead but of the living. Accordingly, Moses, in speaking as he did, indicated that these patriarchs, despite having died long before his time, are nonetheless in some sense alive or will be raised.[65] So again, Moses himself, to whom the Sadducees pay special heed, attests to the existence of resurrection-life.

Jesus' refutation of the Sadducees earns him the commendation of some of the (Pharisaic) scribes. "Teacher," they say in acknowledgment, "you have spoken well" (20:39). More importantly, Jesus' refutation also marks the end of all debate between him and the religious authorities. As Luke observes, "For they no longer dared to ask him any question" (20:40). Regardless, though Jesus has reduced all his opponents to silence, he himself still has words for the very scribes who have just commended him. Addressing them directly, Jesus "corrects" their understanding of the Messiah: While the Messiah is indeed, as they hold, the son of David, he is also "more," for he is the Son of God (20:41-44). And addressing the disciples in the hearing of the people, Jesus warns both disciples and people about the scribes (20:45-47). In words reminiscent of earlier remarks about the Pharisees, Jesus charges that the scribes exalt themselves over others and are both avaricious and false in their worship.[66] In other words, the scribes, declares Jesus, are self-righteous and stand in a right relationship with neither God nor neighbor.

Apparently, as Jesus assails the scribes in the presence of the disciples and the people, the religious leaders disappear from the scene. They relinquish the temple to Jesus, and early each day all the people gather about him to hear his teaching (21:37-38). On this note, the middle of Luke's gospel story gives way to the end.

THE RESOLUTION OF THE CONFLICT: JESUS' DEATH, RESURRECTION, AND ASCENSION

The end of Luke's gospel story tells at last of the "exodus" Jesus is to accomplish in Jerusalem: his suffering, death, resurrection, and ascension (22:1—24:53). In Jesus' death, resurrection, and ascension, the conflict he has with Israel, and especially with the religious authorities, comes to fundamental resolution. The final resolution, however, must await Jesus' Parousia and the final judgment (Acts 3:20-21).

The Final Onslaught against Jesus

In the end of Luke's gospel story (22:1—24:53), the religious authorities, along with Satan and aided by Judas, mount their final onslaught against Jesus (22:2-6, 53). Unable to defeat Jesus in debate, the authorities concentrate on having him put to death. Still, as the end begins the authorities are yet looking for a way to accomplish their goal because of their chronic fear of the people (22:2). By the time Jesus appears before Pilate, however, the mood of the people will have changed and they will have joined with the authorities in opposing Jesus (23:4, 13). Together, leaders and people will coerce Pilate into ordering the crucifixion of Jesus (23:13-25).

In the final onslaught against Jesus, Luke contrasts Jesus' rectitude with the authorities' wickedness. On the one hand, Jesus is "innocent" and "righteous" (23:47). On the other hand, the authorities show themselves to be "unjust" men committing unjust acts. Being unjust, they are also "deceitful" and, ironically, "deluded." They are deceitful, for they willfully lie. And they are deluded, for when confronted with the truth, they cannot discern it.

Luke projects this picture of the religious authorities as unjust men who lie and deny the truth in both obvious and subtle ways. Thus, when Judas comes to the chief priests and officers of the temple and discusses with them how he might betray Jesus, they rejoice and agree to give him money (22:4-5). When the chief priests, officers of the temple, and elders come to arrest him, Jesus delivers himself to them even as he declares that they have allied themselves with Satan, the "power of darkness" who blinds humans to the light and truth of God (22:52-53; Acts 26:18). In commanding Jesus to prophesy so as to mock and blaspheme him, the underlings of the Sanhedrin unwittingly bring to fulfillment the prophecies Jesus has already made concerning his righteous suffering.[67] After Jesus has confronted the members of the Sanhedrin in the first trial-scene with the truth that he is the Messiah Son of God (22:66-71), they turn this into the lie before Pilate that he "perverts our nation" and is a revolutionary (23:2,5).[68] At Jesus' appearance before Herod

Antipas, the chief priests and the scribes again falsely accuse him of sedition (23:10). At Jesus' second appearance before Pilate, the chief priests and the rulers, with the people, make a complete mockery of justice by calling for the release of Barabbas, a certified revolutionary and murderer, and for the crucifixion of Jesus (23:18-25). And at the cross, the leaders of the Jews ridicule as a lie the truth that Jesus is "God's Messiah" (23:35).[69] To repeat, at the end of his gospel story Luke matches his characterization of Jesus as "innocent" and "righteous" with a corresponding characterization of the religious authorities as "unjust" ("deceitful" and "deluded"). Injustice, therefore, becomes the hallmark of the authorities' final onslaught against Jesus.

The Irony of the Conflict

While the religious authorities are ironic characters throughout the whole of Luke's gospel story, nowhere is this more apparent than here in the end. The acts of injustice the authorities perpetrate stand in glaring contrast to their perception of themselves as being righteous in the sight of God and neighbor.[70] It is this discrepancy between what the authorities are ("self-righteous" and "unjust") and what they perceive themselves to be ("righteous") that makes of them ironic characters.

For example, while perceiving themselves to be righteous, the authorities nonetheless make themselves guilty of all of the following: They resort to betrayal to accomplish their aims; ally themselves with Satan; subject God's supreme agent to mockery and blasphemy; deny Jesus' true identity as the Messiah Son of God; lodge false accusations against Jesus before both Pilate and Herod Antipas; call for the release of a bona fide revolutionary and the crucifixion of the innocent Jesus; and ridicule God's chosen Messiah as he hangs upon the cross in the mistaken belief that his obedience unto death is merely a sign of helplessness.

What is most fateful, however, is that the authorities, as ironic characters, cannot discern the salvation-historical significance of the events surrounding their conflict with Jesus. In their eyes, Jesus is, as we know, a false messiah who perverts Israel by undermining their authority, stirring the people to rebellion, and violating law, tradition and rules of purity, and temple cult. Although Jesus may have defeated them in debate and enjoyed great popularity with the people, the authorities are utterly convinced that the final victory in their conflict with him has gone to them. As they ridicule Jesus from beneath the cross in the last scene in which they appear[71] in the gospel story, they believe that his ostensible helplessness in the face of death proves that, far from being God's chosen Messiah, he is a fraud without authority (23:35). In their conflict with Jesus over who will rule God's people, they, not he, have won.

What the authorities do not perceive, however, is that God is at work in Jesus to accomplish his plan of salvation. Accordingly, the authorities are, or will be, oblivious to those crucial events we cited at the end of last chapter: that Jesus, too, wills his death, in obedience to God (22:42); that through Jesus' death, God will establish a new covenant (22:20); that to put Jesus in the right in his conflict with Israel, God will raise him from the dead (24:4-7); and that to exalt Jesus (who they think is without authority) to universal authority, God will take him to heaven in the ascension (22:69; Acts 1:2). For all the authorities' blindness, however, there is yet another irony attending their conflict with Jesus: the irony of grace. Already from the cross, Jesus forgives them their "ignorance" (23:34). And on Pentecost, both they and the Jewish people will again be summoned to repentance, belief on Jesus' name, and salvation (Acts 2:38; 3:17-20). Still, because of their repudiation of Jesus the authorities will also, by Pentecost, have been supplanted by the twelve apostles as the leaders of God's (reconstituted) people (20:16; 22:28-30). More distantly, the responsibility for Jerusalem's destruction and the terrible fate that will befall the populace will likewise be theirs.[72] In Jesus, God has visited Israel to grant it peace (19:41-42). Blind to God's gracious visitation, Israel will be visited again, by gentile armies.

Before taking leave of Luke's gospel story, the reader confronts one last figure from among the religious authorities: Joseph of Arimathea, who is a member of the Sanhedrin (23:50-54). As we noted in chapter 1, Joseph stands out as a foil ("contrast") for his "colleagues": Whereas his fellow Sanhedrists ruled against Jesus (22:71) and led him to Pilate to be sentenced to death (23:1-5), Joseph consented to neither their intent nor their deed (23:51). Accordingly, whereas they were "unjust" in their treatment of Jesus, Joseph attested to Jesus' innocence and is consequently "upright" (23:50). Equally remarkable, Joseph does not hesitate to act on his conviction about Jesus: Doing what even Jesus' disciples will not do, Joseph goes to Pilate, requests the body of Jesus, and buries him (23:52-53).

In serving as a foil for the religious authorities at the end of Luke's gospel story, Joseph is the counterpart to Zechariah at the beginning.[73] Like Zechariah, Joseph is "righteous," one who upholds the law of Israel.[74] Like Zechariah, who prayed for God to act decisively on behalf of Israel and himself, Joseph awaits the kingdom of God.[75] And like Zechariah, Joseph is not a disciple of Jesus. Nevertheless, just as Zechariah rejoiced over the imminent coming of Jesus, Israel's "horn of salvation" (1:67-75), so Joseph is "ripe" to become Jesus' disciple. As such, he foreshadows in his person those religious authorities in Acts—priests, Pharisees, the Pharisee Paul, and a ruler of a synagogue—who will turn and become followers of Jesus.[76]

SUMMARY

At the human level, the conflict in Luke's gospel story is above all between Jesus and Israel. Within Israel, the religious authorities, not the people, are Jesus' chief antagonists. In characterizing the authorities, Luke tends to stereotype them as a single group, and his portrait of them is strongly polemical.

At root, Jesus' conflict with the religious authorities is over "authority." It is a question of who will rule God's (reconstituted) people. Progressively, Luke leads the reader to view the authorities as morally unqualified to exercise such authority and rule. Fundamentally, the authorities "serve the purposes not of God, but of humans." Though they look upon themselves as "righteous," in reality they are "self-righteous," wrongly related to both God and humans. As a result, they are ironic characters, unable to perceive reality aright. They reject the baptism of John, repudiate Jesus as Israel's Messiah-King in whom God's end-time rule is a present reality, and despise the people, especially the "poor." As they interact with Jesus, they grow to regard him as a false messiah who undermines their authority, misleads the people, and violates law, traditional values, and temple cult. To preserve Israel as the nation of the covenant and their position as Israel's leaders, they decide they must kill him.

Except for the teachers in the temple with whom the twelve-year-old Jesus has to do (2:46), the religious authorities make their debut in the middle of Luke's gospel story (3:1—21:38). Throughout the first two phases of the middle (3:1—19:46), Jesus reaches out to Israel (4:14—9:50) and journeys to Jerusalem (9:51—19:46). In these phases, his conflict with the religious authorities assumes the form of a lengthy but intermittent "conversation." Jesus remains open to the authorities because he would summon them to repentance. The authorities, though they are perplexed by Jesus and early on feel intense animosity toward him (6:11), nonetheless grant him the respect due a teacher and deal with him as a social equal. Also, fierce as Jesus' clashes with the authorities are, almost none of them is "acutely confrontational" in nature: Only rarely does any of the authorities confront Jesus directly over a matter pertaining strictly to him.[77]

The climactic episode in Jesus' journey to Jerusalem is his entry into the temple (19:45-46). Cleansing the temple, Jesus takes possession of it to teach there. In so doing, he challenges the authority of the religious authorities at the very center of their power and rule.

In phase three of the middle of Luke's gospel story (19:47—21:38), Jesus discharges a ministry of teaching in the temple. At this point, his conflict with the religious authorities intensifies dramatically, for now the authorities are out to destroy him (19:47). Still, because the people throng to Jesus to hear him (19:48; 21:38), the authorities are unclear how to move against him. Nevertheless, they challenge his authority to teach and clash with him in debate (20:1-40). At every turn, however, Jesus outwits them, so that they finally fall silent (20:40). Leaving the temple for the time being to Jesus, they henceforth concentrate on one objective, to bring about his death.

The fundamental resolution of Jesus' conflict with the religious authorities comes in the end of Luke's gospel story (22:1—24:53). The final resolution must await the Parousia. In bringing about Jesus' death, the authorities prove themselves to be unjust, deceitful, and deluded. In the last scene in which they appear in Luke's gospel story, they confront Jesus as he hangs on the cross (23:35). As they see it, Jesus' crucifixion betokens his powerlessness and is proof that they are the ones who have won out in their conflict with him. What they do not perceive, however, is the irony that God and Jesus, too, have willed the death of Jesus. Indeed, to vindicate Jesus in his conflict with Israel, God raises him from the dead (24:5-7). Further, to confer on Jesus lordship over all and therefore also over his people, God exalts him to his right hand in the ascension (22:69; 24:51). In point of fact, far from triumphing over Jesus, the authorities set the stage for their own demise: Under the lordship of the exalted Jesus, the apostles, not they, will be the leaders of God's reconstituted people,[78] and they make themselves responsible for the destruction of Jerusalem.[79] This notwithstanding, Jesus forgives the authorities their "ignorance" already from the cross (23:34). Moreover, come Pentecost God and the risen Jesus will grant them a "second chance" to repent, believe on Jesus' name, and become heirs of salvation. On this score, the figure of Joseph of Arimathea already invites the reader to anticipate that there will be those authorities in Acts who will turn to Jesus and be saved.

4 THE STORY OF THE DISCIPLES

The third major story line in Luke's Gospel features the disciples. Because the disciples are Jesus' followers, their story is closely tied to his and they exert no great influence on the plot, or flow of events. Even Judas, who betrays Jesus, does so as one doing the bidding of Satan (22:3).

Like the religious authorities, the disciples make their debut in the middle of Luke's gospel story. To a far greater extent than either Mark or Matthew, Luke associates Jesus with diverse numbers of disciples. The reader encounters, for example, a great crowd, or even multitude, of disciples (6:17; 19:37), women disciples (8:2-3), the twelve (9:1), the seventy-two (10:1), groups of three disciples (Peter, John, and James)[1] or of two disciples (Peter and John; James and John),[2] and individual disciples: Levi, who is not one of the twelve (5:27-28); and Peter,[3] John (9:49), and Judas (22:3, 47-48). Among these many disciples, however, the twelve, or individuals among them, receive the lion's share of attention.

Although Jesus' major conflict in Luke's gospel story is with Israel, whether people or authorities, he must also struggle with the disciples. The nature of each of these conflicts, however, is profoundly different. Jesus' conflict with the religious authorities is over "authority" and who will rule God's people. Jesus' conflict with the people is to win their allegiance. In the case of the disciples, however, Jesus' conflict is with those who already follow him. But though they follow Jesus, the disciples nonetheless disclose that they are of two minds: On the one hand, they "serve the purposes of God." On the other hand, they "serve the purposes of humans." At root, the cause of the disciples' double-mindedness is that they do not understand the plan of salvation God is accomplishing in Jesus.[4] The upshot is that they often view reality not

109

from a divine perspective as Jesus does, but from a human, this-worldly perspective. Viewing reality from a human perspective, the disciples show themselves to be spiritually immature. Frequently, their immaturity manifests itself as incomprehension. Fundamentally, therefore, the conflict Jesus has with the disciples is to bring them to spiritual maturity and enlightenment. Not until the disciples comprehend the saving purposes that God brings to realization in Jesus will they be in any position to be Jesus' witnesses and to undertake the worldwide ministry he has in store for them (24:44-49).

WITH JESUS IN GALILEE

We recall that in the first phase of the middle of Luke's gospel story (3:1—9:50), Jesus reaches out to Israel while wandering primarily in Galilee (4:14—9:50). Although Peter speaks globally in Acts 1:21-22 of the disciples as being with Jesus from "John's baptism to the ascension," in reality Jesus calls the first disciples at a later point in his ministry in Luke than he does in either Mark or Matthew.[5] Also, Peter is, in all three Gospels, the first disciple to be called. Luke alone, however, depicts a scene in which Peter appears as an acquaintance of Jesus even prior to his call. Before he calls Peter, Jesus has already visited Peter's house in Capernaum and healed his mother-in-law (4:38-39).

The Call, Mission, and Confession
of the Disciples

In the episode in which Jesus calls his first disciples (5:1-11),[6] the first two scenes set the stage for the critical third scene. In the first scene (5:1-3), the crowds who have come to Jesus at Lake Gennesaret press in on him so closely that he boards Simon Peter's boat so he can teach the people from out on the water. In the second scene (5:4-7), Jesus, having finished teaching, commands Simon to launch out into the deep for a catch. Although Simon believes that this will prove futile, he nevertheless does as Jesus commands. Significantly, even in expressing his doubts to Jesus, Peter addresses him as "master." "Master" in Luke's gospel story is a designation used exclusively by such as the disciples or those like the ten lepers.[7] As a term that befits subordinates addressing a superior,[8] "master" carries with it the acknowledgment that Jesus is a figure of authority.[9] Narratively, what prompts Simon to address Jesus as "master" was his earlier experience of the miracle Jesus performed in curing his mother-in-law of a great fever (4:38-39). In obedience to Jesus' command, Simon launches out and suddenly catches so many fish that he must beckon James and John in their boat to come to his aid. In the end, both boats become so swamped with fish that sinking seems imminent.

In the crucial third scene (5:8-11), Simon, astonished at the enormity of the miracle he has just witnessed, falls before Jesus and confesses his sinfulness. Equally astonished are James and John. Focusing his attention on Simon, Jesus absolves him of his sins[10] even as he commissions him[11] to ministry: "Fear not!" Jesus declares, "From now on you will be catching humans" (5:10). In directing his words to Simon, Jesus ensures that he will be the first of the disciples to be called. As such, Simon becomes both "spokesperson"[12] for the others and "typical"[13] of them in faith and in weakness. Still, though Jesus focuses on Simon, James and John, too, share in Simon's commissioning. They, too, respond to Jesus' words exactly as Simon does, by leaving behind everything and following after Jesus (5:11).

This episode goes far to apprise the reader of the nature and purpose of discipleship.[14] The nature of discipleship is giving to Jesus one's loyalty, and this, in turn, involves several factors. To begin with, the enabling power to become Jesus' disciple comes from Jesus himself: It is Jesus who commissions one to ministry or calls one to follow him. Second, discipleship involves "leaving behind everything." Because disciples become members of a new community led by Jesus, persons called to discipleship must be prepared to relinquish possessions and even family, if need be.[15] Indeed, "forsaking all" means that the disciples of Jesus have their rightful place among the "poor" (6:20). And discipleship involves "following" Jesus, going after him as an eye- and ear-witness to what he says and does and as one who internalizes the "way" of Jesus.[16]

Correspondingly, the purpose of discipleship is "mission." Here in 5:1-11, Jesus is still in the beginning stages of his ministry to Israel. Regardless, his commission to Peter is thoroughly universal in scope: Peter is commissioned not to catch Israelites, but human beings. Already at this juncture, therefore, Jesus envisages that the people of God he will gather through the agency of the disciples will be a people comprising both Jews and gentiles (2:27-32). Eventually, this people will also be a "great people," as is suggested by the great catch of fish the boats take and the great crowds Jesus teaches (5:1-3, 6-7).

On another day, Jesus again summons a person to discipleship, a toll collector[17] named Levi (5:27-28). As Jesus is "underway," he "sees" Levi at a toll office and "summons" him to follow him. Immediately, Levi gets up and "leaves everything" and "follows" Jesus. In other words, with authority Jesus calls Levi to become his disciple and Levi, forsaking everything to follow Jesus, gives to Jesus his loyalty. The importance of Jesus' call of Levi has to do with the latter's social standing. Since Levi is a toll collector, other Jews regard him as being of the same ilk as robbers and those prone to dishonesty (3:12-13).[18] Indeed, he is despised by both people and authorities.[19] In calling Levi, therefore, Jesus ignores prevailing rules of purity. Graciously, he invites one to become his follower who, despite whatever wealth he may possess, is nonetheless an outcast living on the margins of society (5:29-32). By breaking down social barriers, Jesus is enlarging the boundaries of the people of God he gathers.

Luke moves swiftly in his gospel story to depict the circle of the twelve as complete. To underscore the importance of the formation of the twelve (6:12-16), Luke notes that Jesus ascends a mountain the evening before and remains throughout the night in prayer. The mountain is a place of divine revelation, and in prayer Jesus communes with God. In Jesus' choosing of the twelve, therefore, God is at work guiding the history of salvation. When day arrives, Jesus summons disciples to him and selects from among them the twelve, naming them "apostles." For Luke, the peculiarity of the twelve resides in at least three factors: (a) They become eye- and ear-witnesses of Jesus' public ministry and therefore guarantors of "Christian" tradition (Acts 1:21-22); (b) they are persons who will have seen the risen Jesus (Acts 1:22); and (c) they will become, in Acts, the leaders of God's reconstituted people.[20] In a special sense, therefore, the twelve apostles are destined to be empowered by Jesus to represent him and to act in his name.[21] In this same episode, Luke also notes that Simon receives the name "Peter"; henceforth, this becomes the name by which Simon will chiefly be known.[22] Further, Judas is referred to as the one who will betray Jesus. In the pleasing portrait of the disciples Luke has thus far sketched, this reference to Judas is the first unseemly line Luke has drawn.

Descending from the mountain to a nearby plain, Jesus delivers his first major discourse, the Sermon on the Plain (6:20-49). As the multitude listens, Jesus addresses the great crowd of disciples standing about him (6:20; 7:1). His topic is the nature of disciple-ship, and he deals with it in three parts:[23] (a) pronouncements of beatitudes and woes (6:20-26); (b) declarations on love as supersed-ing reciprocity (6:27-38); and (c) statements on the moral character of the disciple (6:39-49).

To capture the sense of each of these parts, Jesus announces the end-time reversal of fortunes in his beatitudes and woes. In the four beatitudes, Jesus "congratulates" the disciples who, in the present, are poor, hungry, grief-stricken, and persecuted; even now, he an-nounces, they live in the sphere of God's end-time rule and God will, at the future appearance of the glorious kingdom, reverse their lot (6:20-23).[24] In the four woes, Jesus "laments" the self-sufficient and self-satisfied of this world who presently live in disregard of both God and neighbor; they have, Jesus declares, already received their consolation and God will, at the coming of the glorious kingdom, also reverse their lot (6:24-26).[25]

In part two of the sermon (6:27-38), Jesus teaches the disciples that the system of reciprocity,[26] whereby "you only do for those who do for you," is not the way of discipleship. Instead, disciples are to act to benefit others just as they would have others act to benefit them ("And as you wish that others would do to you, do so to them" [6:31]). More than this, disciples are, in fact, to love as God loves (6:36). This means loving one's enemy, doing good, and giving to others with no expectation of return (6:35). Doing the latter is what it means to lead a life well-pleasing to God and to be a child of God (6:35).

In the last part of the sermon (6:39-49), Jesus narrates a series of "parables" touching on the moral character of the disciple. Of particular importance are two sayings of Jesus. In the one saying, Jesus declares, "A disciple is not above his teacher; but when he is fully trained, he will be like his teacher" (6:40). Within Luke's gospel story, Jesus, of course, is the teacher each disciple is ultimately to be like. Jesus serves as a "model" for disciples, and disciples are to emu-late him. And the second saying is the parable of the house built upon the rock (6:46-49), with which Jesus closes the sermon. In this parable, Jesus enjoins the disciples not simply to hear his words but to "hear and do" them. Luke's view of the exemplary disciple is sum-marized in these two parables: The disciple is to emulate Jesus and to internalize his words and be guided by them.

Some time after delivering the Sermon on the Plain, Jesus goes about the villages of Galilee proclaiming the kingdom of God (8:1-3).

Altogether striking is Luke's notation that Jesus is accompanied not simply by the twelve, but by many women disciples. Among them are such personages as Mary Magdalene, the wealthy Joanna, and Susanna.[27] Historically, in fact, Jewish rabbis did not have women as disciples, and for a teacher to travel with women was scandalous. Accordingly, in that Jesus not only has women as disciples but is also accompanied by them, Luke presents him as removing social barriers and fashioning a community in which membership is not determined by gender. Moreover, by making mention of women disciples in this first phase of Jesus' ministry, Luke emphasizes that women, too, are among the "Galileans"[28] Jesus calls to discipleship and that they, too, are eye- and ear-witnesses of his ministry. On a related note, Luke furthermore prepares the reader for the significant role that women disciples will play at the end of his gospel story: They will be "last at the cross, first at the tomb" (23:49; 24:8).[29] More conventionally, Luke's statement that the women disciples support Jesus and the twelve from their means points to a form of service that women, as well as men, were known in the ancient world to perform (8:3).[30]

Still touring Galilee and drawing crowds, Jesus next narrates the parable of the sower (8:4-8). Asked by the disciples what this parable means, Jesus interprets it and instructs the disciples on the importance of "hearing" (8:9, 11-18). As a first remark, Jesus makes a programmatic statement in which he contrasts "disciples" with "others" (8:10). In principle, he asserts, God grants disciples to know the secrets of his kingdom, which is a gift not imparted to others (8:10). Within the story world of Luke, the secrets God makes known to the disciples are ultimately as all-encompassing as the plan of salvation God is bringing to realization in and through his Son, Jesus. In Jesus, God in his end-time rule is present among humans (8:1; 11:20). In Jesus, God graciously reaches out to summon humans to repent, be saved, and live in the sphere of God's rule. To lead life in the sphere of God's rule, however, is to lead life in accord with God's rule. To lead such a life, one must "hear and do" what Jesus says. Those who do "hear and do" what Jesus says constitute Jesus' true family (8:21). In point of fact, "hearing and doing" is what the parable of the sower is about (8:11-15). Thus, for one not to hear the word Jesus proclaims is for one not to believe and be saved (8:12). For one to hear the word and believe but then fall away after a time owing to persecution or entanglement with the cares, riches, and pleasures of life is no less tragic (8:13-14). What is essential is that one hear the word, hold it fast, and bear fruit with endurance (8:15). Or to put it another way: Part and parcel of hearing and doing the word is persevering in the face of persecution and the allure of riches or the perceived need to secure one's future.

After further travels and healings, Jesus sends the twelve apostles out on their first mission, to Israel (9:1-6, 10). Patterned after Jesus' own mission, the mission of the twelve becomes an extension of his. Himself endowed with power and authority by the Spirit,[31] Jesus gives power and authority to the twelve. Himself sent to proclaim the kingdom of God and to heal,[32] Jesus sends the twelve to proclaim the kingdom and to heal. Himself under the care of God during his public ministry (13:32-33), Jesus enjoins the disciples to expect care during their mission from those who will receive them. Himself repudiated both by the people of Nazareth and the persons of this generation,[33] Jesus forewarns the twelve that they, too, will experience repudiation. In obedience to Jesus' instructions, the twelve go out and discharge their mission, wandering through the villages of Galilee preaching and healing everywhere.

Following the return of the twelve and against the backdrop of Jesus' having fed the five thousand, Luke rehearses the episode of Peter's confession (9:18-22). In this confession, Luke brings the story of the disciples in the first phase of Jesus' ministry to its culmination. Indeed, the opening narrative comment depicting "Jesus at prayer" alerts the reader to the singular importance of this episode: Through his questions, Jesus will bring the disciples to new insight. Addressing the disciples, Jesus first asks them who the Jewish public thinks he is. In echo of the reports Herod Antipas, too, has heard (9:7-8), the disciples reply that whereas some think he is John the Baptist, others think he is Elijah, and still others that he is one of the ancient prophets come back to life (9:18-19). None of these answers, we know from chapter 1, is correct. Jesus then asks the disciples who they, in contrast to the Jewish public, think he is. Responding on behalf of all, Peter declares, "The Messiah of God!" (9:20). Because Peter's answer tallies both with God's understanding of Jesus (2:11) and with Jesus' understanding of himself (4:18), we recognize that it is correct. Accordingly, the disciples, in contrast to "others" (8:10), know that Jesus is God's Messiah.

In the wake of Peter's climactic confession, three events occur. First, Jesus' immediate reaction to Peter's confession is both to command the disciples not to divulge his identity and to deliver to them his first passion-prediction (9:21-22). At first glance, Jesus' suppression of Peter's confession seems strange. If Peter's confession is correct, why does Jesus suppress it? Jesus does so, we recall from chapter 1, because although the disciples have been led to perceive his identity, they have not as yet been told that suffering and death will be his destiny. To inform the disciples of this, Jesus delivers forthwith his first passion-prediction. As Luke points out in a later passage, however, the disciples do not comprehend it (9:44-45). Still, until the disciples can comprehend Jesus' destiny, they cannot properly proclaim his identity. So again, Jesus commands the disciples to silence about his identity.

The second event following Peter's confession comprises the sayings that Jesus directs to "all" (the crowd as well as the disciples). In them, Jesus describes discipleship in light of his suffering and death (9:23-27). The first saying is the key one: "If anyone would come after me, let one deny oneself and take up one's cross daily and follow me" (9:23; 14:27). In addressing this saying to the crowd, Jesus summons the people to become his disciples. In addressing it to the disciples, he elaborates on the nature of discipleship. In the saying itself, Jesus describes discipleship, or "coming after him," in terms of three essentials, to wit: (a) One must "deny oneself," that is, surrender one's own will in favor of giving complete loyalty to Jesus; (b) one must "take up one's cross daily," that is, persevere as a disciple amid the routines of life no matter what the cost; and (c) one must "follow" Jesus, that is, witness his "way" and internalize it, so that one's own life becomes conformed to his. Then, continuing his sayings, Jesus in effect asserts: Those who attempt to secure their lives on their own terms will ultimately lose them; and those who lose their lives out of loyalty to him will ultimately save them (9:24). In the final analysis, Jesus declares, discipleship has to do with the utterly precious commodity of "life" (9:25). At the latter day, when he returns in glory, what will ultimately count is whether or not a person has rejected him (9:26). Nevertheless, even now he can affirm that the disciples standing here will not die before they have seen the kingdom of God, whether in the events of the resurrection or of Pentecost (9:27).[34]

The third event following Peter's confession is the confirmation his confession receives from God himself at Jesus' transfiguration (9:35). In the hearing of Peter, John, and James atop the mountain, God announces from the cloud, "This is my chosen Son, hear him!" Since in Luke's gospel story the "Messiah" is the "Son" whom God has "anointed" with his Spirit,[35] God's announcement that Jesus is his chosen "Son" confirms Peter's confession that Jesus is God's "Messiah" ("Anointed"). Thus, God's announcement from the cloud also points to the climactic character of Peter's confession.

Spiritual Immaturity and Incomprehension

In tracing Luke's account of the disciples in the first phase of the middle of his gospel story (3:1—9:50), we have thus far concentrated on those aspects that cast the disciples in the role of "serving the purposes of God" by serving God's plan of salvation: their obedient response to Jesus' call; their reception of the secrets of God's kingdom; the mission they undertake to Israel; and Peter's climactic confession that Jesus is God's Messiah. These aspects draw the reader to the side of the disciples and elicit approval. By the same token, one discovers that there are also those instances in this phase where the disciples assume the opposite role and "serve the purposes of humans." In these instances, the disciples view reality not from a divine perspective, but from a perspective that is human, self-centered, or this-worldly. In great measure, the disciples are still spiritually immature, and they often attest to this by showing themselves to be uncomprehending. Although Jesus teaches them and serves as a model to be emulated, the disciples all too frequently do not hear, know, or do as he expects or would want.

Luke depicts one display of spiritual immaturity and lack of perception on the part of the disciples in the episode of the stilling of the storm (8:22-25). One day, not long after the disciples have heard Jesus tell the parable of the sower, Jesus commands them to sail across the Sea of Galilee. Underway, while Jesus is asleep, the disciples get caught in a storm. As the boat fills with water and their situation becomes precarious, they rush to him, arouse him, and cry out that they are perishing. Jesus rebukes wind and wave and restores calm. Yet he also chides the disciples: "Where," he demands to know, "is your faith?" Narratively, Jesus' question alludes to the interpretation of the parable of the sower. In it, he told the disciples that the seed falling into good soil stands for those who receive God's word with a faith that holds firm and brings forth fruit with endurance, or perseverance (8:15). Out here on the water, the disciples have just faced their first test. But far from exhibiting a "persevering faith," they forgot Jesus' word and lost all courage when confronted with danger. In time of trial, their faith did not sustain them. In response to Jesus' miracle and admonishing question, the disciples, full of fear and amazement, query themselves:

"Who then is this that he commands even wind and water, and they obey him?" At this point in the story prior to Peter's confession, it is apparent that the disciples have not yet perceived that Jesus is God's Messiah.

In the episode of the feeding of the five thousand (9:10b-17), Jesus again struggles with the disciples' incomprehension. At this juncture, the twelve have just returned from their mission to Israel and are with Jesus in a desert place as he preaches the kingdom to the crowds and heals. Shortly before, as Jesus sent out the twelve, he endowed them, too, with power and authority to preach the kingdom and to heal (9:1-2). Be that as it may, as day ebbs the twelve approach Jesus and suggest that he send the crowd(s) away so that they can secure lodging and provisions. Ignoring their suggestion, Jesus commands the twelve, "You give them something to eat!" Precisely because the twelve have been endowed with power and authority, Jesus expects them to do as he has commanded and feed the five thousand. Still, as the twelve view the situation from a human standpoint, they find Jesus' command perplexing: "We have no more than five loaves and two fish," they object, "unless we are to go and buy food for all these people." Taking charge himself, Jesus makes do with the loaves and fish and, using the twelve as assistants, miraculously provides a meal for all five thousand persons.

Within this episode, the twelve fall short of Jesus' expectations because they fail to view the situation as he does and to comprehend it aright: They do not realize that they have at their disposal the authority to do as Jesus does. For his part Jesus, in performing the miracle, does not exclude the twelve but has them assist him. This, in turn, foreshadows the coming time of the church, when the exalted Jesus will preside over God's end-time people and the twelve will function under his lordship as leaders. In addition, the very incomprehension of the twelve serves, ironically, as a literary device both to underscore the enormity of the miracle Jesus performs and to enable Jesus to reveal anew his awesome authority. In performing this miracle in the sight of the twelve, therefore, Jesus paves the way for Peter's confession.

Peter's confession, in fact, follows almost immediately (9:20). Its significance is that it marks the point at which Jesus leads the disciples to overcome their incomprehension concerning his identity. Out on the water, the disciples wondered who Jesus is (8:25). In the feeding of the five thousand, they participated in the miracle through which he revealed his divine authority and prepared them to perceive his identity (9:10b-17). In the confession itself, Peter, on behalf of all the disciples, at last names the one who calms wind and wave and wondrously feeds the people: He is the Messiah of God (9:20). In perceiving this, the disciples have learned from Jesus and grown in spiritual stature.

This notwithstanding, the disciples show almost immediately that they are uncomprehending about another crucial matter, that concerning Jesus' suffering and death. Jesus responds to Peter's confession, we remember, by commanding the disciples to silence concerning his identity (9:21): Not until the disciples are in a position to proclaim Jesus' destiny will they also be in a position to proclaim his identity. At the heart of Jesus' destiny, however, lie suffering and death. To apprise the disciples of this, Jesus delivers his first passion-prediction (9:22). Later, Luke bluntly states that the disciples do not comprehend such predictions (9:44-45; 18:31-34). This inability on the part of the disciples carries with it enormous consequences. Because the disciples are unable to grasp the essential truth that at the heart of Jesus' ministry lie suffering and death, neither are they able to grasp essential truths about the meaning of discipleship. To underscore this, Luke lays particular stress at the end of Jesus' Galilean ministry on both the incomprehension afflicting the disciples and their spiritual immaturity.

Thus, in the episode featuring Jesus' transfiguration, Peter, John, and James become so dull with heavy sleep that they miss out on Jesus' conversation with Moses and Elijah about his "exodus" and see only the glory of the three figures (9:31-32). Moreover, Peter, desiring to prolong the transfiguration experience, speaks nonsense when, as Moses and Elijah take their departure, he suggests to Jesus that they build three booths in which Jesus and the heavenly visitors can dwell (9:33). Again, central to God's injunction that the three disciples "hear him [Jesus]" is the total failure of all the disciples to comprehend Jesus' first passion-prediction.[36] And finally, the primary effect of Luke's comment at the end that the three disciples "kept silence and told no one in those days anything of what they had seen" (9:36) is simply to reinforce the reader's impression that the transfiguration experience has been beyond the comprehension of the disciples.

Meanwhile, the nine disciples below have shown that they are just as uncomprehending (9:37-43). On descending from the mount the next day, Jesus and the three disciples are met by a great crowd and a father with an epileptic boy possessed of a demon. During Jesus' absence, the father brought his boy to the nine and implored them to cast out the demon. Earlier, when Jesus commissioned the twelve to their mission to Israel, he had endowed them with power and authority over "all demons" (9:1). Regardless, the nine have not availed themselves of this authority and have been ineffectual in their attempt to heal the boy. The father puts it this way: "I begged your disciples to cast [the demon] out, but they could not" (9:40). Exasperated, Jesus, with an eye to the nine, exclaims, "O faithless and perverse generation, how long am I to be with you and bear with you?" (9:41). Then, rebuking the demon, Jesus heals the boy himself. The point is, because Jesus commissioned the twelve to preach and to heal, the nine disciples had it within their power to perform the exorcism and Jesus fully expected them to do so.

Following this exorcism, Jesus delivers his second passion-prediction to the disciples (9:43b-45). In doing so, he urges the disciples to internalize it: "Let these words," he enjoins them, "sink into your ears!" (9:44). Jesus' injunction, however, goes for naught, for once again the disciples are unable to comprehend his prediction (9:45). This time, however, Luke informs the reader why: The inability of the disciples to comprehend Jesus' passion-predictions is attributable both to failure on their part and to divine intention. On the one hand, the disciples are themselves at fault for not comprehending. Thus, when Jesus uttered this second passion-prediction and the disciples did not understand it, "they were [nonetheless] afraid," Luke remarks, "to ask him about [it]." On the other hand, it belongs to God's purposes that the disciples do not comprehend Jesus' passion-predictions. In the case of this second one, for example, although Jesus delivers it to the disciples, Luke states that "it was concealed from them, that they should not perceive it." Luke's position on the inability of the disciples to comprehend Jesus' passion-predictions, therefore, is plain: On the one hand, the disciples are not to be absolved of responsibility; on the other hand, their incomprehension is to be understood as part of a larger plan God is carrying out. Whatever the tension between the two parts of this construct, each part must be given its due.

The disciples' inability to comprehend Jesus' second passion-prediction has immediate consequences: In stark contrast to Jesus' firm will to humble himself to suffer, the disciples show themselves to be both "status-conscious" and "exclusive." As a symptom of their status-consciousness, the disciples fall to quarreling over who among them is greatest (9:46-48). To settle the quarrel, Jesus takes a child, who is among the humblest of persons, and places it at his side, that is, identifies with it. To receive this humblest of persons and to serve it as though it were he, Jesus insists, is to receive him, and to receive him is to receive God. Paradoxically, the disciple who most humbles himself to serve is, like Jesus himself, truly great.[37]

Desirous of greatness, the disciples also reveal that they are exclusive and unwilling to share with others the prerogatives that they believe are theirs by virtue of being Jesus' disciples (9:49-50). No sooner has Jesus finished speaking about true greatness than John informs him that the disciples have discovered and tried to thwart a man who is not one of his followers but who nevertheless exorcises demons in his name. Jesus' immediate reply is to charge the disciples not to hinder such a one, "for he who is not against you is for you." Clearly, Jesus' contention is that one mark of his disciples is not exclusivity but openness toward anyone genuinely acting in his name.[38]

ON THE WAY TO JERUSALEM

In looking back over the first phase of the middle of Luke's gospel story (3:1—9:50), one is struck by the grand note on which the story of the disciples began and the low note on which it ended. Initially, the disciples stood out with great reader approval as those who "serve the purposes of God." Seemingly, they grasped and embraced the plan of salvation God is accomplishing in Jesus. After a time, however, the disciples revealed that they were also prone to "serve the purposes of humans": Falling victim on occasion to spiritual immaturity, the disciples embroiled themselves in conflict with Jesus.

Here in the second phase of the middle of Luke's gospel story (9:51—19:46), Jesus journeys toward Jerusalem. On the journey, he schools the disciples in the ways of discipleship. While the disciples learn from Jesus and hence "serve the purposes of God," they continue to show, by their spiritually immature behavior and incomprehension, that they are yet inclined to "serve the purposes of humans."

Dispatching Messengers, Encountering Would-be Disciples, and the Mission of the Seventy-two

As Jesus sets out on his journey toward Jerusalem, Luke recounts, as we noted in chapter 2, a series of events that parallel earlier events: Just as God sent John as a messenger before Jesus,[39] so Jesus now sends disciples as messengers before him (9:52). Also, just as Jesus, variously, was rejected by the people of Nazareth, called his first disciples, and sent the twelve out on a mission, so now he is rejected by Samaritans,[40] impresses upon would-be disciples the demands of discipleship,[41] and sends the seventy-two out on a mission.[42] At this juncture, our interest is in the prominence with which the disciples stand out in these latter events.

On his way up to Jerusalem, Jesus sends disciples as messengers before him so that people will be prepared to receive him (9:52-56). In heralding Jesus' coming, the messengers visit a Samaritan village. The moment the villagers learn that Jesus' destination is Jerusalem, however, they flatly refuse him entrance. Observing this, James and John immediately ask Jesus whether he does not want them to do as Elijah had once done, call down fire from heaven to consume the people (2 Kings 1:9-15). Because Jesus has already counseled love of enemy and empowered the disciples for ministry and not for performing vindictive acts,[43] Jesus rebukes James and John for their display of spiritual immaturity. Instead of compelling the Samaritans to receive him, Jesus directs his entourage toward another, Israelite village (9:56).

As Jesus continues his way, he exchanges words with three would-be disciples (9:57-62). Through these exchanges, he teaches those with him about the demands of discipleship. The larger point Jesus drives home is that discipleship, or loyalty to him, is intolerant of all competing loyalties: attachment to home, obligation to family, or anything that might infringe upon one's total commitment to him (9:57-62). In the first scene (9:57-58), a man who would become Jesus' disciple approaches him and roundly declares, "I will follow you wherever you go!" Jesus' reply is such as to urge the man not to pledge loyalty to him without first counting the cost: Unlike even fox and bird, he is completely without home. In other words, discipleship, Jesus asserts, involves one in sharing in his homelessness.

In the second scene (9:59-60), Jesus himself seizes the initiative and authoritatively calls a man to discipleship. In principle, the man accepts Jesus' call. Still, in the same breath in which he accepts the call, he requests that the start of his life of discipleship be delayed: "Permit me," he pleads, "first to go and to bury my father." This plea is no ordinary one: It carries with it the full weight of sacred obligation and is based on Moses' command to honor one's father and mother.[44] Indeed, this plea is rooted in patriarchal example: At death, Jacob made Joseph swear to see after his burial (Gen. 50:5-6). To this man's way of thinking, therefore, his sacred obligation to family takes precedence over Jesus' call to discipleship. Responding to the man with a harsh retort and a command—"Leave the dead to bury their own dead; but as for you, go and proclaim the kingdom of

God"—Jesus gives him to understand that discipleship involves placing loyalty to Jesus above all other loyalties, even sacred obligation to family. Giving to Jesus absolute loyalty is of the essence of discipleship.

In the third scene (9:61-62), yet another man addresses Jesus. This man, like the first one, is ready to follow Jesus but, like the second one, is eager to delay the start of his life of discipleship: "Let me first say farewell to those at my home." This man's request is an echo of that of Elisha (1 Kings 19:19-21). Summoned to discipleship by Elijah, Elisha accepts the call but delays following Elijah until after he has first returned home to kiss his parents goodbye. As with the second man, this man views family obligation as taking precedence over the obligations of discipleship. Moreover, he can justify this by alluding to the notable example of Elisha. For his part, however, Jesus regards the man's request as a delaying tactic and evidence of a lack of resolve. Just as no farmer, he tells the man, can plow a straight furrow by looking backward instead of forward, so no person who is irresolute about following him is fit to be his disciple. Discipleship involves total dedication to Jesus and his cause.

Following these three exchanges, Jesus commissions seventy-two disciples and sends them out in pairs to every place in Israel where he is about to come (10:1-16). Earlier, Jesus had sent out the twelve, to expand his outreach to Israel (9:1-6). Now he expands his outreach even more. The large group of seventy-two, which is still insufficient for the task (10:2), calls attention to the great harvest awaiting the missionaries. It foreshadows the universal mission the church will undertake in Acts. Sending the disciples out "two by two" alludes to the role they will play at the latter day as witnesses on behalf of, or against, those to whom they go.[45] It also prefigures the practice of the church in Acts.[46] Like the twelve before them, the seventy-two are to undertake a ministry of word and deed: They are to heal the sick and proclaim the (nearness of) the kingdom (10:9). In so doing, they proffer peace, or salvation, throughout Israel (10:5-6). In the discharge of their mission, urgency is the order of the day. For this reason, they are to travel speedily and lightly and to rely on the hospitality of those who receive them (10:4, 7-8). By the same token, they can anticipate that they will also encounter hostility (10:3). Regardless, they go out as accredited ambassadors: To accept or reject them is to accept or reject Jesus and, finally, God himself (10:16). For all those they meet, therefore, the decision to accept or reject carries with it ultimate consequences (10:10-15).

The return of the seventy-two becomes an occasion for joy and congratulations (10:17-24). As they report to Jesus, the seventy-two are ecstatic: By virtue of the authority Jesus gave them, demons were subject to them (10:17). Jesus concurs: In their ministry he saw Satan suffering swift defeat;[47] and because they preached and healed under the umbrella of his protection, no harm came to them (10:18-19). Nevertheless, what is infinitely more important than that they have power over demons is that they have been granted the gift of life, or salvation (10:20; Rev. 3:5).

In this moment of high joy, the Holy Spirit also moves Jesus himself to exult (10:21-22). Jesus gives God thanks for having revealed "these things" not to the wise and understanding (i.e., to such as the religious authorities), but to "infants" (i.e., to such as his disciples). The "things" God reveals have to do with knowledge of his plan of salvation: that God in his end-time rule is present in the ministry of Jesus and his disciples to vanquish Satan and to save (10:17-20). Indeed, Jesus continues, God has entrusted "all things" (i.e., all knowledge and authority) to him, who is God's Son (10:22). It is he, therefore, who reveals "who the Father is" (i.e., Jesus, in his person and ministry, makes known to humans the saving presence, rule, purpose, and will of God).

After giving thanks to God, Jesus turns to the disciples and pronounces a beatitude (10:23-24). He declares the disciples to be "blessed," or fortunate, because they are eye- and ear-witnesses to the things that not even prophets and kings were privileged to see and hear, to wit: the time of salvation and the signs that, in him, God in his end-time rule is present in the midst of Israel (10:23-24; 17:20-21).

Instruction on Discipleship

As Jesus moves toward Jerusalem, he addresses, in rotating fashion, the disciples, the people, and the religious authorities. In addressing the disciples, Jesus for the most part instructs them in the ways of discipleship. While the disciples are attentive to Jesus, they continue to exhibit spiritual immaturity and incomprehension. This especially seems to be the case as they draw near to Jerusalem.

On the way to Jerusalem, the disciples attest to their spiritual immaturity by showing that they are both "status-conscious" and "anxious about the future." Because of their concern for status, the disciples do all they can to turn away those bringing infants to Jesus that he might bless them (18:15-17). Their reasoning is apparent: In their view children, because they are totally dependent upon their parents, have no standing of their own in society and hence are of little consequence.[48] Or again, in looking to the future Peter speaks for all the disciples when he expresses his anxiety about what will become of them (18:28-30). After all, from a human perspective their anxiety is justified: So as to follow Jesus, the disciples have left behind everything and made themselves "poor."

In two instances, the disciples also fail to measure up because of incomprehension. Near Jericho, Jesus takes the twelve aside and delivers the most extensive of his passion-predictions (18:31-33). As Luke remarks, however, Jesus' words are lost on the disciples: "But they understood none of these things . . . and they did not grasp what was said" (18:34). Moreover, despite having been given knowledge of the secrets of God's kingdom (8:9-10), the disciples, too, are apparently among those who mistakenly suppose that Jesus' nearness to Jerusalem means that the kingdom of God is about to arrive in splendor (19:11).[49] One reason Jesus tells the parable of the pounds (19:11-27) is to teach that the disciples' first priority is not to look for the final manifestation of the kingdom but to be faithful in doing the work with which Jesus has entrusted them.

Notwithstanding the disciples' failings, Jesus' principal interest on the way to Jerusalem is to instruct them so that they gain a clear picture of the life of discipleship. Typically, Jesus couches his instruction in the form of clusters of sayings, some of which virtually become speeches,[50] and he also tells many parables. Key topics that occur or recur in Jesus' instruction have to do with being on guard against the hypocrisy of the Pharisees;[51] rebuking and forgiving one another;[52] availing oneself of the incomparable power of faith;[53] cultivating the life of prayer;[54] trusting in God to provide the necessities of life;[55] relinquishing one's goods so as to benefit others;[56] being faithful in doing Jesus' will;[57] being steadfast in time of persecution and unafraid to confess Jesus;[58] being watchful and prepared for Jesus' return;[59] and placing loyalty to Jesus above loyalty to all else, including family.[60]

One topic deserving special mention is that of prayer. In reply to the disciples' request that he teach them to pray (11:1), Jesus both invites them to approach God as Father[61] and to use in their life together the model prayer he gives them, the Lord's Prayer (11:2-4). In addition, Jesus enjoins the disciples to submit their needs to God and to expect God to meet them, to be persistent in offering their petitions, and to ask God above all for the gift of the Holy Spirit (11:5-13).

IN THE TEMPLE IN JERUSALEM: WARNINGS AND PREDICTIONS

Jesus' teaching in the temple constitutes the final phase of the middle of Luke's gospel story (19:47—21:38). As Jesus descends from the Mount of Olives to enter Jerusalem, the whole multitude of his disciples burst forth in shouts of joy as they praise God and acclaim him as King (19:37-38). It is Jesus' disciples, therefore, who instill the note of triumph into his entry into Jerusalem.

Once Jesus undertakes his ministry in the temple (19:47—21:38), however, the disciples fade from view until toward the end. In cleansing the temple and taking possession of it to teach the people, Jesus provokes the religious authorities to do what they heretofore have not done: look for a way to destroy him (19:47). Still, after Jesus has finished with the authorities, he again concerns himself, in the hearing of the people, with the disciples (20:45—21:36). As the reader looks on, Jesus warns the disciples about the scribes, extols the poor widow, and predicts events leading up to the end of the age.

The warning Jesus directs against the scribes (20:45-47) and the praise he has for the poor widow (21:1-4) have to do, negatively and positively, with the fundamentals of true discipleship. Negatively, the scribes stand out in Jesus' words as quintessential examples of the dictum that "every one who exalts oneself will be humbled."[62] The reason is that the scribes are right with neither God nor neighbor. The scribes are not right with God, for their religion is false and inauthentic (20:47). And neither are they right with the neighbor, for they are "self-important," exalting themselves over others, and "avaricious," devouring the houses of widows (20:46-47). Positively, the poor widow stands out in Jesus' words as a quintessential example of the dictum that "the one who humbles oneself will be exalted,"[63] for she is right with God. In casting the whole of her subsistence into the temple treasury, the widow entrusts her life to God and lives in total dependence upon him (12:22-34). In this way, she lays up treasure in heaven and is rich toward God.[64] Just as Jesus holds up the scribes as models the disciples are to shun, so he holds up the widow as a model they are to emulate.

Prompted by the comments of some near him about the beauty of the temple, Jesus next launches into an eschatological discourse full of predictions about events leading up to the end of the age (21:5-36). In substance, this discourse is not new but replete with themes Jesus has earlier dealt with, to wit: Jesus enjoins the disciples to beware of false messiahs (21:8-11); to anticipate persecution and to persevere in it (21:12-19); to be on the lookout for signs portending the destruction of Jerusalem[65] and, later, his coming at the end of the age to redeem them;[66] and to be prepared for his sudden appearance in glory (21:34-46). By returning to these themes, Jesus both stresses their importance and elaborates on them.

Plainly, the role the disciples play during Jesus' ministry in the temple in Jerusalem is that of passive onlookers and listeners. With the onset of the passion, however, this will change noticeably.

EVENTS SURROUNDING THE PASSION, RESURRECTION, AND ASCENSION OF JESUS

As Luke begins his account of Jesus' passion, his gospel story takes another major turn so that the middle gives way to the end and the culmination of the story (22:1—24:53). In the passion account as in earlier phases of the story, the disciples continue to serve the purposes of both God and humans. On the one hand, the disciples "serve the purposes of God": Except for Judas, they do not break their bond of loyalty to Jesus and forsake him.[67] On the other hand, the disciples "serve the purposes of humans": They give no indication that they understand at all the plan of salvation God pursues in the suffering and death of Jesus. Indeed, the result of the disciples' manifest failure to grasp the passion-predictions of Jesus now becomes apparent: They are unable to perceive aright the true nature of the events in which they are enmeshed. Although they believe that they "see," in reality they are "blind." They therefore prove themselves in the passion account to be ironic characters and amply attest to their spiritual immaturity and incomprehension.

The Passion: Spiritual Immaturity and Incomprehension

As Jesus enters upon his passion, he, not his opponents, is in control of events. To set the stage for these events, Luke takes note of the time and of the gathering of the "coalition of darkness": The Passover, Israel's celebration of its liberation from Egypt, is at hand;

and Judas, who becomes Satan's pawn, makes common cause with the religious authorities against Jesus (22:1-6).

Of significance is the participation of Judas in this coalition. The first time Luke referred to Judas in his gospel story, he remarked that he would become a "traitor" (6:16). As Satan now takes control of Judas, Luke's narrative prediction comes true. To signal this, Luke chooses words echoing the earlier passage: "Satan entered into Judas called Iscariot, who was of the number of the twelve" (22:3). Then, too, as Judas confers with the chief priests and temple officers how he might betray Jesus, Luke points out that the bond sealing their agreement is "money" (22:5-6). United in the bond of money, both Judas and the authorities show themselves to be allies of Satan and enemies of God, for in Luke's story world one "cannot serve God and mammon" (16:13; 4:5-8).

To all intents and purposes, Judas's participation in the coalition of darkness removes him from the circle of the twelve. This is clear from both the episode of Jesus' arrest and the way in which Peter describes Judas in Acts. In the episode of Jesus' arrest, Luke reports: "While [Jesus] was still speaking, there came a crowd, and the man called Judas . . . was leading them" (22:47). And in reflecting on this selfsame scene in Acts, Peter says of Judas: ". . . who was guide to those who arrested Jesus" (Acts 1:16). Still, if Judas, in becoming a leader within the coalition of darkness, removes himself from the twelve, why does Luke have Jesus allude to Judas at the Passover meal and thus indicate that Judas is yet present with the others (22:21)?

The answer lies in the purpose this meal-scene serves (22:21-23). Its purpose is to permit Jesus, and in part the disciples, to place Judas's treachery in proper perspective. In alluding to Judas, Jesus speaks in fact of his betrayal: "But behold the hand of him who betrays me is with me on the table" (22:21). Having now mentioned his betrayal, Jesus makes two related observations. The first is that although he will indeed suffer betrayal, the disciples are to understand that it is not this but the definite plan and foreknowledge of God that ultimately determines his fate (22:22; Acts 2:23). Jesus' second observation is that notwithstanding God's plan, the one who betrays him is without excuse and will not escape the dire consequences: ". . . but woe to that man by whom 'this man' is betrayed" (22:22). For their part, the disciples, in reacting to Jesus' words by querying one another about which of them could possibly do such a thing as betray him, indicate how abhorrent one is to regard Judas's act: The disciples are distressed to think that any of them could conceivably share the religious intimacy of celebrating the Passover meal with Jesus and then turn and betray him (22:23).

Apart from Judas, Luke depicts the rest of the disciples, or apostles (22:15), as "loyal" to Jesus during his passion but heavily encumbered by "spiritual immaturity" and "incomprehension." Out of loyalty to Jesus, Peter and John readily obey him when he dispatches them to prepare for the celebration of the Passover meal (22:7-13). Also, during Jesus' farewell discourse both he and the apostles repeatedly point to the apostles' loyalty to him. For example, the apostles are profoundly distressed, as we mentioned, by the thought that Jesus will suffer betrayal by one of his own (22:21-23). Moreover, Jesus himself baldly declares in view of the apostles, "You are those who have continued with me in my trials [i.e., throughout my ministry]" (22:28). In fact, Jesus asserts that owing to such fidelity he, as the one in whom God in kingly rule is present,[68] will share his rule with the apostles (beginning already in Acts) (22:29). The upshot is that they will have table fellowship with him in the sphere of both his present[69] and future rule and will themselves rule over Israel (the reconstituted people of God) both in this age[70] and in the age to come (22:30).[71] Again, Jesus promises Simon Peter—and indirectly all the apostles—that because of his own supplication Satan will not take control of Peter as he did of Judas (22:31-32). Just the opposite, Jesus assures Peter that his faith will not fail (22:32). Technically, of course, Peter's faith does fail, since he denies Jesus. Regardless, Jesus' assurance to Peter remains valid, for Peter repents of his sin and his faith revives.[72] Envisaging this, Jesus tells Peter that after he has repented, he is to "strengthen the brothers" (22:32); as a leader of the church in Acts, Peter does just this.[73] Last, as one looks beyond Jesus' farewell discourse, one observes that Luke also pays at least tepid tribute to the apostles' loyalty to Jesus even in a scene at the crucifixion: The apostles, too, are among the acquaintances of Jesus who stand, albeit "from afar," watching the fateful proceedings (23:49).

Despite their loyalty, the apostles call most attention to themselves during Jesus' passion because of their "spiritual immaturity" and "incomprehension." This is already the case in Jesus' farewell discourse. Thus, it is a sign of the apostles' spiritual immaturity that their distress over the thought that one of them could be so "low" as to betray Jesus should rekindle their old sense of "status-consciousness": They fall to quarreling among themselves over which of them is "greatest" (22:24-27; 9:46-48). To squelch this quarrel, Jesus instructs the apostles about true greatness by comparing the kings and leaders of the gentiles with himself. The way of gentile kings and leaders is to "lord it over" their subjects. In contrast, he is among them not after the manner of one of privilege who reclines at table, but after the manner of one who waits at table and thus "serves." So it is to be with the apostles, whom he has already chosen to rule over God's reconstituted people. They are to emulate not gentile authorities, but him. With him as their model, he who is the "greatest" among them will become as the "youngest" (one who serves others as if they were one's seniors),[74] and he who is the "leader" as the one who "serves." Accordingly, the hallmark of apostleship is "service," not "status."

In two later scenes during Jesus' farewell discourse, the spiritual immaturity of Peter and the incomprehension of all the apostles tarnish the apostles' image still further. In immediate response to Jesus' promise that his faith will not fail and to the command to strengthen the brothers, Peter, aglow with the zeal of false confidence, pledges to Jesus: "Lord, I am ready to go with you to prison and to death!" (22:33). In Acts, Peter will in fact be cast into prison for Jesus' sake.[75] Here, however, Jesus exposes Peter's confidence as false by predicting that he will deny him: "I tell you, Peter, the cock will not crow this day, until you three times deny that you know me" (22:34). Then, addressing all the apostles, Jesus attempts to prepare them for the new situation of persecution they will face (in Acts) (22:35-38). Thus far, the apostles have been untouched by persecution. When Jesus sent them out on an earlier mission in Israel, he not only endowed them with authority but placed them under the shield of his divine protection (9:1; [10:19]). Reminding the apostles of this, Jesus asks them whether they lacked anything that previous time. "Nothing," they acknowledge (22:35). At the present, however, a new situation looms, before both him and them. The new situation for him is that he must soon face his persecutors (23:32-33). The new situation for them is that henceforth they, too, must be prepared to face persecutors. To dramatize the apostles' need for such preparedness, Jesus urges them, "So now, let him who has a purse take it, and likewise a bag; and let him who has no sword sell his mantle and buy one" (22:36). Seizing on Jesus' command to buy a "sword" and misconstruing the intention of his words, the apostles exclaim, "Look, Lord, here are two swords!" (22:38). In swift reply to their incomprehension, Jesus ends the conversation:[76] "It is enough," he asserts (22:38).

Following Jesus' farewell discourse, the spiritual immaturity of the apostles becomes even more pronounced. At the Mount of

Olives, Jesus enjoins the apostles to pray so as not to succumb to temptation (i.e., commit apostasy)[77] (22:40). They, however, "fall asleep for grief" (22:45). Because the grief the apostles experience is symptomatic of fear and cowardice,[78] the sleep they take amounts to blatant disobedience to Jesus' injunction to pray. Again, at Jesus' arrest the two apostles with the swords, still thinking that Jesus' word about buying a sword advocated armed resistance, now press him to know: "Lord, shall we strike with the sword?" (22:49). Indeed, one of them even takes action and with a swing cuts off the right ear of the high priest's slave (22:50). To end such doings and correct the apostles' misguided notions about defending him, Jesus shouts aloud at the sword-wielding apostle, "No more of this!" and restores the slave's ear (22:51). And finally, after Jesus has been arrested and brought to the house of the high priest, Peter confronts his hour of testing only to fail: Because he did not pray at the Mount of Olives, Peter cannot withstand testing. Hence, while sitting in the courtyard of the high priest's house where Jesus is also present, Peter fulfills Jesus' prediction and denies three times that he ever knew him (22:34, 54-60). Even at this, however, Jesus' promise to Peter that his faith would not fail also proves true: Peter, seeing Jesus turn and look at him, remembers Jesus' prediction of denial and "goes out and weeps bitterly." In this act, Peter repents of his sin (22:61-62).

As we observed above, the apostles in Luke's gospel story do not abandon Jesus but stay on with the women disciples to watch the crucifixion, even if only "from afar" (23:49). That the apostles watch "from afar" is suggestive of their plight: As Jesus wends his way to the cross, none of them walks behind him carrying his cross, and neither does any of them bear public witness to his righteousness or look after his burial. Those performing these acts and hence functioning as foils for the apostles are Simon of Cyrene (23:26), the Roman centurion (23:47), and Joseph of Arimathea (23:50-54). In themselves, the apostles have shown themselves to be anything but staunch followers: Spiritually immature and uncomprehending, Judas has betrayed Jesus and fallen away; none of them has perceived what Jesus was about; and Peter, though repentant, has denied him.

Resurrection Appearances: Enlightenment and Spiritual Maturity

In the passion account, Luke narrowed his story of Jesus' disciples to focus almost exclusively on the apostles. Now, as he turns to the resurrection and ascension episodes, other disciples, such as the women and the two men from Emmaus, also stand out prominently (23:56b—24:53). Although at the outset spiritual immaturity in the form of incomprehension still characterizes all the disciples, gradually incomprehension gives way to enlightenment and spiritual maturity. As the gospel story draws to a close, the disciples worship the risen and ascending Jesus and joyfully return to Jerusalem to spend their time in the temple praising God.

In contrast to Matthew, who locates Jesus' resurrection appearance to the disciples on a mountain in Galilee,[79] Luke locates all the events surrounding Jesus' resurrection and ascension in and around Jerusalem (chap. 24). Also, Luke gives no hint in his gospel story that the risen Jesus appears to the disciples over a period of forty days (Acts 1:3). On the contrary, Jesus' resurrection, his appearances to the disciples, and his ascension all take place on the single day of Sunday, "the first day of the week" (24:1).[80]

In the first of Luke's resurrection episodes (23:56b—24:12), his primary concern is to stress the sheer reality of Jesus' resurrection by pointing to the emptiness of the tomb. Correlatively, Luke also contrasts the enlightenment of the women disciples with the incomprehension of the other disciples, especially Peter and the other apostles.

The women disciples who make their way to Jesus' tomb at dawn to anoint his body are no strangers to Luke's story: They are the selfsame persons who wandered with Jesus in Galilee (8:1-3); witnessed his crucifixion (23:49); followed Joseph of Arimathea to see Jesus' tomb and how his body had been placed (23:55); and, having prepared spices and ointments for Jesus' anointing, first observed the law by resting on the Sabbath before setting out on their journey (23:56; 24:1, 10). To call attention to the emptiness of Jesus' tomb, Luke stipulates what the women both "find" and "do not find" upon their arrival there: What they find is the stone rolled away from the tomb (24:2). What they do not find in the tomb is Jesus' body (24:3). Because the women had earlier followed Joseph, not to find Jesus' body perplexes them (23:55; 24:4). When, however, two message-bearing angels appear to them (24:4, 23), their perplexity turns to enlightenment and they comprehend that Jesus has in fact been raised.[81] To impart this truth to the women, the angels do two things. First, they explain the emptiness of Jesus' tomb in such fashion as to announce at the same time his resurrection: "Why do you seek the living among the dead? He is not here but has been raised [by God]" (24:5-6). Second, the angels summon the women to "remember" that Jesus himself had already announced his resurrection, in the passion-predictions he uttered while still in Galilee (24:6-7; 9:22, 44). To underline the angels' success in leading the women to comprehend the reality of Jesus' resurrection, Luke himself remarks: "And they 'remembered' [Jesus'] words" (24:8; Acts 11:16). Also, the women act on their "remembrance," for they immediately leave the tomb and go and report their experience to the eleven apostles and the other disciples with them (24:9; Acts 1:15). Unfortunately, the eleven give no credence to the women's report, preferring to believe that they talk nonsense (24:10-11). Nevertheless, Peter, his curiosity peaked, runs to the tomb and peers in (24:12). What he sees, however, is not Jesus' body but only the linen cloths in which he had been wrapped. Hence, Peter, too, becomes witness to the emptiness of Jesus' tomb. Regardless, Peter does not infer from this that Jesus has been raised. Instead, he simply leaves Jesus' tomb bewildered by what he has seen.[82]

The first disciples to be enlightened about God's plan of salvation are Cleopas and his companion. In the episode featuring them (24:13-35), the poles between which the action moves have to do with "not recognizing" Jesus (24:16) and "recognizing" him (24:31).[83] The episode itself contains four scenes: (a) The two disciples describe the ministry of Jesus from their own "human point of view" (24:13-24); (b) Jesus interprets his suffering and entry into glory from his "divine point of view" (24:25-27); (c) at the breaking of the bread, the incomprehension of the disciples gives way to enlightenment (24:28-32); and (d) that same night, the two disciples return to Jerusalem to share their story with the eleven apostles and the other disciples (24:33-35).

As the episode begins, the two disciples, on their way to Emmaus, converse with each other about recent events involving Jesus. As they walk and talk, the risen Jesus joins them, but they do not recognize him. At Jesus' instigation, the two disciples tell him how they understand the things that have happened to him these last days. Noteworthy about the two disciples' understanding is that they perceive these things wholly apart from the perspective of resurrection faith. This means, in effect, that they perceive them from a "human point of view." Indeed, Luke highlights this both by what he himself says of them and by what they say of Jesus and of recent events. Thus, Luke describes the two disciples as taking leave of Jerusalem, which is already a sign of despair on their part (24:13).[84] Moreover, when Jesus asks them what they are talking about, Luke relates that they stand still and "look sad (gloomy)"

(24:17). The reason Luke takes note of the "look" of the two disciples is that it serves as a forecast of the tenor of the report they will
give Jesus: It, too, will be "gloomy," that is to say, untouched by
resurrection faith.

With this in mind, the reader listens in as the risen but unrecog-
nized Jesus engages the two disciples in dialogue. As was mentioned,
Jesus first asks them what they are discussing as they walk (24:17).
By way of reply, Cleopas asks Jesus how it can possibly be that he
does not know of the things that have recently taken place in
Jerusalem; in point of fact, everyone there knows of these things
(24:18). As Jesus, feigning ignorance, presses to know "What things?"
the two disciples tell him of himself and his fate. Specifically, they
tell Jesus all of the following: They tell him who he "was"—signaling
by their use of the past tense that they think of him as dead—from
the standpoint of Jewish public opinion: ". . . a prophet mighty in
deed and word before God and all the people" (24:19).[85] They tell him
who was responsible for his death: ". . . how our chief priests and
rulers delivered him up to be condemned to death, and crucified him"
(24:20). They tell him of the hope his disciples had placed in him:
"But we had hoped that he was the one to redeem Israel [i.e., that he
was the Messiah]"[86] (24:21). They tell him how the crucifixion has all
but destroyed their hope: "Yes, and besides all this, it is the third day
since these things [suffering and crucifixion] happened" (24:21). And
they tell him that although the story the women disciples had told
after returning from Jesus' tomb had checked out, the fact remains
that those confirming the women's story still "did not see him [Jesus]"
(24:24). In other words, the sadness and hopelessness that have overtaken the two disciples ultimately stem from the fact that they do not
believe that Jesus has been raised from the dead.

Having listened to their woeful tale, Jesus himself seizes the
word (24:25-27). He chides the two disciples for their ignorance
("O foolish men") and reluctance to believe the words spoken by
the prophets. He stresses that divine necessity ordained that it was
precisely through suffering that the Messiah should enter into the
glory of his resurrected state. Through suffering, the Messiah's life
was made to conform to that of the prophets.[87] Through suffering,
the Messiah established a new covenant whereby he will, in glory,
preside over the reconstituted people of God (22:20). Working
through the scriptures, Jesus interprets for the two disciples the
plan of salvation God accomplishes in him.

With the aid of scripture, Jesus has now explained to the
two disciples God's plan of salvation. Nevertheless, Luke does

not yet describe the two as enlightened. To be sure, Luke will later make a point of having them attest to the enlightening power of Jesus' instruction: "Did not out hearts burn within us while he talked to us on the road, while he opened to us the scriptures?" (24:32). For the time being, however, Luke delays this special moment. His purpose in doing so is that Jesus might have opportunity to combine the instruction he has given the two disciples with the sharing of table fellowship (24:28-32). At the passover meal, Jesus promised the apostles that they would eat and drink at his table in his kingdom (22:30). As a "connecting link" to the meals that the followers of the risen, exalted, and reigning Jesus will share with him in Acts,[88] Jesus reclines at table with these two disciples. In a manner reminiscent especially of the feeding of the five thousand and of the Passover meal, Jesus takes the bread and blesses it, and breaks it and gives it to them.[89] Suddenly, in Jesus' act of breaking the bread, the incomprehension beclouding the two disciples dissipates and they become enlightened (24:35). As Luke himself puts it: "And their eyes were opened and they recognized him!" (24:31). At this, the risen Jesus vanishes from sight (24:31).

Enlightened, the two disciples return at once to Jerusalem (24:33-35). There they find the eleven apostles and other disciples assembled and asking, "Has the Lord really been raised?" "Did he appear to Simon?"[90] Following the earlier example of the women (24:9), the two disciples tell those assembled about the instruction they received on the road and how Jesus became known to them at the breaking of the bread (24:35).

While the apostles and other disciples are still busily discussing the report of the Emmaus disciples, Jesus himself suddenly appears in their midst (24:36-49). With this final appearance in the gospel story, Jesus leads the apostles and other disciples to believe that he has in fact been raised. He also opens their minds to a full understanding of the plan of salvation God accomplishes in him (24:36-49).

At the sudden appearance of Jesus before them, the apostles and other disciples become terrified. They suppose that it is not Jesus but a spirit, or ghost (24:37). To convince them that it is he himself raised from the dead, Jesus invites them to look at his hands and feet and to touch him and observe that he has flesh and bones (24:38-39). What the reader learns from this is that the resurrection-state does not obliterate corporeality. Although the prospect that what they see is indeed Jesus himself fills the apostles and other disciples with joy, they nonetheless remain captive to their unbelief (24:41). Jesus, however, finally overcomes this, by eating before them a piece of broiled fish (24:42-43).

Still in their midst, the risen Jesus next opens the minds of the apostles and other disciples to comprehend the plan of salvation God accomplishes in him (24:44-49). To do this, Jesus leads them to understand the scriptures. In particular, however, he mentions three things: that the Messiah must suffer; that he must rise; and that repentance for the forgiveness of sins must be proclaimed in his name to all the nations (24:46-47). In citing the latter, Jesus teaches the apostles and other disciples something new: that from of old God ordained that the word of repentance, forgiveness, and salvation should be proclaimed not only in Israel but also among the gentiles (2:30-32). Beyond this, the risen Jesus also speaks a new word to the apostles and other disciples about themselves (24:48-49): He declares that they are "witnesses" of God's plan of salvation accomplished in him; he assures them that he will empower them with the Spirit for the mission to the nations they are to undertake (Acts 1:4-5); and he commands them to remain in Jerusalem until the Spirit has descended upon them.

As Jesus falls silent at the close of this episode, the reader has arrived at that place in Luke's gospel story where the whole assemblage of disciples can, in principle, be said to be fully enlightened about God's plan of salvation in Jesus. The disciples now comprehend that the life and ministry of Jesus are in fulfillment of the scriptures. They comprehend that the suffering and death of Jesus Messiah attest not to the victory of the religious authorities over him, as the Emmaus disciples dejectedly thought, but to God's purpose in establishing a new covenant and saving humankind. They comprehend that Jesus Messiah has in fact been raised from the dead by God and vindicated in his conflict with Israel. And they comprehend that it will be their task to proclaim, in the name of Jesus and as an extension of his ministry, repentance and forgiveness to gentiles as well as to Jews. As Jesus declares the disciples to be the "witnesses" of God's plan of salvation in him, he in effect declares them to be spiritually mature.

The Ascension: Worship and the Mission to Come

As Jesus completes his "exodus" by ascending to universal rule, he leaves the disciples to anticipate the outpouring of the Spirit and the commencement of the worldwide mission with which he has entrusted them. As he begins his ascent, Jesus blesses the disciples as a priest would bless the people, commending them to the care of God (24:50).[91] As the disciples receive Jesus' blessing, they bow down in worship (24:52).[92] In this act of worshiping the risen and ascending Jesus, the conflict between Jesus and the disciples formally comes to resolution. Through their worship, the disciples outwardly manifest that they are enlightened about God's plan of salvation in Jesus and that they have attained to spiritual maturity. In addition, the disciples' worship marks the point in the gospel story at which Luke has now mediated to Theophilus and the reader, those to whom he has narrated the story, the "certainty" ("assurance") concerning the "things which have been accomplished among us" (1:1-4).

Having worshiped Jesus, the disciples return to Jerusalem with great joy and spend their time in the temple blessing God (24:52-53). By bringing his gospel story to a close[93] with just this picture, Luke trumpets the same themes at the end as he did at the beginning (chaps. 1–2). At the beginning, the time of prophecy gave way to the time of salvation: Scenes of great joy abounded; God was richly praised for acting to save through John and especially Jesus; and the temple in Jerusalem figured prominently as a setting. Here at the end, the time of Jesus and of the accomplishment of salvation gives way to the time of the church. In the time of the church, the disciples will proclaim salvation in Jerusalem, in all Judea, in Samaria, and to the end of the earth (Acts 1:8). In joyful anticipation of this, they spend their time in the temple in Jerusalem praising God for the new thing God is about to do.

SUMMARY

The disciples make their debut in the middle of Luke's gospel story (3:1—19:46), after Jesus has begun his ministry. In characterizing the disciples, Luke shows that they are of two minds and hence inwardly divided: On the one hand, they "serve the purposes of God" and view reality from a divine perspective. On the other hand, they "serve the purposes of humans" and view reality from a human perspective. The reason the disciples are inwardly divided is that although they are the followers of Jesus, they do not comprehend the plan of salvation God is accomplishing in him. The upshot is that they tend to be spiritually immature, and this immaturity often manifests itself as incomprehension. Spiritually immature, the disciples not infrequently set themselves at odds with Jesus, and this, in turn, leads to conflict. Fundamentally, therefore, Jesus' struggle with the disciples is to guide them to spiritual maturity, and to do this he must enlighten them about God's ways and purposes.

Throughout the three phases of the middle of Luke's gospel story (3:1—9:50; 9:51—19:46; 19:47—21:38), the disciples give ample evidence of their double-mindedness. To their credit, they stand in the service of God's purposes. When Jesus summons them to be with him, they hear his call, leave behind everything, and pledge to him their loyalty (5:11, 27-28). God gives them to know the secrets of his kingly rule (8:10). Both the twelve and the seventy-two undertake ministries in Israel (9:1-6; 10:1-16). As spokesperson for the disciples, Peter correctly confesses Jesus to be "the Messiah of God" (9:20). And at every turn, the disciples readily give ear to Jesus' teaching and obey his commands (e.g., 19:29-35).

On a negative note, the disciples fail at critical times to demonstrate the kind of spiritual maturity Jesus expects of them. Out on the sea, their faith does not sustain them (8:25). Though endowed with authority, they are perplexed by Jesus' command to feed the five thousand (9:13). Taught by Jesus that he is constrained by divine necessity to suffer and die, they cannot fathom his words (9:44-45; 18:31-34). Atop the mount of transfiguration, Peter, John, and James are made dull by sleep and Peter talks nonsense (9:32-33). While Jesus and the three are away, the nine disciples below are ineffectual in trying to heal a demon-possessed boy (9:40). And on other occasions, one or some or all of the disciples prove themselves to be "status-conscious" (9:46-48; 18:15-17), "exclusive" (9:49-50), "vindictive" (9:52-56), inclined to "temporize" (9:59-60), "anxious about the future" (18:28-30), and "misguided" in their understanding about when God will establish his kingdom in glory (19:11; Acts 1:6).

The spiritual immaturity of the disciples exacts its greatest toll at the end of the gospel story (22:1—24:53). True, both the apostles and other disciples remain steadfast in their loyalty to Jesus, for they do not forsake him during his passion (22:28; 23:49). Regardless, from the hour Jesus and the apostles celebrate the Passover to the time he is arrested and later crucified, the apostles attest in word and deed to their spiritual immaturity. They quarrel over who is greatest (22:24-27). Peter exudes false confidence (22:33). They misconstrue Jesus' exhortation to buy a sword (22:36, 38). At the Mount of Olives, they sleep for grief, which is a symptom of cowardice and fear (22:45). At Jesus' arrest, the two apostles with the swords delude themselves into believing that Jesus would have them defend him (22:49-50). And at the last, Judas not only betrays Jesus but also dies as an apostate (22:47-48; Acts 1:18-19); Peter, despite repenting afterwards, denies Jesus (22:54-62); and all the apostles, though they watch the crucifixion, nonetheless do so "from afar" (23:49).

Although the disciples especially have behaved dismally, Luke's final word on the assemblage of Jesus' disciples is still one of triumph and not defeat. On Easter Sunday, the women disciples are enlightened by two angels concerning Jesus' resurrection (24:4-8). Also, the risen Jesus himself enlightens both the Emmaus disciples and the apostles and those with them about the plan of salvation God accomplishes in him (24:25-27, 32, 44-49). Finally, therefore, Jesus brings the disciples to spiritual maturity, and it is a mark of their maturity that they worship him as he ascends to heaven (24:52). This act of worship, in fact, is the point in Luke's gospel story at which Jesus' conflict with the disciples comes to resolution. Once the Spirit has been poured out upon them, they will be prepared to undertake the worldwide mission Jesus has entrusted them. In Jerusalem and to the end of the earth, they will proclaim to Jew and gentile the salvation God has accomplished in Jesus.

ABBREVIATIONS

NIGTC	New International Greek Testament Commentary
NovT	*Novum Testamentum*
NTL	New Testament Library
NTS	*New Testament Studies*
OBT	Overtures to Biblical Theology
PC	Proclamation Commentaries
PRS	*Perspectives in Religious Studies*
PRSSSS	Perspectives in Religious Studies Special Studies Series
PThS	Paderborner Theologische Studien
RNT	Regensburger Neues Testament
RSV	Revised Standard Version
SANT	Studien zum Alten und Neuen Testament
SB	Sources bibliques
SBLDS	SBL Dissertation Series
SBLMS	SBL Monograph Series
SBS	Stuttgarter Bibelstudien
SJLA	Studies in Judaism in Late Antiquity
SNTSMS	Society for New Testament Studies Monograph Series
SNTU	Studien zum Neuen Testament und seiner Umwelt
SNTW	Studies of the New Testament and Its World
StBT	*Studia Biblica et Theologica*
TDNT	G. Kittel and G. Friedrich, eds., *Theological Dictionary of the New Testament* (Grand Rapids, Mich.: Wm. B. Eerdmans, 1964–76)
TI	Theological Inquiries
TynBul	*Tyndale Bulletin*
VMAB	Veröffentlichungen des Missionspriesterseminars St. Augustin bei Bonn
WF	Wege der Forschung
WS	Walberberger Studien
ZNW	*Zeitschrift für die neutestamentliche Wissenschaft*

NOTES

(Works referred to earlier in the notes for a given chapter or listed in the Selected Bibliography are cited by name and title only)

1. INTRODUCTION

1. The notion that Luke's Gospel is "the most beautiful book there ever was" was first expressed by the French scholar E. Renan (*Les évangiles et la seconde génération chrétienne*, 2d ed. [Paris: Michel Lévy, 1877] 283) and has since been repeated countless times, especially in the early part of this century.

2. The view that Luke is both "artist" and "theologian" is one that Karris has captured well in the title of his book: *Luke: Artist and Theologian.*

3. Scholars do not know where Luke's Gospel was written, but I. H. Marshall (*Commentary on Luke*, NIGTC [Grand Rapids, Mich.: Wm. B. Eerdmans, 1978] 35) seems to show some slight preference for Antioch of Syria, and this, in turn, is the strong choice of J. A. Fitzmyer (*The Gospel according to Luke I–IX*, AB 28 [Garden City, N.Y.: Doubleday, 1981] 44–47, 57). However, in his book *Lokalisation der Lukas-Leser* (forthcoming from J. C. B. Mohr), P. Lampe shows that Luke's Gospel was most likely written in Ephesus in Asia Minor.

4. Concerning the likelihood that the evangelist Luke wrote his Gospel for "residential believers," see John Koenig, *New Testament Hospitality: Partnership with Strangers as Promise and Mission*, OBT (Philadelphia: Fortress, 1985) 103–7, 119.

5. On the "world view" of contemporary apocalyptic literature, see J. J. Collins, *The Apocalyptic Imagination: An Introduction to the Jewish Matrix of Christianity* (New York: Crossroad, 1984) 4–6.

6. Whereas the term "Hades" occurs four times in Luke (10:15; 16:23) and Acts (2:27, 31), the term "Gehenna" occurs only once (Luke 12:5). Regarding the notion of Gehenna and how it relates to Hades, see T. H. Gaster, "Gehenna," *IDB* 2:361–62.

7. See Luke 10:21; 21:35; Acts 4:24; 17:26.

8. H. Sasse, "*Gē*," *TDNT* 1 (1964): 678.

9. See Luke 1:31-32; Acts 7:2-53. While Jesus' genealogy extends to Adam and therefore embraces the "history of the world," it also quickly narrows to Abraham and the history of Israel (3:23-38).

10. See Matt. 12:40; also J. Jeremias, "*Hadēs,*" *TDNT* 1 (1964): 148.

11. See, e.g., T. H. Gaster, "Dead, Abode of The," *IDB* 1:787–88.

12. See, e.g., 2 Esd. 8:59; *2 Enoch* 10.

13. See Sir. 21:9-10; *1 Enoch* 10:13; also Rev. 20:14-15.

14. See Luke 2:14; 19:38.

15. See Luke 1:19, 26; 2:15.

16. See Luke 12:8; 22:69; Acts 1:9-11; 2:32-35; 3:20-21; 5:31; 7:56.

17. See Luke 6:23; 10:20; 12:8; 13:29; 18:22.

18. See Luke 10:21; Acts 4:24; 17:24, 26.

19. The expression "peace in heaven" in 19:38 seems to suggest that there exists in heaven the state, or condition, of salvation (see, e.g., W. Foerster, "*Eirēnē,*" *TDNT* 2 [1964]: 413). By the same token, "peace," or "salvation," is the gift that God, through Jesus Christ, would bestow on Israel and the gentiles (Luke 2:14; Acts 10:34-36).

20. See Luke 11:20; 17:20-21.

21. On "word and deed," see Luke 4:43; 8:1; 9:11; 10:13; 11:20; Acts 10:38. On "repentance," see Luke 5:32; 10:13; 11:32; 13:3, 5. On "discipleship," see Luke 9:23; 14:25-27. On "peace" and "salvation," see Luke 19:9-10, 42; Acts 10:36; 13:23, 26.

22. See Luke 21:27, 29-31; Acts 3:20-21.

23. See Luke 3:38; 21:27; Acts 17:24-26, 31.

24. See, e.g., N. A. Dahl, "The Story of Abraham in Luke-Acts," in *Jesus in the Memory of the Church* (Minneapolis: Augsburg, 1976) 66–86.

25. Concerning Luke's view of salvation history, see F. Bovon, *L'oeuvre de Luc: Études d'exégèse et de théologie,* LD 130 (Paris: Cerf, 1987) esp. 19–21. For a different view, which reckons with three phases instead of two and takes its inspiration from Hans Conzelmann, see Fitzmyer, *Luke I-IX,* 179–92, esp. 185.

26. See M. H. Abrams, *A Glossary of Literary Terms,* 4th ed. (New York: Holt, Rinehart and Winston, 1981) 175.

27. See Mark 7:31; 8:27-30.

28. "And": Luke 3:23; 4:14, 16, 31; 8:26; 11:14. "And when": Luke 2:21, 22; 23:33. "And behold": Luke 2:25; 10:25; 23:50.

29. See, e.g., Luke 9:18 (RSV); also 3:21; 5:1, 12, 17; 9:51.

30. For a detailed portrayal of "Galilee" in Luke's Gospel, see S. Freyne, *Galilee, Jesus and the Gospels: Literary Approaches and Historical Investigations* (Philadelphia: Fortress, 1988) 90–103.

31. On the importance Luke attaches to the word "beginning," see F. W. Danker, *Jesus and the New Age: A Commentary on St. Luke's Gospel,* rev. ed. (Philadelphia: Fortress, 1988) 96–97.

32. Cf. Acts 10:38 with Luke 23:2-5; also Danker, *Jesus and the New Age,* 364–65.

33. See, e.g., Acts 1:21-22.

34. See Luke 8:2-3; 23:49, 55; 24:6.

35. See, e.g., E. Hilgert, *The Ship and Related Symbols in the New Testament* (Assen: Van Gorcum, 1962) 43–49, 106; O. Eissfeldt, "Gott und das Meer in der Bibel," *Kleine Schriften* (Tübingen: J. C. B. Mohr, 1966) 3: 261–64.

36. See Luke 11:43; 20:46.

37. See Luke 4:15, 44.

38. See Luke 6:6-11; 13:10-17.

39. See Luke 12:11; 21:12.

40. See R. L. Cohn, *The Shape of Sacred Space: Four Biblical Studies,* AARSR 23 (Chico, Calif.: Scholars Press, 1981) chap. 3.

41. See Luke 6:12; 9:28; 22:39-46 (esp. v. 39).

42. For a sampling of scholarly views on "Jerusalem" and the "temple" in Luke-Acts, see K. Baltzer, "The Meaning of the Temple in the Lukan Writings," *HTR* 58 (1965): 263–77; R. Glöckner, *Die Verkündigung des Heils beim Evangelisten Lukas,* WS 9 (Mainz: Matthias-Grünewald, 1976) 68–90; F. D. Weinert, "The Meaning of the Temple in Luke-Acts," *BTB* 11 (1981): 85–89; Tyson, *Death of Jesus,* chap. 4; Esler, *Community and Gospel,* chap. 6; Chance, *Jerusalem, the Temple, and the New Age.*

43. See, e.g., 2 Chron. 33:4; Ezra 7:15; Pss. 46:4-5; 135:21; Zech. 8:3-8.

44. See Luke 6:4; 19:46.

45. See, e.g., Luke 19:45-46; 1 Kings 8:10-13; Isa. 6:1; Ezek. 43:6-9; also Baltzer, "Meaning of the Temple," 265–67.

46. See Luke 1:10; 18:10; 19:46.

47. See Luke 24:53; also 2:28, 38; 18:11.

48. See Luke 2:46-47; also 19:47; 21:37.

49. See also Weinert, "Meaning of the Temple," 86–88.

50. See Luke 9:53; 13:22, 33; 17:11, 25; 18:31-33; 19:28.

51. Regarding the term "type-scene" and the number and salient features of such scenes, see Tannehill (*Narrative Unity of Luke-Acts,* 170–72). One may question, however, whether one is justified in grouping 19:1-10 with 5:29-32 and 15:1-32: (*a*) The depiction of Jesus at meal is only indirect (19:5, 7); (*b*) those who grumble are not the Pharisees and scribes but "all"; and (*c*) Jesus directs his closing words, not to the grumblers, but to Zacchaeus (19:9-10). In other respects, the setting of the meal also appears in connection with the story of Mary and Martha (10:38-42), Jesus' eating the Passover with the apostles (20:14-23), and Jesus' sitting at table with the two disciples from Emmaus (24:30).

52. See Luke 5:29-32; 15:1-32.

53. See Luke 7:36-50; 11:37-54; 14:1-24.

54. On the Lukan motif of "prayer," see, e.g., P. T. O'Brien, "Prayer in Luke-Acts," *TynBul* 24 (1973): 112, 121, 127; A. Trites, "The Prayer Motif in Luke-Acts," *Perspectives on Luke-Acts,* ed. C. H. Talbert, PRSSS 5

(Danville, Va.: Association of Baptist Professors of Religion, 1978) 169; L. Feldkämper, *Der betende Jesus als Heilsmittler nach Lukas*, VMAB 29 (St. Augustin: Steyler Verlag, 1978).

55. See further, C. H. Talbert, "The Way of the Lukan Jesus: Dimensions of Lukan Spirituality," *PRS* 9 (1982): 237–49.

56. See, e.g., Luke 22:41-44; 23:46.

57. On characterization, see Abrams, *Glossary of Literary Terms*, 20–22.

58. For a defense of the traditional view that the author of the Third Gospel and Acts was "Luke," the companion of Paul, see Fitzmyer, *Luke I–IX*, 35–53.

59. One who dissents from this commonly acknowledged view is Dawsey (*The Lukan Voice*, 110, 122, chaps. 7–8). As Dawsey sees it, the narrator of Luke's gospel story is unreliable, for in significant respects the narrator's point of view differs from that of Jesus, and Jesus is the one whom the implied author shows to be reliable. To date, however, Dawsey's position has not won the assent of other scholars.

60. Abrams, *Glossary of Literary Terms*, 143.

61. Ibid.

62. See Luke 1:31; 4:34; 8:28; 17:13; 18:37-38; 23:42; 24:19. At 3:29, the Greek name "Jesus" refers to the Old Testament figure of Joshua.

63. See Luke 1:6, 9, 11, 58, 66; 2:9, 22, 23a-b, 24, 26, 39; 3:4; 5:17.

64. See Luke 7:13, 19; 10:1, 39, 41; 11:39; 12:42; 13:15; 17:5, 6; 18:6; 19:8; 22:61; 24:3.

65. See, e.g., Luke 10:21; Acts 4:24; 17:26.

66. See, e.g., Acts 2:23-24; 4:27-28; 5:38-39; also Luke 7:30.

67. See Luke 22:42; Acts 21:14; 22:14-15.

68. See, e.g., Luke 22:22; Acts 10:42; 17:26, 31.

69. See Acts 4:27-28.

70. See Acts 3:20.

71. See Acts 10:41.

72. See, e.g., Luke 4:18, 43; 9:48; 10:16; 13:34.

73. See Luke 1:8-20, 26-38; 2:8-20; [22:43]; 24:4-9, 23.

74. See Luke 1:21-23; 24:22-23.

75. See Luke 1:41-45, 67-79; 2:25-35.

76. See Luke 5:25-26; 7:16; 13:13, 17; 17:15; 18:43.

77. See Bovon, *L'oeuvre de Luc*, 226.

78. For an insightful exposition of the role Satan plays in Luke's Gospel, see Garrett, *Demise of the Devil*, chap. 2.

79. See, e.g., Luke 10:17-19; Acts 13:10.

80. See Luke 13:11, 16; Acts 10:38.

81. Brown, *Apostasy and Perseverance*, 10.

82. Ibid., 7. See Luke 11:17-23.

83. The term Danker (*Luke*, chap. 3) has coined for Jesus as the supreme agent of God is "benefactor." Through the use of this term, Danker masterfully places Luke's understanding of Jesus within the context of contemporary Greco-Roman thought.

84. See Luke 1:30-35; 2:11; 3:22, 38; 4:18.

85. See Luke 4:32, 36; 5:24; 20:1-8; 20:19; Acts 1:1-2; 10:37-38.

86. See Luke 10:22; 22:42. Jesus as "Servant": Luke 2:43, 49; Acts 3:13, 26; 4:25, 27, 30; 20:12. Jesus as the "Righteous One": [Luke 23:47]; Acts 3:14; 7:52; 22:14 (F. Matera, "The Death of Jesus according to Luke: A Question of Sources," *CBQ* 47 [1985]: 479–84).

87. On "praying," see Luke 11:1-13. On "forgiving," cf. Luke 11:4; 17:3-4; with 23:34. On "renouncing (surrendering) possessions," cf. Luke 14:33 with 23:34b. On "taking up (enduring) the cross," cf. Luke 9:23; 14:27; with 23:33.

88. See Luke 5:27-29; 9:23; 14:27; 18:22.

89. See, e.g., Luke 6:13-16; 8:1-3.

90. See Luke 9:1-6; 10:1-16.

91. For further details, see C. H. Talbert, "Discipleship in Luke-Acts," in *Discipleship in the New Testament,* ed. F. F. Segovia (Philadelphia: Fortress, 1985) 67–73.

92. See Luke 5:15, 19; 8:4, 19; 12:1; 14:25; also 7:9, 11; 9:11; [23:27].

93. See, e.g., Luke 4:15; 5:3, 15; 6:17-18; 7:1; 9:11; 19:47-48; 21:37-38.

94. See, e.g., Luke 8:4-8; 12:13-21; cf. 13:1 with 13:6-9; cf. 14:25 with 14:28-32; cf. 19:2 with 19:11-27; 20:9-18.

95. See Luke 4:40-41; 5:15; 6:17-19; 7:21; 11:20; 13:32.

96. See Luke 9:23; 14:25-27.

97. See Luke 11:29-32; cf. 12:54a with 13:3, 5.

98. See Luke 11:29; 7:31-35.

99. See Luke 7:36; 11:37; 14:1.

100. See, e.g., Luke 4:18-19; 9:22; 11:2, 13; 22:20, 27, 42; 24:44-49. Also C. H. Talbert, *Reading Luke: A Literary and Theological Commentary on the Third Gospel* (New York: Crossroad, 1982) 209.

101. On this point, see chap. 4.

102. Cf., e.g., Luke 8:1 with 8:22 (also 8:9 [?]); 9:14, 16, 18 with 9:10, 12; 9:40 (= nine disciples) with 9:37 (= Jesus and Peter, John, and James); 17:1 with 17:5; 22:11 with 22:14; 22:39, 45; also 7:11; 18:15. At 8:1-2, Luke remarks that the twelve are with Jesus, and some women disciples as well. Is one to suppose that these women disciples remained with Jesus on a "continuous" basis? Whereas Danker (*Jesus and the New Age,* 173) would deny this, B. Witherington ("On the Road with Mary Magdalene, Joanna, Susanna, and Other Disciples—Luke 8:1-3," *ZNW* 70 [1979]: 244–45) affirms it.

103. See Luke 22:59; Acts 1:11; 2:7.

104. See, e.g., Luke 5:11, 27-28; 18:28; Acts 9:2; 19:9, 23; 22:4; 24:14, 22; also Talbert, "Discipleship in Luke-Acts," 66–67.

105. See, e.g., Luke 24:48; Acts 1:22; 10:36-41; 13:23-31.

106. See Luke 9:1-6, 10; 10:1-16, 17-19; 22:35; also Talbert, "Discipleship in Luke-Acts," 71.

107. See, e.g., Luke 9:14-15, 21, 36; 19:28-35.

108. See, e.g., Luke 5:29-32, 33-35; 6:1-5.

109. See J. Neyrey, "The Absence of Jesus' Emotions—the Lukan Redaction of Lk 22,39-46," *Bib* 61 (1980): 158.

110. Historically, the "captain of the temple" (Acts 4:1; 5:24, 26), who was a "chief priest" second in rank only to the "high priest," supervised the sacrificial system in the temple and commanded the temple guard. He, in turn, was assisted by seven high officers ("proctors," "overseers") who bore the same title as he; that is, they were called "captains of the temple." The question that Luke's use of the expression "captains (of the temple)" in 22:4, 52 raises is whether it refers more narrowly to these high officers (see J. A. Fitzmyer, *The Gospel according to Luke X–XXIV*, AB 28A [Garden City, N.Y.: Doubleday, 1985] 1375, 1451) or more broadly to the temple guard (see B. Reicke, *The New Testament Era: The World of the Bible from 500 B.C. to A.D. 100* [Philadelphia: Fortress, 1968] 148; Marshall, *Luke*, 838). Perhaps one does best simply to refer to these "captains" as "officers of the temple." See further J. Jeremias, *Jerusalem in the Time of Jesus: An Investigation into Economic and Social Conditions during the New Testament Period* (Philadelphia: Fortress, 1969) 165–66, 179-80; F. D. Gealy, "Captain of the Temple," *IDB* 1:535–36.

111. For a discussion of these various groups, see, e.g., Reicke, *New Testament Era*, 141–68; A. J. Saldarini, *Pharisees, Scribes and Sadducees in Palestinian Society: A Sociological Approach* (Wilmington, Del.: Michael Glazier, 1988).

112. The notion that Luke looks kindly on the Pharisees in contradistinction to the other groups of religious leaders actually has its point of departure in Acts. The major arguments supporting this view, which has almost become commonplace in Lukan scholarship, can conveniently be found in the article by J. A. Ziesler ("Luke and the Pharisees," *NTS* 25 [1979]: 146–57). When one examines these arguments, they are not nearly so compelling as they are usually made out to be. Allegedly, the reasons Luke shows partiality toward the Pharisees are that both Christians and Pharisees believe in resurrection and that it is in this common belief that one finds continuity between Judaism and the church (ibid., 147). This line of argument, however, is specious. It assumes that Luke takes the position that Pharisees, who already believe in resurrection, will have little difficulty in becoming Christians because all they must do is take the "small step" of believing in the resurrection of Jesus Christ. In point of fact, Luke's position is that the key to becoming a Christian is repentance for the forgiveness of sins, faith in Jesus as Savior, and the reception of the Holy Spirit, as these are preached in Acts (e.g., 2:37-38; 3:19; 4:12; 8:22; 17:30; 20:21). When it comes to bringing persons to repentance, faith, and the reception of the Spirit, however, belief in resurrection as such is never said to be an advantage. For further reading on the Pharisees in Luke-Acts, see J. T. Sanders, "The Pharisees in Luke-Acts," in *The Living Text: Essays in Honor of Ernest W. Saunders*, ed. D. E. Groh and R. Jewett (New York: University Press of America, 1985) 141–88; Tyson, *Death of Jesus*, 64–72; R. L. Brawley, *Luke-Acts and the*

Jews: Conflict, Apology, and Conciliation, SBLMS 33 (Atlanta: Scholars Press, 1987); J. T. Carroll, "Luke's Portrayal of the Pharisees," *CBQ* 50 (1988): 604-21; Saldarini, *Pharisees, Scribes and Sadducees,* chaps. 9, 12; Moxnes, *Economy of the Kingdom.*

113. See Luke 5:21, 30; 6:7; 11:53; 15:2; also 5:17; 7:30; 14:3.

114. See Luke 19:47; 20:1, 19; 22:2, 66; 23:10.

115. See, e.g., Luke 23:35; Acts 3:17; 13:27.

116. That the religious authorities in Luke's gospel story are at root "self-righteous" is the central thesis of the article by M. A. Powell ("The Religious Leaders in Luke: A Literary-Critical Study," *JBL* 109 [1990]: 95).

117. These points, too, are aptly stressed by Powell, "Religious Leaders in Luke," 96, 98.

118. On the role that Zechariah and Joseph of Arimathea play in Luke's story, see also Powell, "Religious Leaders in Luke," 97, 103, 107–8.

119. This expression is one that Danker (see, e.g., *Luke,* 94) has coined and popularized in his work on Luke.

120. See Luke 5:29-32; 15:1-32; 16:19-31; 18:11.

121. See Luke 12:1; also 11:39, 44; 20:47.

122. Powell ("Religious Leaders in Luke," 99) speaks of Jesus as being an "enigma" to the authorities.

123. See Luke 7:40; 10:25; 11:45; 18:18; 19:39; 20:21, 28, 39.

124. See Luke 7:36; 11:37; 14:1.

125. See Luke 5:29-30, 33; 6:1-2.

126. The religious authorities are elitist and "unloving" because they are disposed to "mix" only with those whom they consider to be their equals (14:12). They disdain those beneath them living on the margins of society (5:29-30; 14:13-14; 15:1-2; 16:19-31; 18:11). They advocate rigorous adherence to law and tradition, irrespective of human need, and burden the people with regulations hard to bear (5:29—6:11; 11:46; 13:14; 14:1-6). Though entrusted with the key of knowledge, they have enlightened neither themselves in the wisdom of scripture nor the people (11:52).

127. The religious authorities are "hypocritical" because, while they appear righteous on the outside, inwardly they are wicked (11:39; 16:15).

128. Symptomatic of the "avariciousness" of the religious authorities is their greed and eagerness to devour the houses of widows (11:39; 20:47).

129. The "self-importance" of the religious authorities expresses itself in their desire to garner for themselves recognition and esteem by wearing long robes, accepting deferential greetings in the market places, occupying the best seats in the synagogues, assuming the places of honor at banquets, and putting their religiosity on public display (11:43; 20:46-47).

130. Cf., e.g., 6:17 with 6:19; 7:24 with 7:29; 9:12 with 9:13; 18:36 with 18:43; also 23:4 with 23:13.

131. See P. S. Minear, "Jesus' Audiences, According to Luke," *NovT* 16 (1974): 81-87; J. Kodell, "Luke's Use of *Laos,* 'People,' especially in the Jerusalem Narrative (Lk 19,28—24,53)," *CBQ* 31 (1969): 327.

132. See, e.g., Luke 3:10-11, 15, 18; 3:21; 7:29.

133. See Luke 4:14; 5:15; 7:17.

134. See Luke 5:15; 6:17; 8:4; 12:1.

135. See Luke 5:1, 3, 19; 8:19; 12:1; 19:3.

136. See Luke 7:9, 11; 14:25; 18:36-37; 19:1-3.

137. See Luke 5:1; 8:42, 45.

138. See Luke 1:16; 3:10; 7:29.

139. See Luke 4:15; 5:3; 7:1; 19:47; 20:1.

140. See Luke 4:43-44; 7:22; 9:11; 20:1.

141. See, e.g., Luke 8:4-8; 20:9-18.

142. See Luke 4:22, 32; 19:48; 21:38.

143. See Luke 4:40; 5:15, 17; 6:18-19; 7:21-22; 9:11.

144. See Luke 4:41; 6:18; 7:21.

145. See Luke 7:11-17, 22; also 8:41-42, 49-56.

146. See Luke 6:19; 7:16; 8:42-48; 9:43, 44; 11:14.

147. See Luke 19:47-48; 20:19; 22:2.

148. See Luke 1:6, 28; 2:25, 37.

149. See Luke 1:32-35, 43, 68-75; 2:26, 38.

150. For a detailed, insightful discussion of this group of minor characters, see Tannehill, *Narrative Unity of Luke-Acts*, 111–27.

151. "Quest stories" is Tannehill's term (ibid., 111–12).

152. Significantly, Joseph of Arimathea functions within Luke's gospel story as a foil, or contrast, for two group characters: As a member of the Sanhedrin who is nonetheless "righteous," Joseph is a foil for the religious authorities, who are "self-righteous." As the one who "serves" Jesus by looking after his burial, Joseph is a foil for the disciples, who should have served their master in this way but do not.

153. E. Käsemann, "Begründet der neutestamentliche Kanon die Einheit der Kirche?" *EvT* 11 (1951): 14.

154. See, e.g., S. M. Praeder, "Luke-Acts and the Ancient Novel," *Society of Biblical Literature: 1981 Seminar Papers*, ed. K. H. Richards (Chico, Calif.: Scholars Press, 1981) 269–92.

155. See, e.g., C. H. Talbert, *What is a Gospel? The Genre of the Canonical Gospels* (Philadelphia: Fortress, 1977) esp. chap. 4.

156. See, e.g., D. E. Aune, *The New Testament in Its Literary Environment*, LEC (Philadelphia: Westminster, 1987) chaps. 3–4.

157. For a helpful discussion of "plot," see F. J. Matera, "The Plot of Matthew's Gospel," *CBQ* 49 (1987): 235–40.

158. As is apparent, I take the section 9:51—19:46 to be presented by Luke as a "journey to Jerusalem." Also, I construe this journey as ending, not at 18:14; 19:27; or 19:44, but at 19:46. At 19:41, Jesus is still "near" Jerusalem. Luke's comment at 19:45, "And he [Jesus] entered the temple," marks Jesus' entry into both Jerusalem and the temple. On the question of the length of Luke's so-called "central section," see J. L. Resseguie, "Interpretation of Luke's Central Section (Luke 9:51—19:44) since 1856," *StBT* 5 (1975): 3 n. 2.

2. THE STORY OF JESUS

1. The premier commentary on the infancy narrative of Luke remains that of R. E. Brown, *The Birth of the Messiah: A Commentary on the Infancy Narratives in Matthew and Luke* (Garden City, N.Y.: Doubleday, 1977) 235–496.

2. For an insightful exposition of these two canticles, or hymns, see Farris, *Hymns of Luke's Infancy Narratives*, 127–150.

3. On this point, see, e.g., A. George, *Études sur l'oeuvre de Luc*, SB (Paris: Gabalda, 1978) 45–47; Brown, *Birth of the Messiah*, 156, 297; Tannehill, *Narrative Unity of Luke-Acts*, 15.

4. On several of the points cited below in illustration of this, see George, *L'oeuvre de Luc*, 64–65.

5. On the Magnificat, see Farris, *Hymns of Luke's Infancy Narratives*, 108–26.

6. George, *L'oeuvre de Luc*, 64.

7. See Luke 3:2; also Jer. 1:1 (LXX); Hos. 1:1; Joel 1:1.

8. See Matt. 11:14; 17:10-13; also Mark 9:11-13.

9. See Luke 1:15-17, 76-79; 3:4-6; 7:27. For two contrasting views on the person and role of John the Baptist in Luke, see Danker (*Luke,* 69–71) and Fitzmyer (*Luke the Theologian,* 86–116).

10. See Luke 1:17, 76; 3:4.

11. See Luke 3:16; 7:27.

12. See Acts 1:21-22; 10:37-38; 13:24-25; 19:4.

13. Although it is not apparent from 3:15-17, Luke bases the messianic designation "the Coming One," which becomes prominent later in his gospel story, on the statement John makes here in 3:16: "But he who is mightier than I is coming." See, e.g., Luke 7:19-20; 13:35; 19:38.

14. See, e.g., Isa. 4:4; B. Reicke, "Die Verkündigung des Täufers nach Lukas," in *Jesus in der Verkündigung der Kirche,* ed. A. Fuchs, SNTU 1 (Linz: A. Fuchs, 1976) 58–59.

15. See Luke 24:49; Acts 1:5; 2:1-4, 33; 11:16.

16. See Luke 3:17; Acts 10:42; 17:31; 24:25.

17. Since John is the one who baptizes "all the people" in Luke's gospel story, Luke intimates that John also baptizes Jesus when he remarks: "When all the people had been baptized and Jesus had been baptized. . . ." On Jesus' baptism by John in Mark and Matthew, see Mark 1:9; Matt. 3:13-15.

18. See, e.g., Acts 10:37; Luke 23:5; also 3:23.

19. By contrast, D. L. Bock (*Proclamation from Prophecy and Pattern: Lucan Old Testament Christology,* JSNTSup 12 [Sheffield: JSOT, 1987] 102–4) argues that the term "beloved" in the baptismal words God utters is derived not from Gen. 22:2 but Isa. 41:8 and connotes not the "uniqueness" of Jesus but Jesus as "chosen Servant."

20. For a succinct, insightful treatment of Luke's genealogy of Jesus, see W. S. Kurz, "Luke 3:23-38 and Greco-Roman and Biblical Genealogies," in *Luke-Acts: New Perspectives from the Society of Biblical Literature Seminar,* ed. C. H. Talbert (New York: Crossroad, 1984) 169–87.

21. See Luke 3:23; Gen. 41:46; 2 Sam. 5:4; Ezek. 1:1.

22. For a penetrating analysis of Luke's portrayal of Satan, see Garrett, *Demise of the Devil*, esp. chap. 2.

23. See Brown, *Apostasy and Perseverence*, 5–7.

24. See Luke 4:14-15; Acts 10:37; also Luke 23:5.

25. In reality, the order in which the two activities are cited by Luke is "deed" and "word."

26. See also Acts 13:14-15. For an analysis of Jesus' behavior as part of the liturgical action of a synagogue service, see B. Chilton, "Announcement in *Nazara*: An Analysis of Luke 4:16-21," in *Gospel Perspectives: Studies of History and Tradition in the Four Gospels*, ed. R. T. France and D. Wenham (Sheffield: JSOT, 1981) 154–61.

27. See also Acts 4:26-27; 10:36-38.

28. For an informed discussion not only of Luke 4:19 but of Jubilee images and traditions in the synoptic Gospels in general, see S. H. Ringe, *Jesus, Liberation, and the Biblical Jubilee*, OBT 19 (Philadelphia: Fortress, 1985).

29. On "Jubilary Theology" in Luke's Gospel, see R. B. Sloan, Jr., *The Favorable Year of the Lord: A Study of Jubilary Theology in the Gospel of Luke* (Austin, Tex.: Schola Press, 1977).

30. The term "forgiveness" includes, of course, remission of sins, but used as a virtual synonym for salvation, it connotes release from all forms of social, economic, and political oppression (see Ringe, *Biblical Jubilee*, 65–66).

31. See Luke 6:20-23; 7:22; 14:13, 21; also U. Busse, *Das Nazareth-Manifest Jesu: Eine Einführung in das lukanische Jesusbild nach Lk 4, 16-30*, SBS 91 (Stuttgart: Katholisches Bibelwerk, 1978) 33–34. For an excellent discussion on "recognizing 'the poor,'" see Ringe, *Biblical Jubilee*, 51–60.

32. See Luke 5:18-25; 11:14-22; 13:16; Acts 10:38. Also Tannehill, *Narrative Unity of Luke-Acts*, 65–66.

33. See Luke 1:79; 2:30-32; 3:6; Acts 26:17-18; Tannehill, *Narrative Unity of Luke-Acts*, 66–67.

34. The expression is that of J. A. Sanders, "From Isaiah 61 to Luke 4," in *Christianity, Judaism and Other Greco-Roman Cults: Studies for Morton Smith at Sixty*, ed. J. Neusner, SJLA 12 (Leiden: E. J. Brill, 1975) 93.

35. F. W. Danker (*Jesus and the New Age: A Commentary on St. Luke's Gospel*, rev. ed. [Philadelphia: Fortress, 1988] 107–8) points out that Luke, in depicting Jesus as uttering "gracious words" (4:22), is portraying him as one graced with God's wisdom (i.e., as a "wise person" who knows and observes God's will).

36. Scholars argue over whether the "rejection" of Jesus at Nazareth is first expressed by the people in 4:22 or by Jesus in 4:24. The inclination among scholars nowadays is to defend the latter position. For a strong defense of the former position, see F. O'Fearghail, "Rejection in Nazareth: Lk 4:22," ZNW 75 (1984): 60–72; also Tiede, *Prophecy and History*, 33–39.

37. See Danker, *Jesus and the New Age*, 108.

38. See ibid., 108–9.

39. See, e.g., Luke 4:14, 37; 5:15; 7:17; 8:40.

40. Cf. Luke 9:23 with 6:17.

41. For a treatment of this motif in Mark and Matthew see, respectively, J. D. Kingsbury, *The Christology of Mark's Gospel* (reprint; Minneapolis: Fortress, 1989) chap. 3; idem, *Matthew as Story,* 2d ed., rev. and enl. (Philadelphia: Fortress, 1988) 74–75, chap. 4.

42. As we mentioned in n. 13, the words John utters in 3:16, "but he who is mightier than I is coming," become the source in Luke's gospel story for the messianic designation "the Coming One" (see Luke 7:19-20; 13:35; 19:38).

43. Narratively, the background for Simon's remark at Luke 7:39 is the crowd's acclamation of Jesus as a "great prophet" in 7:16. On the interpretation of 7:16, see below.

44. See, e.g., H. Schürmann, *Das Lukasevangelium: Kommentar zu Kap. 1,1—9,50,* HTKNT 3 (Freiburg: Herder, 1969) 1: 506–7; R. J. Dillon, *From Eye-Witnesses to Ministers of the Word: Tradition and Composition in Luke 24,* AnBib 82 (Rome: Biblical Institute, 1978) 121 n. 154.

45. See Luke 1:32-35, 69; 2:11, 25, 38.

46. See Acts 1:5; 2:33; 11:16.

47. Cf. Luke 3:17 with Acts 10:42; 17:31.

48. For succinct statements on how Jesus is "like" Moses and Elijah, see Franklin, *Christ the Lord,* 68; Tiede, *Prophecy and History,* 60-61; Tannehill, *Narrative Unity of Luke-Acts,* 96-99. For a discussion of the thesis that Luke presents Jesus' journey to Jerusalem as recapitulating and consummating the career of Moses in Deuteronomy, see D. P. Moessner, "Luke 9:1-50: Luke's Preview of the Journey of the Prophet like Moses of Deuteronomy," *JBL* 102 (1983): 575–604; idem, *Lord of the Banquet.*

49. Cf., e.g., Acts 3:22 with Acts 3:20.

50. Concerning this "pattern," see, e.g., Dillon, *From Eye-Witnesses to Ministers of the Word,* 119–21; Tannehill, *Narrative Unity of Luke-Acts,* 96–99.

51. Cf. Luke 4:24 with Acts 7:27, 35.

52. The expression "prophetic Messiah" is also used occasionally by Johnson (e.g., *Possessions in Luke-Acts,* 95, also 85 n. 2). So as to avoid misunderstanding, however, it should be noted that Johnson's position, contrary to mine, is that Luke does present Jesus as the Prophet.

53. "This is my chosen Son" is the way the NABR renders the first part of God's declaration in 9:35. The question posed by both 9:35 and 23:35 is whether the participle and the adjective are being used more grandly as christological titles ("the Chosen One") or more modestly to connote that God has "chosen" Jesus for his mission. In following the NABR, I have decided in favor of the latter. If Luke intended for the word "chosen" to be understood as a christological title, one would expect that the pertinent words in such key passages as 3:22; 9:35; and 23:35 would exhibit a more uniform reading.

54. On the significance of Luke's reference to "Jerusalem" at 9:51, see J. A. Fitzmyer, *The Gospel according to Luke I-IX*, AB 28 (Garden City, N.Y.: Doubleday, 1981) 166–67, 828.

55. See Luke 3:16; 7:27.

56. See Luke 5:1-11, 27.

57. Johnson, *Possessions in Luke-Acts*, 107–8.

58. The following list of passages featuring Jesus' words to the disciples has been conveniently compiled by Johnson (*Possessions in Luke-Acts*, 108 n. 2): Luke 10:1-12, 17-23; 10:38—11:13; 12:1-12, 22-53; 16:1-13; 17:1-10; 17:22—18:8. Generally speaking, Jesus' teaching concerns religious, ethical, or relational matters having to do with God, Jesus himself, worship, life together, mission, the use of goods, times of persecution, and the Parousia.

59. On Jesus' encounters with the religious authorities while journeying to Jerusalem, Johnson (*Possessions in Luke-Acts*, 109 n. 1) cites these passages: Luke 10:25-37; 11:37-53; 13:31—14:24; 15:1-32; 16:14-31; 17:20-21; 18:9-14. In one or two instances, it appears that Jesus may assume the role of teacher (e.g., 17:20-21). By and large, however, he calls the authorities to repentance by threatening them with judgment or strongly condemning them them for their self-righteousness, exclusiveness, lovelessness, and all-around false values.

60. As passages in which Jesus addresses the people on his way to Jerusalem, Johnson (*Possessions in Luke-Acts*, 108 n. 3) lists the following: Luke 9:57-62; 10:13-15; 11:14-36; 12:13-21; 12:54—13:30; 14:25-35.

61. On Jesus' attempts to gather specifically the people of Jerusalem to himself, see Luke 5:17; 6:17.

62. That Jerusalem's "house" refers to the "temple" (see, e.g., E. E. Ellis, *The Gospel of Luke*, NCB [London: Oliphants, 1974] 191) or to the "city" itself (see, e.g., Marshall, *Luke*, 576) is a common interpretation of this term. Another interpretation to be considered, however, is that of F. D. Weinert ("Luke, the Temple, and Jesus' Saying about Jerusalem's Abandoned House [Luke 13:34-35]," *CBQ* 44 [1982]: 76), who argues that "house" in 13:35 connotes "Israel's Judean leadership" and the people falling under their authority.

63. See Marshall, *Luke*, 576; J. Ernst, *Das Evangelium nach Lukas*, RNT (Regensburg: Friedrich Pustet, 1977) 434.

64. See Luke 3:17; 7:18-20.

65. See Acts 3:19-21; 10:42.

66. See, e.g., Luke 1:32-33, 69; 2:4; 3:32.

67. See Luke 3:22; 9:35; also D. M. Hay, *Glory at the Right Hand: Psalm 110 in Early Christianity*, SBLMS 18 (Nashville: Abingdon, 1974) 115–16.

68. See 1 Sam. 8:10-11, 16-17. J. D. Derrett, "Law in the New Testament: The Palm Sunday Colt," *NovT* 13 (1971): 243–49.

69. The "colt" is the "messianic mount" par excellence: See Zech. 9:9; Gen. 49:11; also H.-W. Kuhn, "Das Reittier Jesu in der Einzugsgeschichte des Markusevangeliums," *ZNW* 50 (1959): 86–89.

70. See Fitzmyer, *The Gospel according to Luke X–XXIV*, AB 28A (Garden City, N.Y.: Doubleday, 1985) 1251.

71. See Tiede, *Prophecy and History*, 79.

72. See Chance, *Jerusalem, the Temple, and the New Age*, 56–58.

73. So Fitzmyer, *Luke X–XXIV*, 1265–66. C. H. Talbert (*Reading Luke: A Literary and Theological Commentary on the Third Gospel* [New York: Crossroad, 1982] 188) speaks of the religious leadership as permitting the temple's purpose to be "perverted."

74. On the notion of "shame," see B. J. Malina, *The New Testament World: Insights from Cultural Anthropology* (Atlanta: John Knox, 1981) chap. 2.

75. So A. Plummer (*A Critical and Exegetical Commentary on the Gospel according to S. Luke*, ICC [Edinburgh: T. & T. Clark, 1896] 456) and, more cautiously, Fitzmyer (*Luke X–XXIV*, 1273).

76. More exactly, since the Jewish day began at sundown, Passover was celebrated during the evening that marked the beginning of the fifteenth day of the month of Nisan. The feast of Unleavened Bread followed the day of Passover and lasted for another seven days (see 2 Chron. 35:17). In the course of time, people tended not to distinguish between the two celebrations, as Luke does not (22:1). Popularly, the two were simply referred to as "Passover." See, e.g., Fitzmyer, *Luke I–IX*, 439–40.

77. For a detailed discussion of the "Last Supper" in Luke, see Fitzmyer, *Luke X–XXIV*, 1386–92. On the meaning of Luke 22:19-20, see Talbert, *Reading Luke*, 208–10.

78. For succinct treatments of this address, see Karris, *Luke: Artist and Theologian*, 64–70; Neyrey, *Passion According to Luke*, chap. 1; Matera, *Passion Narratives*, 164–66; M. L. Soards, *The Passion according to Luke: The Special Material of Luke 22*, JSNTSup 14 (Sheffield: JSOT, 1987) esp. 56–57.

79. Matera, *Passion Narratives*, 169.

80. Fitzmyer, *Luke X–XXIV*, 1461.

81. See F. J. Matera, "Luke 22,66-71: Jesus before the *Presbyterion*," *ETL* 65 (1989): 57–58.

82. The translation of the Greek is that of Danker, *Luke*, 64.

83. Regarding the "evasiveness" of Jesus' answer, see Talbert, *Reading Luke*, 215–16.

84. The concurrence of 23:2 ("misleading [perverting] our nation") with 23:14 ("misleading the people") may be taken to mean that one major charge (reinforced by three "explanations") is brought against Jesus in 23:2, 5. See, e.g., Matera, *Passion Narratives*, 176–77. In contrast, Tyson (*Death of Jesus*, 129–33), followed by Senior (*Passion of Jesus*, 107), understands Jesus to be accused in 23:2, 5 of four separate charges.

85. So also Tyson, *Death of Jesus*, 128.

86. On the notion of "seeing," as opposed to spiritual "blindness," in Luke's story, Karris (*Luke: Artist and Theologian*, 87) is to the point when he writes: "To see is to see deeply, to see with the eyes of faith, to be converted and to walk in the light."

87. Cf. Luke 23:11 with 9:22; 17:25; also 18:32.

88. On this fourth, climactic part of Jesus' trial, see Neyrey, *Passion According to Luke,* 80–84.

89. As F. G. Untergassmair (*Kreuzweg und Kreuzigung Jesu: Ein Beitrag zur lukanischen Redaktionsgeschichte und zur Frage nach der lukanischen "Kreuzestheologie,"* PThS 10 [Paderborn: F. Schöningh, 1980] 13–33) and J. H. Neyrey ("Jesus' Address to the Women of Jerusalem [Lk. 23.27-31]—A Prophetic Judgment Oracle," NTS 29 [1983]: 82) correctly point out, Luke 23:27-31 is "a prophetic oracle of judgment" against Jerusalem. The purpose this oracle serves is, as Danker (*Jesus and the New Age,* 372) and Karris (*Luke: Artist and Theologian,* 93–94) correctly point out, to call the inhabitants of Jerusalem to repentance.

90. For a review of varying interpretations of this proverb, see Fitzmyer, *Luke X–XXIV,* 1498.

91. See Mark 15:29-30; Matt. 27:39-40.

92. In Luke's theology as in that of Mark and Matthew, Jesus is the supreme agent of salvation by virtue of the fact that God is at work in him (cf. Luke 20:17 with Acts 4:10-12).

93. For a discussion of the meaning of "today" and "Paradise" in Luke 23:43, see J. Jeremias, *"Paradeisos,"* TDNT 5 (1967): 765–73; Fitzmyer, *Luke the Theologian,* 203–33.

94. Danker, *Jesus and the New Age,* 379.

95. The "temple curtain" in question could either be that hanging before the "holy of holies" or that hanging before the "holy place." Fitzmyer (*Luke X–XXIV,* 1518) and Danker (*Jesus and New Age,* 379) identify it with the latter.

96. See, e.g., Luke 13:34-35; 19:41-44; 23:28-31; also 21:20-24. For a succinct review of various meanings associated with the tearing of the temple curtain, see Senior, *Passion of Jesus,* 139–43.

97. On this theme of Jesus' "oneness with the Father" at death, see F. Matera, "The Death of Jesus according to Luke: A Question of Sources," CBQ 47 (1985): 476–77.

98. On Luke's understanding of Jesus both as "righteous" and as the "Righteous One," see Matera, "Death of Jesus according to Luke," 479–84; R. J. Karris, "Luke 23:47 and the Lucan View of Jesus' Death," JBL 105 (1986): 65–74. See also Acts 3:13-15; 7:52; 22:14.

99. According to 23:55, the women follow Joseph of Arimathea and observe "how" Jesus' body "is placed." When this comment is read in light of 23:56a ("they [the women] returned and prepared aromatic oils and perfumes"), it suggests that Joseph of Arimathea placed the body of Jesus as he did because he had too little time properly to wash and anoint it (see, e.g., Fitzmyer [*Luke X–XXIV,* 1530]). To wash and anoint Jesus' body, then, is why the women come to the tomb.

100. See, e.g., Luke 9:22, 44; also 17:25; 18:31-34.

101. Cf. Luke 9:44-45; 18:31-34 with 24:25-27, 44-47.

102. For an insightful treatment of Jesus' ascension in Luke, see Parsons, *Departure of Jesus,* chap. 3.

103. Ibid., 103–4.

104. Cf. Acts 10:37 with Luke 3:23; 23:5.

105. In light of especially such passages as Luke 1:32-33, 35; 4:41 (also, cf. 3:22 with 4:18; 20:9-18 [esp. v. 13] with 24:26, 46; 22:67 with 22:70), I take "Son of God" in Luke's gospel story to be "messianic" in nature, i.e., the Son of God is a royal, or kingly, figure.

106. See, e.g., Luke 1:30-35; 2:10-11; 3:22; 4:3, 9; 4:33, 34, 41; 9:35.

107. Cf., e.g., Luke 6:22 with 6:20.

108. Cf., e.g., Luke 6:22 with 7:1; 7:34 with 7:31, 29, 24.

109. Cf. Luke 5:24 with 5:17; 6:5 with 6:2; 22:69 with 22:66.

110. Cf. Luke 21:27 with 22:69; see also Acts 1:11; 3:21; 10:40-42.

3. THE STORY OF THE AUTHORITIES

1. See, e.g., 4:16-30; 11:14-16; 19:3, 7; also 11:29-32; 12:54-56; 13:3, 5.

2. Luke seems to equate "lawyers" and "teachers of the law" with "scribes," as is evident from a comparison of 5:17 with 5:21 on the one hand and of 11:45, 46, 52 with 11:53 on the other.

3. For a sampling of scholarly opinion on one or all of these groups, see B. Reicke, *The New Testament Era: The World of the Bible from 500 B.C. to A.D. 100* (Philadelphia: Fortress, 1968) 141–74; J. Neusner, *From Politics to Piety: The Emergence of Pharisaic Judaism,* 2d ed. (New York: KTAV, 1979); E. Rivkin, *A Hidden Revolution: The Pharisees' Search for the Kingdom Within* (Nashville: Abingdon, 1978); M. Goodman, *The Ruling Class of Judea: The Origins of the Jewish Revolt against Rome A.D. 66–70* (Cambridge: University Press, 1987) chap. 4; A. J. Saldarini, *Pharisees, Scribes and Sadducees in Palestinian Society: A Sociological Approach* (Wilmington, Del.: Michael Glazier, 1988); also S. Freyne, *Galilee, Jesus and the Gospels: Literary Approaches and Historical Investigations* (Philadelphia: Fortress, 1988) 96–115.

4. For a summary treatment of the Sadducees as a social group, see Saldarini, *Pharisees, Scribes and Sadducees,* chap. 13.

5. For a summary treatment of the Pharisees as a social group, see ibid., chap. 12.

6. See Reicke, *New Testament Era,* 156–57.

7. Neusner (*From Politics to Piety,* 80, 83, 91) in particular has stressed these acts as the marks of early first-century Pharisaism.

8. The "captain of the temple" (Acts 4:1; 5:24, 26) was himself a chief priest and second in rank only to the "high priest." It was his duty to supervise the sacrificial system of the temple and to command the whole of the temple guard. This chief captain, in turn, was assisted by seven high officers who bore the same title as he ("captains of the temple"). For their part, the captains commanded corps of Levite guards who served, in effect, as temple police. On the meaning of the term "captains of the temple" in Luke 22:4, 52, see chap. 1, n. 110.

9. Relative to the Jewish leaders, Luke employs the term "ruler(s)" to refer, respectively, to the high priest (Acts 23:5), to an official in charge of a synagogue (8:41; 14:2), to a leader of the Pharisees (14:1), and in several passages to members of the Sanhedrin (e.g., [18:18]; 23:13, 35; 24:20). When referring to members of the Sanhedrin, the term "rulers" can refer to all the members (23:35; Acts 3:17; 13:27), to all the members except the chief priests (23:13; 24:20), and to the chief priests (Acts 4:5, 8). In other words, "rulers" tends to be a term that, though not always referring to the same exact persons, does envisage members of the governing class who most often belong to the Sanhedrin.

10. For a brief description of the "governing class," see Saldarini, *Pharisees, Scribes and Sadducees*, 40–41.

11. See, e.g., Reicke, *New Testament Era*, 146–49.

12. See, e.g., R. W. Corney, "Zadok the Priest," *IDB* 4:928–29.

13. For a summary treatment of the scribes as a class of professionals, see Saldarini, *Pharisees, Scribes and Sadducees*, chap. 11.

14. See Luke 5:17, 21, 30; 6:7; 7:30; 10:25; 11:45, 46, 52, 53; 14:3; 15:2.

15. See Luke 19:47; 20:1, 19, 46; 22:2, 66; 23:10.

16. See Luke 20:1; 22:52; also 19:47.

17. See, e.g., Mark 1:22; 11:27-33; Matt. 7:29; 21:23-27.

18. As we noted in chap. 1, this is the central thesis of the insightful article by M. A. Powell ("Religious Leaders in Luke: A Literary-Critical Study," *JBL* 109 [1990]: 3).

19. See, e.g., Luke 5:39; 11:39, 42-43, 46; 12:1; 16:15; 18:9, 11; 20:46-47.

20. See Luke 17:20-21; 19:38-39; 20:9-19; 22:66-71; 23:35.

21. See Luke 1:31-33; 19:37-39; 20:13-14; 22:66-71; 23:3, 35.

22. See Luke 1:5-25, 57-79.

23. Powell, "Religious Leaders in Luke," 6, 21.

24. Note that at Acts 2:12, the verb "to be amazed" is used in conjunction with the verb "to be perplexed": "And all were amazed and perplexed, saying to one another, 'What does this mean?'" The notion of "perplexity" also inheres in the term "to be amazed" in Luke 24:22-24; Acts 2:7-8; 9:21; 10:45; 12:16. Further, lest one think that to be "amazed" or "astonished" at something always connotes a positive reaction, it is noteworthy that on one occasion the crowds, having witnessed Jesus cast out a demon, are astonished at this only to have some of them charge him with casting out demons on the authority of Beelzebul while others put him to the test by demanding of him a sign from heaven (11:14-16). See as well Luke 1:59-63; 8:25; 11:38; 24:41.

25. On this point, Tannehill (*Narrative Unity of Luke-Acts*, 170) correctly notes: "Through much of the gospel the two sides remain in conversation."

26. See ibid., 170–71.

27. See esp. Luke 5:29-32; 15:1-32.

28. See Luke 7:36-50; 11:37-54; 14:1-24.

29. See Luke 6:6-11; 13:10-17; 14:1-6.

30. Powell ("Religious Leaders in Luke," 8–9) speaks of the authorities as being confused by Jesus.

31. Cf. Luke 5:17 with 5:26; 6:7; 7:3-5; cf. 19:47-48 with 20:1-8; 20:26, 39; 23:35.

32. See Luke 7:40; 10:25; 11:45; 18:18; 19:39; 20:21, 28, 39.

33. On this matter of social equality, which involves the values of "honor and shame," see B. J. Malina, *The New Testament World: Insights from Cultural Anthropology* (Atlanta: John Knox, 1981) chap. 2.

34. See Luke 7:36; 11:37; 14:1.

35. As illustrative of the view that sin could cause sickness, see, e.g., Luke 13:3-5 and John 9:1-2, 34.

36. See, e.g., Exod. 34:6-7; Pss. 103:2-3; 130:3-4; Isa. 43:25; Dan. 9:9. Also Beyer, *"Blasphēmeō,"* TDNT 1 (1964): 623.

37. See Neusner, *From Politics to Piety*, 67, 73, 80.

38. See J. Jeremias, *Jerusalem in the Time of Jesus: An Investigation into Economic and Social Conditions during the New Testament Period* (Philadelphia: Fortress, 1969) 310-11.

39. See K. H. Rengstorf, *"Hamartōlos,"* TDNT 1 (1964): 327.

40. Tannehill (*Narrative Unity of Luke-Acts*, 173) aptly puts it this way: The disciples are seen to be "feasting instead of fasting."

41. For a trenchant discussion of Luke 5:36-38, see F. W. Danker, *Jesus and the New Age: A Commentary on St. Luke's Gospel*, rev. ed. (Philadelphia: Fortress, 1988) 128–29.

42. In an otherwise helpful discussion of Luke 6:1-5, Wilson (*Luke and the Law*, 31–35) insists that "[human] need" plays no role in Luke's understanding of this controversy. Jesus, however, pointedly refers to the "hunger" of David and his men (6:3), and this, in turn, invites the reader to draw an analogy on this score between David and his men and the disciples (6:1).

43. As numerous commentators point out, one can best make sense of this story if one assumes that the sinful woman, prior to the moment she approaches Jesus in Simon's house, has already experienced the gift of God's forgiveness. See, among others, J. J. Kilgallen, "John the Baptist, the Sinful Woman, and the Pharisee," *JBL* 104 (1985): 675–79.

44. J. Jeremias, *The Parables of Jesus*, NTL (Philadelphia: Westminster, 1963) 126.

45. See Deut. 6:5; Lev. 19:18.

46. For an exposition of the parable of the good Samaritan in light of Luke's theological program, see Donahue, *Gospel in Parable*, 128–34.

47. In the Matthean parallels to Luke 11:39-52, the scribes and Pharisees are explicitly attacked as "blind leaders" (see Matt. 23:16, 24).

48. The justification for understanding Luke to be describing the Pharisees as "hypocrites" comes from Luke 12:1.

49. On the meaning of 11:39-41, see Moxnes, *Economy of the Kingdom,* 111–23.

50. Ibid., 124-25.

51. T. W. Manson, *The Sayings of Jesus* (London: SCM, 1949) 99.

52. Ibid., 103.

53. For an extended treatment of this topic within the social context of the first century, see Malina, *New Testament World,* chap. 2.

54. For a brief but pertinent discussion of the kind of social interaction the parable of Luke 14:7-11 presupposes, see Moxnes, *Economy of the Kingdom,* 134–36.

55. See ibid., 129–34.

56. On these three parables as presenting Luke's "gospel within a Gospel," see Donahue, *Gospel in Parable,* 146–62.

57. See Luke 15:6-7, 9-10, 23-24, 28, 32.

58. See Moxnes, *Economy of the Kingdom,* 148–50.

59. On the meaning of the parable of the rich man and Lazarus against the broad backdrop of "rich and poor in Luke," see Donahue, *Gospel in Parable,* 169–80.

60. In his discussion of this parable, Donahue (*Gospel in Parable,* 189) points to the Pharisee's persistent reference to "I" and observes that his language is that of "egocentric achievement."

61. See J. A. Fitzmyer, *The Gospel according to Luke X–XXIV,* AB 28A (Garden City, N.Y.: Doubleday, 1985) 1265–66; also C. H. Talbert, *Reading Luke: A Literary and Theological Commentary on the Third Gospel* (New York: Crossroad, 1982) 188; I. H. Marshall, *Commentary on Luke,* NIGTC (Grand Rapids, Mich.: Wm. B. Eerdmans, 1978) 720–21.

62. See 1 Kings 18:31; Isa. 54:11-13; Lam. 4:1-2; M. Black, "The Christological Use of the Old Testament in the New Testament," *NTS* 18 (1971/72): 1–14.

63. On this point, see Fitzmyer, *Luke X–XXIV,* 1296.

64. In explanation of this saying, Talbert (*Reading Luke,* 191) observes: "The saying affirms the sovereignty of God. . . . The only areas in which Caesar can expect allegiance from Jesus' disciples are those in which his patterns are in conformity with God's desired patterns."

65. See Talbert, *Reading Luke,* 194–95.

66. Cf. Luke 20:46-47 with 11:39, 43; 18:10-12.

67. Cf. Luke 22:63-65 with 9:22; 17:25; 18:32-33.

68. See further Matera, *Passion Narratives,* 176.

69. Cf. Luke 23:35 with 4:18; 9:20.

70. See, e.g., Luke 5:32; 16:15; 18:9.

71. Technically, the last episode in Luke's gospel story in which one of the religious authorities appears is 23:50-54. This pericope, however, features Joseph of Arimathea.

72. See Luke 13:33-35; 19:41-44; also 21:20-24; 23:28-31.

73. See also Powell, "Religious Leaders in Luke," 21.

74. Cf. Luke 23:50 with Luke 1:6; also Danker, *Jesus and the New Age,* 384.

75. Cf. Luke 23:51 with 1:13-17, 68-75.

76. See Acts 6:7; 15:5; 18:8; 23:6; 26:5.

77. But see Luke 10:25; 11:45, 53.

78. See Luke 20:16; 22:28-30.

79. See Luke 13:33-35; 19:41-44; also 21:20-24; 23:28-31.

4. THE STORY OF THE DISCIPLES

1. See Luke 8:51; 9:28.

2. See, respectively, Luke 22:8 and 5:10; 9:54.

3. See Luke 8:45; 9:20, 33; 12:41; 18:28; 22:54-62.

4. See Luke 24:25-27, 44-47; also 9:44-45; 18:31-34. Perhaps the problem can be stated even more sharply: Despite the fact that God imparts the secrets of his kingdom to the disciples (8:10), the latter still do not comprehend the plan of salvation God has announced in the scriptures and is accomplishing in Jesus, God's Son and Israel's Messiah.

5. Cf. Luke 5:1-11 with Mark 1:16-20; Matt. 4:18-22.

6. Form-critically, B. J. Hubbard ("Commissioning Stories in Luke-Acts: A Study of Their Antecedents, Form, and Content," *Semeia* 8 [1977]: 103–26) points out that Luke 5:1-11 properly constitutes not a "call story," but a "commissioning story."

7. See Luke 5:5; 8:24, 45; 9:33, 49; 17:13.

8. See A. Oepke, *"Epistatēs,"* TDNT 2 (1964): 622–23.

9. Although O. Glombitza ("Die Titel *didaskalos* und *epistatēs* für Jesus bei Lukas," ZNW 49 [1958]: 275–78) may be guilty of reading too much into the term "master," he does correctly see that for one to address another as "master" is for one to acknowledge the other as a figure of superior status and authority.

10. On this, see F. W. Danker, *Jesus and the New Age: A Commentary on St. Luke's Gospel,* rev. ed. (Philadelphia: Fortress, 1988) 117.

11. See, e.g., C. H. Talbert, "Discipleship in Luke-Acts," in *Discipleship in the New Testament,* ed. F. F. Segovia (Philadelphia: Fortress, 1985) 69.

12. See, e.g., Luke 8:45; 9:20, 33; 12:41; 18:28.

13. See, e.g., Luke 9:20 (Peter as typical of the disciples' "insight"); 9:33 (Peter as typical of the disciples' "ignorance").

14. See also Talbert, "Discipleship in Luke-Acts," 62–75.

15. On Jesus as the "leader" of a new community, see ibid., 65; Acts 3:15; 5:31.

16. See, e.g., Luke 6:40; 8:1-3; 24:48; Acts 1:8; also Acts 1:21-22.

17. For a historical study of who "toll collectors" were, see J. Donahue, "Tax Collectors and Sinners," *CBQ* 33 (1971): 39–61.

18. Ibid., 58.

19. See Luke 15:1-2; 18:9-11; 19:2-7.

20. See, e.g., Luke 22:28-30; Acts 6:1-6.

21. See Luke 22:29-30; Acts 1:15—2:4; 2:33, 37.

22. Luke, however, does use the name "Simon" again, at 22:31; 24:34.

23. See Danker, *Jesus and the New Age*, 138.

24. See C. H. Talbert, *Reading Luke: A Literary and Theological Commentary on the Third Gospel* (New York: Crossroad, 1982), 69–72.

25. Ibid.; also Luke 1:51-53; 16:19-31.

26. Ibid., 72–75.

27. For a close study of Luke 8:1-3, see B. Witherington, "On the Road with Mary Magdalene, Joanna, Susanna, and Other Disciples—Luke 8:1-3," *ZNW* 70 (1979): 243–48.

28. On Jesus' followers as being known, or at least recognized, as "Galileans," see Luke 22:59; [23:6]; Acts 1:11; 2:7; also 13:31.

29. Witherington, "Mary Magdalene, Joanna, Susanna," 248.

30. On the ministries of women in Luke-Acts and the New Testament, see Talbert, *Reading Luke*, 90–93.

31. Cf. Luke 4:36 with 4:14; 4:1; 3:22.

32. See esp. Luke 4:43; 5:17; 6:18-19; 8:1.

33. See Luke 4:28-29; 7:31-34.

34. Commenting on Luke 9:27, I. H. Marshall (*Commentary on Luke,* NIGTC [Grand Rapids, Mich.: Wm. B. Eerdmans, 1978] 378) speaks for many scholars when he writes: "In its Lucan form the reference must be to the presence of the kingdom of God as something that can be seen or experienced . . . in the events of the resurrection and Pentecost."

35. Cf. with one another 3:22; 4:18; 9:20; 9:35; also 4:41.

36. Cf. Luke 9:35 with 9:22; see also 9:44-45; 18:31-34.

37. In interpreting Luke 9:46-48, one does best, it appears to me, to take one's clues from Luke 22:24-27. See further Tannehill, *Narrative Unity of Luke-Acts*, 227–28.

38. For a pointed discussion of Luke 9:49-50, see Danker, *Jesus and the New Age*, 206.

39. See Luke 3:2, 16; 7:27; Acts 19:4.

40. Cf. Luke 9:51-56 with 4:16-30.

41. Cf. Luke 9:57-62 with 5:1-11, 27-28; 6:12-16.

42. Cf. Luke 10:1-16 with 9:1-6.

43. See Luke 6:27-30; 9:2.

44. See, e.g., Exod. 20:12; Deut 5:16; Tob. 4:3; 6:14.

45. Cf. Luke 10:5-6, 10-12 with Deut. 19:15.

46. See, e.g., Acts 8:14 (Peter and John); 13:2 (Barnabas and Saul); 15:32-33 (Judas and Silas); 15:39 (Barnabas and Mark); and 15:40 (Paul and Silas).

47. On the meaning of Luke 10:18, the question is whether the "fall of Satan" is to be construed as occurring in the ministry of Jesus and his disciples (so E. E. Ellis [*The Gospel of Luke,* NCB (London: Oliphants, 1974) 157]

and Marshall [*Luke,* 428–29]) or in an apocalyptic vision Jesus has of future victory (so Garrett [*Demise of the Devil,* 50–55]).

48. See, e.g., A. Oepke, *"Pais,"* TDNT 5 (1967): 646, 649; Jeremias, *Jerusalem in the Time of Jesus: An Investigation into Economic and Social Conditions during the New Testament Period* (Philadelphia: Fortress, 1969) 375.

49. See also Luke 24:21; Acts 1:6.

50. See, e.g., Luke 12:1—13:9. For a recent treatment of this speech, see Tannehill, *Narrative Unity of Luke-Acts,* 240–53.

51. See Luke 12:1-3. One will recall that the "hypocrisy" of the Pharisees has to do with an outward show of righteousness that masks inner corruption (cf. 12:1-3 with 11:39; 16:16).

52. See Luke 17:1-4.

53. See Luke 17:5-6.

54. See Luke 18:1-8.

55. See Luke 12:22-31.

56. See Luke 12:33-34; 14:33; 16:1-13; 18:22-30; also 16:19-31.

57. See Luke 12:41-48; 16:10-13; 17:5, 7-10; also 19:12-26.

58. See Luke 12:4-12; 14:27; also 11:49; 17:22.

59. See Luke 12:35-40; 17:22-37.

60. See Luke 12:49-54; 14:26, 28-33; 16:13; 18:28-30; also 9:57-62.

61. See Luke 11:2, 13.

62. See Luke 14:11; 18:14; also 1:52.

63. Ibid.

64. See Luke 12:21, 32-34; 18:22.

65. See Luke 21:20-24.

66. See Luke 21:25-28, 29-33.

67. See, by contrast, Mark 14:50; Matt. 26:56.

68. See Luke 1:32-33; 11:20.

69. See Luke 24:28-35, 36-43; Acts 10:40-41.

70. See Acts 1:15-26.

71. On the meaning of Luke 22:28-30, see Marshall, *Luke,* 816–18; Neyrey, *Passion According to Luke,* 23–28.

72. See R. E. Brown, K. P. Donfried, and J. Reumann, *Peter in the New Testament* (Minneapolis and New York: Augsburg and Paulist, 1973) 122–23.

73. Ibid., 122–24. See, e.g., Acts 1:15.

74. See, e.g., Danker, *Jesus and the New Age,* 349; Marshall, *Luke,* 813; also 1 Pet. 5:5.

75. See Acts 3:1 and 4:1-3, 13; 5:17-18; 12:1-5.

76. See Deut. 3:26; T. W. Manson, *The Sayings of Jesus* (London: SCM, 1949) 342.

77. See Matera, *Passion Narratives,* 168.

78. See Neyrey, *Passion According to Luke,* 65–67.

79. See Matt. 28:7, 10, 16-20; also Mark 14:28; 16:7.

80. The chronology of "Easter Sunday" is clearly documented by Luke: 24:1a, 13, 33, 36, 50.

81. On the women as comprehending that Jesus has been raised, see also J. Plevnik, "The Eyewitnesses of the Risen Jesus in Luke 24," *CBQ* 49 (1987): 91–94.

82. Cf. Acts 2:6-8, 12 with Luke 24:12.

83. R. J. Dillon, *From Eye-Witnesses to Ministers of the Word: Tradition and Composition in Luke 24*, AnBib 82 (Rome: Biblical Institute, 1978) 104.

84. On this point, see Brown, *Apostasy and Perseverance*, 76.

85. See, e.g., Luke 7:16; 9:7-8, 18-19.

86. Brown, *Apostasy and Perseverance*, 75.

87. See Luke 4:24; 13:33-34. As I explained in chap. 2, Jesus' indentity in Luke's gospel story is that of Messiah (e.g., 4:41; 9:20). Exactly as the Messiah, however, his destiny is like that of the prophets. On the latter point, see Dillon (*From Eye-Witnesses to Ministers of the Word*, 139), whom Tannehill follows (*Narrative Unity of Luke-Acts*, 288).

88. See Acts 2:42, 46; 20:7; 27:35; also 10:40-41.

89. Cf. Luke 24:30 with 9:16 and 22:19.

90. Danker (*Jesus and the New Age*, 395) correctly construes the words of Luke 24:34 as constituting a question. When 24:34 is read as a question, one can make better sense of the section 24:36-43.

91. See Lev. 9:22; Sir. 50:20-21.

92. See Sir. 50:21. Also G. Lohfink, *Die Himmelfahrt Jesu: Untersuchungen zu den Himmelfahrts-und Erhöhungstexten bei Lukas*, SANT 26 (München: Kösel, 1971) 172; Dillon, *From Eye-Witnesses to Ministers of the Word*, 184, 223–24.

93. For a detailed study of Jesus' ascension (Luke 24:50-53) as providing closure for Luke's gospel story, see Parsons, *Departure of Jesus*, 96–111.

SELECTED
BIBLIOGRAPHY

Brown, Schuyler. *Apostasy and Perseverance in the Theology of Luke.* AnBib 36. Rome: Pontifical Biblical Institute, 1969.

The thesis Brown advances in this book is that on Luke's view, faith is not predicated to the individual but to the community. Accordingly, just as apostasy connotes falling away from the faith, so perseverance connotes remaining in the faith.

Carroll, John T. *Response to the End of History: Eschatology and Situation in Luke-Acts.* SBLDS 92. Atlanta: Scholars Press, 1988.

Probing the vexing problem of Luke's eschatology, Carroll concludes that Luke's exhortation to faithful living had motivating force for believers exactly because Luke did not abandon the expectation of the imminent return of Jesus.

Cassidy, Richard J. *Jesus, Politics, and Society: A Study of Luke's Gospel.* Maryknoll, N.Y.: Orbis Books, 1978.

In the prologue of his Gospel, Luke declares his intention to write "an orderly account." Appealing to this intention, Cassidy contends that the political and social stance Luke attributes to the earthly Jesus is in fact the stance Jesus actually had.

Chance, J. Bradley. *Jerusalem, the Temple, and the New Age in Luke-Acts.* Macon, Ga.: Mercer University Press, 1988.

Chance explores afresh the prominence that Luke attributes to Jerusalem and the temple. He explains this in large part by postulating that Luke shared Jewish expectations according to which these centers had a crucial role to play in the salvation God would accomplish on behalf of both Israel and the gentiles.

Danker, Frederick W. *Benefactor: Epigraphic Study of A Graeco-Roman and New Testament Semantic Field.* St. Louis: Clayton Publishing House, 1982.

On the basis of the epigraphic data amassed in this book, Danker establishes and describes the model of the Greco-Roman benefactor figure. Danker shows that Luke made extensive use of this model in communicating to both Jewish and Greco-Roman audiences the peculiar significance of Jesus Christ.

———. *Luke.* 2d ed., rev. and enl. PC. Philadelphia: Fortress Press, 1987.

This book, first published in 1976, has served as the standard introduction to Luke's Gospel for well over a decade. Not only revised but also enlarged, it contains additional information about the Greco-Roman cultural environment in which Luke wrote.

Dawsey, James M. *The Lukan Voice: Confusion and Irony in the Gospel of Luke.* Macon, Ga.: Mercer University Press, 1986.

In this controversial study, Dawsey maintains that Luke as author so wrote his gospel story that Jesus' view of events differs markedly from that of the narrator. Through the narrative structure of his gospel story, Luke reveals that he himself sided with Jesus and not with the narrator.

Donahue, John R. *The Gospel in Parable: Metaphor, Narrative, and Theology in the Synoptic Gospels.* Philadelphia: Fortress Press, 1988.

In chapter 4, Donahue discusses the parables of Luke's Gospel. The importance of this chapter for the present study is that Donahue treats the Lukan parables against the background of the shape, direction, and meaning of Luke's own thought.

Esler, Philip F. *Community and Gospel in Luke-Acts.* SNTSMS 57. Cambridge: Cambridge University Press, 1987.

Employing a socio-redaction critical approach, Esler examines the theology of Luke as a response to social and political pressures upon the Christian community for which he wrote. Esler discusses such themes as table fellowship, the law, the temple, the poor and the rich, and politics.

Farris, Stephen. *The Hymns of Luke's Infancy Narratives: Their Origin, Meaning and Significance.* JSNTSup 9. Sheffield: JSOT Press, 1985.

As the subtitle of this book indicates, Farris studies in detail the origin, meaning, and significance of the celebrated songs of praise of God found in Luke 1–2: the Magnificat, the Benedictus, and the Nunc Dimittis.

Fitzmyer, Joseph A. *Luke the Theologian: Aspects of His Teaching.* New York: Paulist Press, 1989.

In this book, which contains eight lectures on Lukan theology, Fitzmyer treats such topics as the following: the authorship of Luke-Acts; problems associated with the infancy narrative; Mary; John the Baptist; discipleship; Satan and demons; the Jewish people and the Mosaic law; and the declaration Jesus makes in Luke 23:43.

Franklin, Eric. *Christ the Lord: A Study in the Purpose and Theology of Luke-Acts.* Philadelphia: Westminster Press, 1975.

On Franklin's view, Luke wrote in a churchly situation in which tension existed between the Christian expectation of the early return of Jesus and the fact that Jesus' return had been delayed. To address this problem, Luke affirmed the imminent return of Jesus even while insisting that Jesus' enthronement as Lord is not contingent upon the End but occurred already at Jesus' ascension.

Garrett, Susan R. *The Demise of the Devil: Magic and the Demonic in Luke's Writings.* Minneapolis: Fortress Press, 1989.

From within the story world of Luke-Acts, Garrett examines the role that magic and the demonic play. She argues that Luke describes Jesus' ministry as a struggle between Jesus and Satan for authority. In deposing Satan at his exaltation, Jesus enables his followers in Acts to triumph over demons and magicians.

Johnson, Luke T. *The Literary Function of Possessions in Luke-Acts.* SBLDS 39. Missoula, Mont.: Scholars Press, 39.

The goal Johnson sets for himself in this published dissertation is that of ascertaining the significance of the motif of community possessions within the literary structure of Luke-Acts.

Juel, Donald. *Luke-Acts: The Promise of History.* Atlanta: John Knox Press, 1983.

Written as an introduction to Luke-Acts, this book touches on theological topics that are of relevance for understanding both documents. The following are the six topics selected for discussion: the infancy narrative; the figure of Jesus; the worldwide mission; the life of faith; the people of God; and the purpose of Luke-Acts.

Karris, Robert J. *Luke: Artist and Theologian. Luke's Passion Account as Literature.* TI. New York: Paulist Press, 1985.

In this study of Jesus' passion, Karris's argument is that, to Luke's way of thinking, the reason for Jesus' death is to be found in the life he led. To explore Jesus' life in Lukan perspective, Karris deals with the three key themes of the faithful God, justice, and food (eating habits).

Maddox, Robert. *The Purpose of Luke-Acts.* SNTW. Edinburgh: T. & T. Clark, 1982.

In delineating the purpose of Luke-Acts, Maddox focuses on the twin themes of ecclesiology and eschatology. The importance of ecclesiology has to do with the pressures that Luke's church encountered from state persecution and Jewish polemic. The importance of eschatology has to do with the Christian need for reassurance concerning the fulfillment of the promises God made in the Old Testament.

Matera, Frank J. *Passion Narratives and Gospel Theologies: Interpreting the Synoptics through Their Passion Stories.* TI. New York: Paulist Press, 1986.

In three chapters, Matera employs Luke's passion narrative to introduce the reader to Lukan theology. Matera provides an overview of Luke's passion narrative, a commentary on each of its segments, and a discussion of major theological themes.

Moessner, David P. *Lord of the Banquet: The Literary and Theological Significance of the Lukan Travel Narrative.* Minneapolis: Fortress Press, 1989.

To explicate the form and content of the travel-section of Luke's Gospel (9:51—19:44), Moessner draws on Old Testament antecedents. He contends that Luke used the Deuteronomic presentation of the person and fate of Moses to give shape to his own presentation of Jesus as the anointed prophet like Moses and of Jesus' journey to Jerusalem.

Moxnes, Halvor. *The Economy of the Kingdom: Social Conflict and Economic Relations in Luke's Gospel.* OBT. Philadelphia: Fortress Press, 1988.

    Using social-scientific method, Moxnes investigates various groups (e.g., the Pharisees) or topics in Luke's Gospel relative to economic matters. Perhaps the main conclusion he reaches is that Luke espouses a divine reversal of socioeconomic relations implying a central, forced redistribution of goods and possessions. In word and deed, Jesus himself manifests such a reversal.

Neyrey, Jerome. *The Passion according to Luke: A Redaction Study of Luke's Soteriology.* TI. New York: Paulist Press, 1985.

    As the title indicates, Neyrey's book is a redaction-critical investigation of Luke's passion narrative (chaps. 22–23). One of the book's distinctive features is that Neyrey, in treating the passion narrative, highlights parallels and lines of development between Luke's Gospel and Acts.

O'Toole, Robert F. *The Unity of Luke's Theology: An Analysis of Luke-Acts.* GNS 9. Wilmington, Del.: Michael Glazier, 1984.

    Employing the method of composition criticism, O'Toole examines the theology of Luke in terms of the overarching concept of salvation. Relative to this concept, O'Toole discusses the activity of God and of Jesus and Luke's notion of discipleship.

Parsons, Mikeal C. *The Departure of Jesus in Luke-Acts: The Ascension Narratives in Context.* JSNTSup 21. Sheffield: JSOT Press, 1987.

    Analyzing the narratives of Jesus' departure in Luke and Acts, Parsons concludes that Luke was moved by both literary and theological considerations to close the Gospel with an "implicit" reference to Jesus' ascension and to open Acts with an "explicit" description of the same.

Pilgrim, Walter E. *Good News to the Poor: Wealth and Poverty in Luke-Acts.* Minneapolis: Augsburg Publishing House, 1981.

    In this study of wealth and poverty in Luke-Acts, Pilgrim understands Luke as advocating a twofold position: first, that possessions pose a radical danger to Christian discipleship; and second, that Christians are to adopt a style of life in which possessions are to be placed radically at the service of those in need.

Powell, Mark Allan. *What are they saying about Luke?* New York: Paulist Press, 1989.

    This survey of Lukan research from the rise of redaction-criticism to the present discusses, in nontechnical language, scholarly views on six topics: approaches to Luke's Gospel; Luke's use of sources; the purpose of Luke's Gospel; major theological topics; the social implications of Luke's Gospel; and Luke's understanding of discipleship.

Sanders, Jack T. *The Jews in Luke-Acts.* Philadelphia: Fortress Press, 1987.

    The purpose of this book is to describe how the author of Luke-Acts portrays the Jews. Since Sanders's position is that Luke-Acts is one major part of the New Testament that promulgates anti-Jewish sentiment, he intends for his study to be historical and to foster both Christian introspection and Jewish-Christian dialogue.

Senior, Donald. *The Passion of Jesus in the Gospel of Luke.* Wilmington, Del.: Michael Glazier, 1989.

As the title reveals, Senior devotes the bulk of his book to a close investigation of Luke's passion account (chaps. 22–23). Before proceeding to this account, however, Senior first situates it within the larger context of Luke's story.

Talbert, Charles H. *Literary Patterns, Theological Themes, and the Genre of Luke-Acts.* SBLMS 20. Missoula, Mont.: Scholars Press, 1974.

Using the method of architecture analysis, Talbert delineates, and discusses the functions of, certain key formal patterns found in Luke-Acts. His aim is to ascertain the relationship of these patterns to the theological perspectives of Luke. In Talbert's view, the way Luke has organized his double work suggests that it conforms to a type of ancient biography according to which the life of a founder of a philosophical school is counterbalanced by the record of his followers.

Tannehill, Robert C. *The Narrative Unity of Luke-Acts: A Literary Interpretation.* Vol. 1: *The Gospel according to Luke.* FFNT. Philadelphia: Fortress Press, 1986.

In this narrative-critical investigation, Tannehill focuses on the characters found in Luke's Gospel and on the development of the Gospel's plot. Tannehill's main argument is that overall, Luke-Acts shows itself to be a unified narrative in which the chief human characters all share in carrying out a mission guided by the single purpose of God. Ultimately, this purpose is one of universal salvation.

Tiede, David L. *Prophecy and History in Luke-Acts.* Philadelphia: Fortress Press, 1980.

One of Tiede's main contentions is that Luke, writing in the turbulent aftermath of the destruction of Jerusalem and of the earlier rejection of Jesus, looks to the scriptures to gain insight into the destiny of Israel and to interpret the time and situation of his own community. As Luke states, it was his conviction that all "the things which have been accomplished among us" were part and parcel of God's (inscrutable) plan of salvation.

Tyson, Joseph B. *The Death of Jesus in Luke-Acts.* Columbia, S.C.: University of South Carolina Press, 1986.

Using literary-critical method, Tyson investigates the ways in which Luke depicts the death of Jesus. He discusses at length such matters as Jesus' interaction with the Jewish public and the leaders; the issues sparking conflict; the trial of Jesus; and the circumstances surrounding Jesus' death.

Wilson, S. G. *Luke and the Law.* SNTSMS 50. Cambridge: Cambridge University Press, 1983.

According to Wilson, central to Luke's view of the law is that it constitutes the ethos of the Jewish nation. In Lukan perspective, therefore, the law applies differently to Jewish and gentile Christians. For Jewish Christians, keeping the law is a legitimate expression of their piety. For gentile Christians, the law has by and large lost its validity.

INDEX

OLD TESTAMENT APOCRYPHA AND PSEUDEPIGRAPHA